RENEWAL APOLOGETICS

RENEWAL APOLOGETICS

The Argument from Modern Miracles

Christopher J. Wilson

☙PICKWICK *Publications* • Eugene, Oregon

RENEWAL APOLOGETICS
The Argument from Modern Miracles

Copyright © 2019 Christopher J. Wilson. All rights reserved. Except for brief quotations in critical publications or reviews, no part of this book may be reproduced in any manner without prior written permission from the publisher. Write: Permissions, Wipf and Stock Publishers, 199 W. 8th Ave., Suite 3, Eugene, OR 97401.

Pickwick Publications
An Imprint of Wipf and Stock Publishers
199 W. 8th Ave., Suite 3
Eugene, OR 97401

www.wipfandstock.com

PAPERBACK ISBN: 978-1-5326-5194-6
HARDCOVER ISBN: 978-1-5326-5195-3
EBOOK ISBN: 978-1-5326-5196-0

Cataloguing-in-Publication data:

Names: Wilson, Christopher J., author.

Title: Renewal apologetics : the argument from modern miracles / Christopher J. Wilson.

Description: Eugene, OR : Pickwick Publications, 2019 | Includes bibliographical references.

Identifiers: ISBN 978-1-5326-5194-6 (paperback) | ISBN 978-1-5326-5195-3 (hardcover) | ISBN 978-1-5326-5196-0 (ebook)

SUBJECTS: LCSH: Miracles. | Supernatural.

Classification: BT97.3 .W62 2019 (paperback) | BT97.3 .W62 (ebook)

Manufactured in the U.S.A. 11/12/19

*This book is dedicated to the two women in my life
who made my PhD journey possible:
my mother (RIP) and my wife.*

Miracles are the original Christian apologetic—
they demonstrate the power of God over creation.

Contents

Preface ix

Acknowledgments xiii

Chapter 1 | Introduction 1
    1.1 Relevance of Study 1
    1.2 Critical Review of Literature 3
    1.3 Outline and Definitions 12

Chapter 2 | Epistemological Concerns 20
    2.1 Introduction 20
    2.2 Worldviews (Overcoming Scientism) 21
    2.3 Reliabilism 32
    2.4 Evidential Apologetics 37
    2.5 Other Concerns 42
    2.6 Michael Polanyi on Epistemology 51
    2.7 Conclusion 55

Chapter 3 | Overview of Special Divine Action Scholarship: Confronting Hume 57
    3.1 Introduction 57
    3.2 David Hume's Argument 59
    3.3 Rebuttals to Hume: (Swinburne/Polkinghorne/Lennox) 62
    3.4 C.S. Lewis and Bertrand Russell 68
    3.5 Joseph Butler's Probabilistic Argument 73
    3.6 Conclusion 75

Chapter 4 | History of Signs and Wonders ... 78
- 4.1 Introduction ... 78
- 4.2 Old Testament Signs and Wonders ... 83
- 4.3 New Testament Signs and Wonders ... 93
- 4.4 Church History Miracles ... 102
- 4.5 Conclusion ... 116

Chapter 5 | Documented Cases of Modern Special Divine Action ... 117
- 5.1 Introduction ... 117
- 5.2 Craig Keener ... 118
- 5.3 Roman Catholic Examples ... 121
- 5.4 Critical Evaluation ... 128
- 5.5 Conclusion ... 131

Chapter 6 | Interpretive Framework ... 133
- 6.1 Introduction ... 133
- 6.2 Jeffrey's "Deeper Meaning" Interpretive Framework ... 134
- 6.3 The Essence of the Gospel (Healing and Salvation) ... 137
- 6.4 Theodicy ... 146
- 6.5 Conclusion ... 157

Chapter 7 | Apologetical Significance of Modern Miracles ... 159
- 7.1 Evidential Value of Modern Miracles ... 161
- 7.2 Miracles as the Foundation of Renewal Apologetics ... 163
- 7.3 Renewal as Polemic ... 172

Conclusion ... 175
- C 1 Theological Implications ... 175
- C 2 Scientific Implications ... 177
- C 3 Future Trajectories ... 178

Bibliography ... 181

Preface

In the fall of 1994 at the age of twenty-two I became a Christian. Although raised as a Roman Catholic, I never knew Jesus Christ as my Lord and Savior until I was witnessed to by a Southern Baptist one night at work. Immediately upon conversion, I began to experience various blessings in my life which were far outside of mere chance. However, I had been so lost due to my agnostic worldview, that it took me a full six months to look back on my decision and to realize that I was now a Christian, and that the Lord had been blessing me. The process of my conversion was one of both intuitive knowledge, as well as of rational and logical conclusion.

After this realization, I began sharing my faith with family and friends and soon discovered that their skepticism went far past critical and amounted to a stubborn belief in secularism which defied all reason. Nevertheless, I remained rock solid in my new-found faith, while disappointed that I lacked the ability to share it effectively with others. This was the beginning of my interest in apologetics.

Over the years I listened extensively to the theology of R.C. Sproul, D. James Kennedy, Tony Evans and others. I also listened to the apologetics of Ravi Zacharias and read Josh McDowell's seminal text *Evidence That Demands a Verdict*. McDowell's text was the first time I had encountered the evidential method of apologetics; and I was hooked. Since my very decision to become a Christian had been rooted in a process of reason and logic; I had now found a method which employed both as a means for answering the reason for the faith which was in me (1Peter 3:15).

While I find value in other areas of apologetics, I believe that the evidential approach is the best approach. It is the method which would have convinced my former agnostic self. I soon discovered that the vast majority of Christian apologists concentrated on classical apologetics. While I found some value to these arguments, I did not find them to be strong enough to overcome the objections which I myself might have raised as a *good faith sceptic*.

I found McDowell's argument from fulfilled prophecy to be the most convincing as he demonstrated that the odds of many of the Bible's prophecies to have occurred by chance alone were infinitesimal. While I still find the argument from fulfilled prophecy to be compelling, some examples of prophetic fulfillment do allow for good faith objections such as vagueness, and ex-post facto fulfillment.

Over time I began to encounter individuals with spiritual giftings. Encountering individuals gifted with the word of knowledge was what finally made me abandon my previously held cessationism. Additionally, I began to hear anecdotal stories of faith healings from various credible people who had served as missionaries in the third world. They themselves were often shocked at what they had witnessed.

Again, just as with my new-found faith, I now had some personal supernatural experience which would be seen as largely anecdotal by sceptics. I began combing the literature to find apologist who argued based upon modern miracles; to my surprise they largely did not exist. The closest I found were Catholic apologist who included such things as Eucharistic miracles, incorruptibility of the Saints, and miracles of the Saints as proof of the Catholic faith. However, none of these Catholic apologists had applied the tool of *good faith skepticism* to their arguments to establish an apologetic based upon modern miracles.

It is with this experience that I set out to see if the phenomenon of modern miracles are of apologetical significance. While I personally believe in and have experienced/ witnessed the power of the supernatural, I realize that my experiences are anecdotal and prone to good faith skeptical objections. This study is geared towards the good faith sceptic; who tends towards naturalistic presuppositions, but does not hold to them against all reason, logic and evidence.

A BRIEF SUMMARY OF THE BOOK

According to Craig Keener there are hundreds of millions of people around the world who believe that they have experienced or witnessed a healing miracle. Unfortunately, the vast majority of these miracles (Special Divine Action) occur in the third world and lack medical and scientific documentation. However, in Craig Keener's text *Miracles: The Credibility of the New*

Testament Accounts (2011), he details over one hundred modern medical miracles which have documentation from American doctors and scientists. In addition to Keener, the Vatican's *Medica Consulta* has also catalogued seventy cases of modern medical miracles originating from the shrine at Lourdes France which meet the Vatican's rigid documentation criteria. Finally, the Renewal linked *Global Medical Research Institute* (GMRI) has begun an extensive study to verify and document claims of personal medical miracles. Thus, there is strong scientific evidence for the occurrence of modern miracles. This scientific evidence are foundational to the thesis of this text: modern medical miracles prove God's existence as more likely than not.

While proving the occurrence of modern miracles is foundational in the development of a Renewal apologetic, the theological implications and meanings of the miraculous are the larger questions according to Polkinghorne, Richard Swinburne, and others. What is ultimately needed in the development of a Renewal apologetic, is a comprehensive theology of the miraculous, which places modern miracles within the larger history of God's interaction with his creation, as a means for the expansion of his kingdom. This will be the focus of the second part of this paper, as modern miracles are shown to be an integral part of the Renewal and expansion of the Kingdom of God; and ultimately the development of a Renewal Apologetic.

Acknowledgments

First, I would first thank my wife who made my progress in this book, the original dissertation, and my PhD program possible. Without her steadfast devotion and sacrifice I could not have done this. Thank you for the hundreds of days and nights where you watched the kids alone while I was buried in books.

Secondly, since this book is largely based upon my dissertation, I would like to thank the members of my committee. First, to Dr. Petrus Grabe, my adviser, to whom I owe my very success in the program. Thank you for being a beacon of light during the darkest of days. To Dr. Peter Prosser, thank you for serving as my outside reader. I am blessed to have had your guidance, insights, and prayers throughout this process. The knowledge and spiritual insights I gained in your classes were invaluable. And finally, to Dr. Corné J. Bekker, thank you for serving as my second reader. I appreciate your willingness to serve on this committee. I know that it was an added burden to your already full schedule. I also appreciate the direction which the program and school have taken under your leadership.

Chapter 1

Introduction

1.1 RELEVANCE OF STUDY

1.1.1 Importance of the Renewal Movement

Renewal theology is an umbrella term for the various Pentecostal and Charismatic movements throughout the world. The twentieth century saw the rise of the Renewal movement with the 1906 Azusa Street Revival in the United States and various other revivals throughout the world. Within one hundred years, the movement claimed 600,000,000 adherents (25% of all Christians), and is currently the fastest growing segment of Christianity.[1]

The Renewal movement places a heavy emphasis on the *gifts of the Holy Spirit* (1 Cor 12: 7–11; Isa 11:1–2) and the immanence of God. Miraculous healings from various medical ailments are an accepted/expected aspect within the various strains of Renewal. Healing miracles are consistent with the biblical witness of the power given to all Christians (Mark 16:15–18).[2]

---

1. Anderson, *Introduction to Pentecostalism*, 1.

2. According to Lunn, the Gospel of Mark's longer ending (Mark 16: 9–20) has been accepted as authentic until the mid-nineteenth century when textual critics came to the consensus that the verses were inauthentic second-century additions. Their argument is largely based upon the absence of the verses in the two earliest manuscripts (Codex Sinaiticus and Vaticanus). However, Lunn makes a very strong case for the inclusion of the longer ending as canonical based upon references from Luke, the early church fathers and various archeological finds. Lund correctly argues that in the argument for the longer ending; nothing short of the belief in the resurrection and biblical inerrancy is at stake. See Lunn, *Original Ending of Mark*, 1–20.

1.1.2 Centrality of Signs and Wonders to Christianity

God's direct interaction with humanity is one of the defining motifs of Christianity. This interaction often occurs through supernatural occurrences such as healings and other signs and wonders. It can be argued that one particular sign and wonder (The Resurrection of Jesus Christ) is the central tenet of Christianity. As Christian apologist/theologian Norman Geisler concluded: "The central claims of Christianity are dependent on the apologetic value of miracles. If miracles have no evidential value, then there is no objective, historical evidence to support the claims of historic, orthodox Christianity."[3]

However, claims of miracles are not unique to orthodox Christians, nor is the discussion of miracles limited to religious circles. A 2003 Harris poll found that 84 percent of Americans, and 74 percent of physicians, believed that miracles still occur today. Fifty-five percent of American physicians claimed to have personally witnessed a medical miracle. This is of importance as orthodox Christians represent a minority in both groups.[4]

1.1.3 Lack of a Renewal Apologetic

Despite the central importance of miracles to the Christian faith, and the persistent belief in modern "post-Christian" America; the scholarship remains sparse in many key areas. For instance, the majority of the existing literature is written by Christian academics relaying testimonials and anecdotal stories of the miraculous. The remaining is written by skeptics such as the *New Atheists* (Richard Dawkins, Christopher Hitchens, Daniel Dennett, and Sam Harris) who attempt to discredit any possibility of the miraculous due to their naturalistic presuppositions. In recent years, Christian scholars such as Craig Keener and Candy Gunther Brown have attempted to rectify this deficit in the academy. They have produced scholarly texts aimed at providing objective studies of the miraculous examining such issues as the problem of defining the miraculous, scientific and philosophical implications, and medical evidence for miraculous occurrences.

However, what has yet to be developed, is a thorough systematic argument for belief in Christianity due to the occurrence of modern miracles: a *Renewal apologetic*. While the texts by Cranston and Duffin are a step in

---

3. Geisler, *Big Book Christian Apologetics*, 319.
4. Ruthven, *Cessation of the Charismata*, 3.

the right direction, as they detail the Catholic authentication process including scientific verification; they serve merely as reference books of these occurrences. Keener's compendium serves as an excellent bibliographic resource and addresses many issues involved in the study of the miraculous within the academy. Keener's assertion is that it is more plausible to believe that some instances of Special Divine Action have occurred (based upon the sheer volume of unexplainable occurrences); rather than to believe in Hume's epistemology, or some other highly implausible, naturalistic argument. This assertion is the very start of an apologetical argument based upon the miraculous. However, Keener's assessment is very brief, only two pages. What is needed is a full 200–300-page book in order to fully answer the question: "Are modern miracles of evidential value in the development of a Renewal apologetic?" That is the purpose of this text.

1.2 CRITICAL REVIEW OF LITERATURE

This review will summarize the current study of the miraculous within the academy and the various difficulties and issues involved. Methodologically, this will be accomplished by first examining the skeptical views of the miraculous contained in the writings of David Hume. Despite being nearly 300 years old, Hume's writings continue to serve as the foundation for the majority of skeptical arguments about the miraculous today.[5]

Next, an examination of the current status of the study of the miraculous within the academy will be given. This will be done by examining the recent comprehensive survey produced by Craig Keener, as well as the texts by Duffin and Cranston on Catholic miracles. Keener's text is of importance as it is very insightful and thorough in its description of numerous possible occurrences of Special Divine Action (events which defy scientific explanation). Duffin's and Cranston's texts are also valuable resources as they reveal occurrences of Special Divine Action which have withstood the Vatican's rigorous authentication process.

The final section (developing an interpretive framework of miracles) will show how the works of Jon Ruthven and Jeffrey John provide excellent starting points towards the development of a Renewal theology of the miraculous. Ruthven's expansion of the *Kingdom of God*, and Jeffrey John's *Deeper Meaning* frameworks will be examined.

---

5. Keener, *Miracles*, 762.

1.2.1 Philosophical Issues and Background (Hume and Butler)

1.2.1.1 David Hume

Hume's most well-known text *An Enquiry Concerning Human Understanding* (1748) is an encapsulation of his much larger work *A Treatise of Human Nature* (1739). Hume is a classical empiricist. Thus, Hume believes that all knowledge is arrived at by checking truth claims against the external world thorough our senses. He does allow for a small body of knowledge which can be obtained by reason alone (e.g., the self-evident proposition that a triangle has three sides). However, for Hume, the overwhelming majority of our knowledge is empirically based and known through our senses.

Hume believed that we must limit the objects of our philosophical inquiries to the natural world as metaphysical systems are like a fine clock, one grain of sand and the whole mechanism ceases to function. Hume further states that if a philosopher is engaged in metaphysics, and has made a mistake at the foundational level, they become like a marathon runner going in the wrong direction, the harder they try, the more lost they become.[6]

Hume's primary objection against miracles is that we cannot have any definitive knowledge through our empiricism. Rather, our empirical observations lead us towards conclusions based upon probabilistic assumptions (e.g., this has always happened this way before; therefore, it probably will happen the same way again). This need to make probabilistic assumptions is Hume's greatest problem with the occurrence of miracles. Hume reasons that since almost all of our knowledge is ultimately based upon probabilities, then when the unexpected occurs, it should be viewed as a mere anomaly, not anything supernatural.

Hume's skepticism of miracles is mostly a byproduct of his overall skepticism on the limits of empirical knowledge. Hume believed that our conceptions of the world, the appearances of causal relationships, and even the scientific method itself, were uncertain. For Hume, believing that nature is uniform to the extent that future events can be predicted by the past (e.g., the sun will rise in the east), is not something empirically verifiable, and thus cannot be definitively known. This is foundational to Hume's problem with induction as well, this will be covered more fully in chapter 3.[7]

---

6. Hume, *Enquiry Concerning Human Understanding*, 42.

7. Many scientists who are skeptics of the miraculous would be surprised if they studied the philosophy of science and saw all of the presuppositions (leaps of faith) necessary in order for the scientific method to be possible. Having said this, Hume's skepticism

Introduction

Hume's work is foundational as he is the most cited sceptic of the miraculous. His philosophical challenge against miracles is based upon the limits of human knowledge. Since the laws of nature and causality are ultimately based upon probabilities (and are not definitively known); any apparent violation of these laws cannot be labeled as a miracle according to Hume.

1.2.1.2 Joseph Butler

Joseph Butler's *The Analogy of Religion* was written in 1736 and remains perhaps both the strongest refutation of Hume, as well as a masterpiece in evidential apologetics. Cardinal John Henry Newman overcame his former skepticism by reading Butler. Hume himself stated that he "castrated" the *Treatise of Human Nature* (1739) in deference to Butler. Butler's argument is very simple. He argues that miracles and fulfilled prophecy are the most direct and fundamental proofs of Christianity (evidences). Additionally, he believes that since miracles can be proven, they are proof of God, as he alone can work miracles.

1.2.1.2.1 Testimony (Christianity vs. Islam)

Interestingly, one of Hume's objections against miracles (the issue of witnesses), is a cornerstone of Butler's argument. Butler argues that the signs and wonders in the Bible were performed in front of unbelievers, causing instant conversions. It is this conversion caused by miracles which separates Christianity from other faiths. For instance, Muhammad had no miracles and thus had to resort to violence and war.

1.2.1.2.2 Collective Whole

Butler argued that although any given miracle or prophecy could be doubted; as a collective whole, they were beyond doubt. The body of evidence for miracles and prophecy is so strong that it serves as the strongest argument for the Christian faith. Butler believes that even if several miracles were to be discounted, it would not change this conclusion. According to Butler, the

---

seems to go too far in disallowing causality as though it might not be 100% predictable of future causality it has worked since the discovery of the scientific method at least and should fit any standard definition and criteria for knowledge.

evidence is so strong that even if it can be diminished, it cannot be destroyed. This is why critics often try to disprove or object to one or two miracles, but they never argue against the collective whole of the evidences for Christianity.

1.2.1.2.3 PROBABILITY

Closely tied to Butler's collective whole argument is his contention that it is more probable than not that miracles did occur. Butler argues that the probability argument must be made with both the miracles and fulfilled prophecies of Christianity as they together establish the evidences for the faith. Butler believes that these evidences (based upon testimony) are strong enough to make them far more probable than not.

Charles Babbage in 1837 concluded that Hume has no good answer to Butler's argument. Babbage states that if independent witnesses can be found who speak more truth than falsehood, it will always be possible to argue in defense of an alleged miracle. This is because you can then argue that is more probable that they are telling the truth than lying.

1.2.2 Documentation of Modern Special Divine Action (Keener, Duffin, Cranston)

1.2.2.1 *Craig S. Keener*

Craig S. Keener's 2011 text *The Credibility of the New Testament Accounts (2 Volume Set)* is a through compendium on the topic of Special Divine Action. The text is divided into four parts. Part one examines the ancient evidences of miracles. Part two asks the question: "are miracles possible?" Part three examines accounts of post-biblical miracles. And, part four examines proposed explanations for miracles.

Of primary importance is the interaction between Keener, the contemporary New Testament scholar, and Hume, the enlightenment philosopher. According to Keener, Hume's arguments form the basis for most modern skeptical arguments against miracles. Yet today there are hundreds of millions of people throughout the world who claim to have had a miraculous experience. Keener states of this dilemma:

> The Western intellectual tendency is to regard most cultures in history and in today's world as precritical, without so much as undertaking a critical analysis of any of their claims. Yet it seems

to me that such disdain for vast numbers of claims (apparently hundreds of millions of them) from other cultures, purely on the basis of unproved presuppositions inherited from the radical wing of the Enlightenment, risks the charge of ethnocentric elitism.[8]

Keener's position in favor of the miraculous is not one of uninformed fideism; rather it is one which is based upon evidence, reasoned deductions, and conclusions. Keener summarizes his observations:

When we have not an isolated instance but a pattern of a number of highly extraordinary events accompanying prayer that do not normally occur without it, it may seem logical to explore prayer as a factor in the anomalous events. I think of circumstances like a number of persons apparently dead for hours abruptly recovering; cataracts immediately disappearing; long-term impaired hearing becoming normal; or the more unusual of the nature miracles I have mentioned. Some of these cases are strongly attested to by reliable eyewitnesses.[9]

Of particular interest to Keener is the fact that these highly extraordinary events are accompanied by prayer and are thus consistent with the character of the biblical God. Keener states:

Since too many of the examples above seem implausible to me as pure coincidence, particularly cumulatively, I prefer a different hypothesis: a personal God ready and able to heal, but one who also often allows created nature to take its own course and who is not manipulated by formulas, as perhaps an impersonal or merely psychological force could be. Although miracles are consistent with the character of the biblical God, we cannot always predict a personal deity's future actions, especially when our knowledge about the factors involved in those actions are limited. If miracles happened with absolute regularity, we would view them as part of the course of nature; their occurrence beyond providence in nature allows them to function more specifically as signs revealing God's activity and character.[10]

These events caused Keener to abandon his natural skepticism and to look towards the occurrence of modern miracles as the most rational explanation. He states that many of the occurrences in his text such as body parts

8. Keener, *Miracles*, 762.
9. Keener, *Miracles*, 762.
10. Keener, *Miracles*, 740–41.

regrowing in public view, blindness cured, broken bones healed and confirmed as undamaged by x-ray; confirms the assessment held by 55% of medical professionals who believe that they have personally witnessed a medical miracle.[11]

Keener's text is of importance to this paper as he lays out the evidences for and against modern miracles. He concludes that it is more probable to believe that these unexplainable events are the result of divine interaction rather than disbelieving in them due to the enlightenment presuppositions held by of Hume and others. This assessment is important as Keener (who was once an atheist), still has an initial knee jerk reaction against the miraculous. Keener looks first for naturalistic explanations. Keener states that this natural skepticism is the byproduct of his academic training, and if anything, he has a bias against believing in individual accounts of the miraculous.[12] However, when looking at the huge number of unusual events defying explanation; he must conclude that they are evidence of Special Divine Action. Keener's initial skepticism, along with his reasoned conclusions, adds considerable value to his views on the topic.

1.2.2.2 Jacalyn Duffin

Jacalyn Duffin's text *Medical Miracles: Doctors, Saints, and Healing in the Modern World* (2009), is a thorough examination of over 1400 miracles examined by the Vatican in the canonization process during the years 1588 to 1999. The vast majority of the miracles included are validated by the attending physicians. Examples include recoveries from paralysis, children being saved from huge falls, and resurrections from the dead. Duffin states that: "For the canonization process, happy outcomes do not automatically qualify as miracles. Even when good evidence establishes that the patient appealed to God or a saint at a crucial moment, recovery is not considered miraculous if any chance remains that it might have occurred naturally or through human intervention."[13] A large percentage of the miracles in the study occurred during the 1600s and 1700s. During the 1800s, there was a steady decline in claims of miracles. Some might interpret this to advances in medicine and science ruling out the supernatural as the cause of healing. However, the prevalence of the enlightenment worldview is more likely the

---

11. Keener, *Miracles*, 721.
12. Keener, *Miracles*, 124.
13. Duffin, *Medical Miracles*, 5.

cause for this reduction in claims. There has been a strong resurgence in the verification of miracles by the Vatican since 1975.[14]

Duffin's text is of value to this endeavor as she has cataloged a large amount of possible miracles which have already withstood the meticulous scrutiny of tests conducted by the Vatican. No miracles are included which do not include outside medical and/or scientific verification. And, as previously noted, cases which might have naturalistic explanations have already been eliminated.

1.2.2.3 Ruth Cranston

Ruth Cranston's text *The Miracle of Lourdes* (1998), examines the phenomenon of miraculous healings in Lourdes France. Each year six million people visit Lourdes in hopes of being miraculously healed by its waters. Of the thousands of claimed miraculous cures, there have only been sixty-nine which have been officially recognized by the Lourdes Medical Bureau. This is not because the Bureau believes that such a small number of cures have actually occurred; rather, it is because of the stringent and lengthy process which it undergoes in authenticating official miracles, which dismisses all but the most verifiable.

Cranston who is a Protestant, developed an interest in these cures and attempted an unbiased ethnographic study of the phenomenon. In the process, she interacted with both cured persons as well as the doctors who staffed the Lourdes Medical Bureau. In her text, she describes the process in-depth of how miracles are officially recognized by the Bureau, and the criteria they must meet:

1. An absence of a curative agent (Such as drugs or injections and special treatments for example).
2. Instantaneousness.
3. Suppression of convalescence.
4. Irregularity of the method of healing.
5. Function restored without function of the organ—still incapable of accomplishing it.[15]

---

14. Duffin, *Medical Miracles*, 115.
15. Cranston, *Miracle of Lourdes*, 126.

According to Cranston, any one of these five characteristics would place a cure outside of the borders of known medical science, and thus, would be sharply challenged by medical sceptics. For instance, Dr. Guinier who worked at the Lourdes Medical Bureau for four years, describes the amazement caused by the *instantaneous* of the Lourdes cases. The cures violate all of the laws of biology which are taught to physicians:

> Microbes are annihilated. . .carcinomas vanish, tubercle bacilli exist no more; gangrenous bones are reformed, severed nerves joined together, wounds cicatrized. Sometimes this happens in a few seconds, sometimes in a few hours, but so rapidly that we can say that factor *time* has disappeared, consequently the cure has operated beyond the laws of biology.[16]

Cranston's account is of value as she does not write as a faithful Catholic blindly believing all of the cures claimed from Lourdes. Rather, as a Protestant attempting an ethnographic approach to the subject, she gives a clear, factual and unbiased rendering of what is occurring. The Lourdes Medical Bureau itself is very thorough in its authentication process. To date, only sixty-nine cases have survived out of the thousands of testimonials. So, what is left are sixty-nine cases documented by medical personnel, which defy naturalistic explanations as the cures have violated the laws of biology. Cranston's account is valuable to this discussion as often the Renewal academy ignores Special Divine Action originating from Catholic sources.

1.2.3 Theology of the Miraculous Ruthven and Jeffrey John

1.2.3.1 Jon Ruthven

Jon Ruthven's *On the Cessation of the Charismata* (1993, 2011) has been an important apologetic for the continuationist position for the past two decades. Ruthven's thesis is that cessationism arose as a post-Calvin polemic against the ongoing miracles within Roman Catholicism. This phenomenon points towards the importance of signs and wonders as a means of establishing the authority of the church, and as the means used by God to authenticate both prophets and doctrines.

Ruthven contends that cessationism reached its fullest form in the writings of B.B. Warfield. Warfield argues that the singular purpose of miracles was to authenticate the gospel message and thus miracles ceased when

16. Cranston, *Miracle of Lourdes*, 127.

the last of the apostles died.[17] Ruthven labels this approach as an *evidentialist* view of miracles. He states that an evidentialist view of miracles ignores their larger role as an important means for the expansion of the *Kingdom of God*. And, this misunderstanding is of major importance as miracles point towards the "central essence of Jesus' being and mission" as the prophetic word (John 1).[18] Ruthven concludes:

> To hold to the cessationist position amounts to a "truncated gospel, this tenet of which could not be more crucially and diametrically opposed to God's central, and biblical, spiritual process for mankind on this earth: the immediate revelation of God's "word" directly into our hearts and experience, in the form of spiritual gifts of divine revelation and power.[19]

In conclusion, while Ruthven's work is largely an apologetic for the continuationist position, his analysis of the meaning and purpose of the miraculous, as a means for the expansion of the Kingdom of God, is important in the development of a Renewal theology of the miraculous. Additionally, Ruthven's historical analysis shows that most objections to the continuation of miracles were ultimately rooted in ecclesiological authority concerns and not developed by sound biblical exegesis nor historical analysis. Today, cessationism is a position largely in retreat within the academy. Cessationism is increasingly seen as an anomaly within church history as it violates 2000 years of tradition. Additionally, the occurrence of modern miracles is seen as a refutation of the position as well.

1.2.3.2 *Jeffrey John*

Jeffrey John's text *The Meaning in the Miracles* (2004), provides a thorough analysis of the meaning and purpose of several New Testament signs and wonders. John's central argument is that Jesus never performed signs and wonders just for the sake of doing signs and wonders. Rather, the performance of a sign and wonder always had a deeper meaning and significance. For instance, throughout the New Testament Jesus repeatedly healed those who were seen as ritually unclean and were thus excluded from the temple. John States:

---

17. Ruthven, *Cessation of the Charismata*, 94.
18. Ruthven, *Cessation of the Charismata*, xxxiii.
19. Ruthven, *Cessation of the Charismata*, xxiii.

> The list of those who suffered some degree of taboo and exclusion contains menstruating women, lepers, Samaritans, Gentiles, tax—collectors, homosexuals, prostitutes, adulteresses, women in general, children, people with withered limbs, the deaf, the dumb, the blind, the lame and the dead. At least one representative from each of these categories is a subject of Jesus' healing in the miracle stories.[20]

Thus, by preforming these signs and wonders, Jesus was pointing both towards the imposition of a new covenant, as well as the need for divine healing of those who were seen as outcasts by society.

However, Jeffrey John does correctly cite that Jesus also performed signs and wonders as a means of authenticating his ministry as he knew that it would take a miraculous sign to make some believe: "'If I am not doing the works of my Father, then do not believe me; but if I do them, even if you do not believe in me, believe in the works, so that you may know and understand that I am in the Father and the Father in me' (John 10:38). In a similar way he says to Philip, 'Believe me that I am in the Father and the Father in me; or else believe me for the sake of the works themselves' (John 14:11–12)."[21] This is why Jesus repeatedly tells those he has healed that their faith has saved them (Luke 17:19, Luke 18:42).

In contrast, despite actually seeing the signs and wonders of Jesus performed in their presence, many opponents of Jesus such as the Pharisees still would not believe, their hearts were too hardened (Mark 8:17–18; Isaiah 6:9–10).[22] This point is of importance as while there is strong evidence of modern Special Divine Action, the hardened sceptic will never be convinced. Even when Jesus preformed miracles in their presence, the Pharisees still refused to believe. This is why the target for apologetics must always be the *good faith sceptic*.

1.3 OUTLINE AND DEFINITIONS

This book is divided into two parts. The first part deals with the question of whether there is enough evidence to conclude that modern miracles occur? And, if so, to what extent is the evidence of apologetical significance? The second section deals with the interpretation and significance of the miraculous.

20. John, *Meaning in the Miracles*, 10.
21. John, *Meaning in Miracles*, 19.
22. John, *Meaning in Miracles*, 20.

Introduction

The second step in this development (interpreting modern miracles in light of Renewal Theology), will ultimately lead towards both an understanding of miracles as a means of the expansion of the Kingdom of God (Ruthven), as well as providing a better understanding of how God, acting as a loving father, chooses to mercifully interact with his children (Keener/Butler). Thus, the project will ultimately provide for an evidential Renewal Apologetic which is biblically based; but offering current theological insights. Currently, Renewal scholarship is almost completely devoid of an evidential apologetic as this has been dismissed as an evangelical endeavor by many Renewal scholars.

Chapter 2 deals with epistemological concerns such as reliabilism, overcoming scientism, and the foundations for an evidential apologetic. This is of importance as a foundational epistemology must be arrived at before any analysis or interpretation can occur.

Chapter 3 gives an overview of the current study of the miraculous. First, by detailing the arguments against the miraculous given by David Hume. Next, the rebuttals of Hume by Swinburne, Polkinghorne, and John Lennox. The chapter concludes with the probabilistic argument of the miraculous given by Joseph Butler. While Hume's arguments are nearly 300 years old, they are of importance as they still form the basis for most modern skeptical arguments.

Chapter 4 deals with the history of the signs and wonders. Accounts are analyzed from both the Old Testament and New Testament. Then accounts from various eras of church history are analyzed as well. By surveying accounts of signs and wonders throughout both the biblical and the post-biblical periods, a better picture of God's usage of signs and wonders develops. This fuller picture is important in laying the foundation for an interpretive framework in chapter 6.

Chapter 5 deals with the existence of documented miracles given by Craig Keener, the Vatican's *Medica Consulta*, as well as various other sources. In this key chapter, the raw data, in the form of several documented miracles, is given and analyzed.

Chapter 6 deals with the interpretive framework of signs and wonders. Polkinghorne's assertion that interpretation is a greater dilemma than evidence is the guiding motif of the chapter. Jeffrey Johns' "Deeper Meaning" interpretive framework is given and analyzed. The chapter concludes with an examination of Ruthven's "Kingdom of God" view of the charismata.

Chapter 7 brings the preceding six chapters into play as the original question of the apologetical significance of modern miracles is answered. This begins by concluding what evidential value is present in the phenomenon of modern miracles. Next, the theological significance of this evidence is presented. Finally, the evidence and its theological significance are used as the foundation for a Renewal apologetic.

1.3.1 Definitions

1.3.1.1 Miracle

The definition of a miracle is one of considerable debate amongst scholars. Historically, enlightenment figures such as Hume defined miracles as a *violation of a law of nature* by a volitional act of a deity. Thomas Aquinas defined three different types of miracles:

1. Acts which are beyond nature (e.g., the sun standing still).
2. Acts of nature out of order (e.g., the healing of the sick).
3. Acts which supersede nature (e.g., the instantaneous healing of a fever).[23]

An additional complication is that many of the world's religions claim to have miracles as well. This will be discussed more fully in chapters 6 and 7. However, I can briefly state that Scripture acknowledges the occurrence of supernatural acts within pagan religions. However, as these acts are demonic in origin, they are limited and inferior to the power of God (Exodus 8:19, Acts 16:16–18, Acts 13:8–11); and thus, do not qualify as biblical miracles.

Since this book is concerned with the ongoing work of the Holy Spirit both today and throughout church history; the definition of a modern miracle adopted will be consistent with that of a biblical miracle. Thus, the three types of miracles categorized by Saint Thomas Aquinas must be remembered in light of those miracles and characteristics exemplified in Scripture. A good brief definition of miracles is "wonders performed by supernatural power as signs of some special mission or gift and explicitly

---

23. Aquinas, *Contra Gentiles*, Book III.

Introduction

ascribed to God".[24] However a more expansive definition is necessary to judge modern miracles in light of Scripture.

Scripture primarily uses three words to describe miracles: sign (semeia), wonder (terata) and power (*dynamis*). While miracles are used throughout Scripture for a variety of reasons; the ultimate goal is for the glory of God. As Geisler notes: "The purposes of a miracle are to glorify the nature of God (John 2: 11; 11: 40) to accredit certain persons as the spokesmen for God (Acts 2: 22; Heb. 2: 3– 4) to provide evidence for belief in God (John 6: 2, 14; 20: 30– 31)."[25] This is what we see throughout Scripture as miracles ultimately serve a deeper purpose. Being divinely ordained by the triune God of Scripture is the one persistent motif.

Miracles also serve the dual purpose of condemning the unbeliever. This is of importance to this paper as there will be no amount of evidence which will satisfy some unbelievers; and thus, the existence of miracles serves to condemn them. As Geisler concludes: "John grieved, "Even after Jesus had done all these miraculous signs in their presence, they still would not believe in him" (John 12: 37). Jesus himself said of some, "They will not be convinced even if someone rises from the dead" (Luke 16: 31). One result, though not the purpose, of miracles is condemnation of the unbeliever (cf. John 12: 31, 37)."[26]

1.3.1.2 *Special Divine Action*

One additional difficulty with using the terms "miracle" or "miraculous" is that since the terms are so overused in modern society, their meanings are often blurred. In this paper, I will try to use the more technical phrase *Special Divine Action* in place of the word "miracle" when referring to post-apostolic phenomena; and *signs and wonders* when referencing Special Divine Action (SDA) within the biblical text. At times, the words "miracle" and "miraculous" will have to be used as they are the words being used by the scholar or referenced by the church.

A short definition of Special Divine Action could be when God interacts within creation in a particular time and place in order to cause a given outcome. This type of action is to be distinguished from the more general

---

24. Driscoll, *The Catholic Encyclopedia*, loc. 436958 of 700382.
25. Geisler, *Big Book Christian Apologetics*, 347.
26. Geisler, *Big Book Christian Apologetics*, 347.

divine actions such as creation and the institution of natural laws. Below is the definition of Special Divine Action given by Oxford's Divine Action Project:[27]

> Although the demarcation of SDA from divine action in general is ancient, the distinction became especially important during the 'deist controversy' (c. 1700–1760) noted previously, when some persons ('deists') accepted the existence of a deity but denied divine action beyond that of creation. The idea of a cosmos closed to divine action remains extremely influential across a spectrum of views generally labelled as naturalism or physicalism. In this context, questions about SDA often focus on the possibility or impossibility of extraordinary events that surpass the productive power of nature and are termed 'miracles.' Nevertheless, within theology, religious studies, various traditions and religious experience, it is common practice to take account of distinct modes of SDA, especially grace, inspiration, miracles, and providence.[28]

Thus, this distinction between divine action and Special Divine Action will be key in many aspects of this book as it separates the biblical worldview from the deistic. Many opponents of Special Divine Action in the enlightenment were deists who believed in general divine action but not in Special Divine Action.

1.3.1.3 Signs and Wonders (Biblical Miracles)

When referring to Special Divine Action in Scripture, the most correct translation of the Hebrew and Greek words are the English words "signs and wonders." In the Old Testament, the word *mopet* is used numerous times and is usually interpreted by the English word "sign." According to John H. Walton:

> The use of the Hebrew term mopet is indicative of an extraordinary event that serves as a sign of God's power, and in this case judgment or punishment (compare the curses in Dt. 28: 45–46). This technical term appears often in the narrative of the plagues in Egypt (e.g., Ex 7: 3 ["wonders]; 11: 9 ["wonders"]), and is used to signal a coming event (1Ki 13: 3, 5). The term does not necessarily designate something supernatural as opposed to natural (i.e., a

---

27. The Divine Action Project is a group of scholars who meet at Oxford on a yearly basis to discuss Special Divine Action. Presentations are given about the philosophy, historicity, and evidences of SDA. Scholars include believers and sceptics alike.

28. Oxford Divine Action Project, "Special Divine Action," lines 6–12.

"miracle"). In the ancient world, people did not consider anything truly "natural"—God was involved in everything and therefore "miracle" was a meaningless designation.[29]

Since the ancient Israelites had no category for natural or supernatural, any translation of the Hebrew words as miracle would be inaccurate as the word miracle "pertains to phenomena without natural explanation."[30] However, the Israelites did believe that some phenomena were beyond their ability to understand and were thus of divine origin and "incomprehensible" to them.[31]

In the New Testament, the "Biblical terms for miracle (sēmeion ["expression," "mark," "sign"], often appearing with teras ["wonder"], dynamis ["power"] and ĕrgon ["action/work"]) stress the acts of power that reveal God in expressing the gospel, which are then usually explained in speech or vice versa (e.g., 1 Thess 1:5; Heb 2:4)."[32] The worldview held by the first century Jewish evangelists was very similar to that of the ancient Israelites. Thus, translating New Testament instances of Special Divine Action as "signs and wonders" is the most accurate.

These terms and concepts will be developed more fully in chapter 4's discussion on the history of signs and wonders. What is important to understand now is that the phrase "signs and wonders" most accurately translates the biblical terms and phrases. And finally, the words "miracles" and "miraculous" in modern English usage often mean something very different from biblical "signs and wonders" and the technical phrase "Special Divine Action."

1.3.1.4 *Global North/Global South*

The terms "global south" and "global north" are often used by scholars in place of the older terms of first world, second world, and third world. Some scholars use the terms "majority world" and "the west" instead of the previously mentioned terms. However, I believe these terms "majority world"

---

29. Walton and Keener, *NIV Cultural Backgrounds Study Bible*, loc. 124194–124201 of 350904.

30. Walton and Keener, *NIV Cultural Backgrounds Study Bible*, loc. 1946–1959 of 350904.

31. Walton and Keener, *NIV Cultural Backgrounds Study Bible*, loc. 1946–1959 of 350904.

32. Dyrness and Karkkainen, *Global Dictionary of Theology*, 549.

and "the west" to be less precise and will only use them when the scholar being quoted has used them. For clarity sake, the term *majority world* can be interpreted as referring to the global south. While *the west* can be interpreted as referring to the global north.

The term global north includes the United States, Western Europe, Japan and Australia. This is largely synonymous with the terms of first world or the west. The term global south refers to the rest of the world which includes second and third world countries many of which happen to also be in the northern hemisphere. These distinctions are of importance for scholars as Christianity in general, and Renewal Christianity in specific, are greatly expanding within the third world; the global south. "A century ago, the Global North (commonly defined as North America, Europe, Australia, Japan and New Zealand) contained more than four times as many Christians as the Global South (i.e., the rest of the world).5 Today, the Pew Forum study finds, more than 1.3 billion Christians live in the Global South (61%), compared with about 860 million in the Global North (39%)."[33] While the global south is growing the fastest and has the highest number of Christians; proportionately the global north is still more Christian at 69% vs. 24% for the global south. This is because the global south has a population 4.5 times greater than the global north.[34]

1.3.1.5 *Statistical Significance = Less Than 5 Percent*

> Significant: has a specialized statistical meaning, which can lead to serious misunderstandings for students who are unaware of this and who use the word in the loose, popular sense. In statistics, 'significant' means 'the likelihood of this happening by random chance is at most 1 in 20'; this is normally accompanied by naming the statistical test which was used. 'Highly significant' and 'very highly significant' involve the same principle, but with odds of 1 in 100 and 1 in 1000 respectively.[35]

---

33. Pew Research Center, "Global Christianity," lines 81–85.
34. Pew Research Center, "Global Christianity," lines 86–91.
35. Petre and Rugg, *Unwritten Rules PhD Research*, 255.

1.3.2 Vatican Criteria

While there are many different criteria which could be used to establish miraculous occurrences, the Vatican Criteria is the most commonly known and is used as an evaluation and elimination tool for all of the Roman Catholic miracles. These criteria will be of value for eliminating miracles both Catholic and otherwise. The five criteria are:

1. An absence of a curative agent (such as drugs or injections and special treatments for example).
2. Instantaneousness.
3. Suppression of convalescence.
4. Irregularity of the method of healing.
5. Function restored without function of the organ—still incapable of accomplishing it.[36]

1.3.3 Good Faith Skepticism

One of the most important concepts in this study is my epistemological tool of *good faith skepticism*. The goal of this study is to first discern if there is enough evidence of modern miracles to overcome objections given by a good faith skepticism towards their occurrence. By good faith skepticism I mean the initial hesitance to accept a supernatural occurrence as it might have naturalistic causes. This type of skepticism rightly places the burden of proof on the apologist to prove their claims as more likely than not (e.g., Bayesian). This is to be distinguished from the posturing positions of the New Atheists and hardened skeptics who insist that claims of the miraculous meet the standard of *extraordinary claims require extraordinary evidences*.

Good faith skepticism initially looks for naturalistic causes, but does not hold onto naturalistic explanations in the face of substantial evidence to the contrary; rather it follows the evidence where it leads. Thus, a good faith skeptic is one who rejects rigidly holding to scientism's naturalistic presuppositions in favor of pure scientific reasoning. This concept will become clearer in chapter 2's discussion on scientism vs. science, and the role of probability and statistical inferencing in scientific reasoning.

36. Cranston, *Miracle of Lourdes*, 126.

Chapter 2

Epistemological Concerns

2.1 INTRODUCTION

"Satan's second strategy is to confuse us, to dim our lights—for instance, by convincing us that truth is negotiable, "nuanced", not ever plain and simple and certain and crude and obvious; that God's revelation is a dark puzzle for theologians, not a bright lamp for travelers."[1]

—Peter Kreeft

"Because faith is the thing that gives us a framework for making decisions in the light of incomplete evidence."[2]

—Troy Van Voorhis

In this chapter, I will examine the current debates within the philosophy of religion and the philosophy of science which are pertinent towards the development of an evidential Renewal apologetic. The adopted epistemology will serve as a methodological framework for this study. The various debates within these disciplines are of importance as they touch on the topics of worldviews, presuppositions, and methods of inquiry. In the next section (2.2 Worldviews), I will examine the differences between scientific inquiry and the naturalistic philosophy of scientism. In Section 2.3 (Reliabilism),

---

1. Kreeft, *Angels and Demons*, loc. 1408–1411 of 1966.
2. Voorhis, *Certainty*, 17.

I will give an overview of the epistemology of reliabilism paying particular attention the question of *justified religious belief*. In the final section 2.4 (Evidential Apologetics), I will discuss probability as an epistemological tool as it relates to various claims of supernatural phenomena. The key question for the evidential apologist is whether there is the possibility in having justified true belief in terms of metaphysics? And, if so, what types of evidences are necessary?

2.2 WORLDVIEWS (OVERCOMING SCIENTISM)

The term worldview is a relatively recent invention;[3] but the concept goes back for millennia. The philosophical systems of Plato and Aristotle can be thought of as worldviews as they sought to provide answers to all of the important questions in life.[4] According to Geisler: "A worldview is how one views or interprets reality. The German word is *Weltanschauung*, meaning a "world and life view," or "a paradigm." It is the framework through which or by which one makes sense of the data of life."[5] Ronald Nash uses the phrase "conceptual scheme" to define how we "consciously or unconsciously place or fit everything we believe and by which we interpret and judge reality."[6]

A worldview seeks to answer several questions about life including: "God, reality, knowledge, morality, and humankind."[7] According to Geisler: "Worldviews influence personal meaning and values, the way people act and think. The most important question that a worldview answers is: "Where did we come from?" The answer to this question is crucial to how other questions are answered."[8, 9] This is the reason why atheists often attack the book of Genesis and the idea of theistic creation so strongly; as the worldview of Christianity is ultimately rooted in creation. Conversely, the worldview of atheism is ultimately rooted in evolution and big bang cosmology.

3. David K. Naugle Jr. traces the concept back to the writings of Kant. See Naugle, *Worldview*. Nagle believes that the usage of the concept has had a profound impact on Christian scholarship during the last 150 years. See also: Sire, *Naming the Elephant*.
4. Nash, *Worldviews in Conflict*, 16.
5. Geisler, *Big Book Christian Apologetics*, 593.
6. Nash, *Worldviews in Conflict*, 16.
7. Nash, *Worldviews in Conflict*, 26.
8. Geisler, *Big Book Christian Apologetics*, 594.
9. Geisler, *Big Book Christian Apologetics*, 593: Geisler also notes that: "A worldview makes a world of difference in one's view of God, origins, evil, human nature, values, and destiny."

Geisler lists the seven major worldviews:

1. Theism—An infinite, personal God exists beyond and in the universe.
2. Deism—God is beyond the universe but not in it. Theism minus miracles.
3. Atheism—No God exists in or beyond the universe.
4. Pantheism—God is the All/Universe.
5. Panentheism—God is in the universe as a mind is in a body.
6. Finite godism—A finite God exists in and beyond the universe.[10]
7. Polytheism—Many gods exist beyond the world and in it.[11]

Next, Geisler compares and contrasts these worldviews:

> Reality is either the universe only, God only, or the universe and God(s). If the universe is all that exists, then atheism is right. If God is all that exists, then pantheism is right. If God and the universe exist, then either there is one God or many gods. If there are many gods, polytheism is right. If there is only one God, then this God is either finite or infinite. If there is one finite god, then finite godism is correct. If this finite god has two poles (one beyond and one in the world), then panentheism is right. If there is one infinite God, then either there is intervention of this God in the universe or there is not. If there is intervention, then theism is true. If there is not, then deism is true.[12]

What is of importance for the agnostic/atheist to recognize is that their worldview is still based upon numerous philosophical presuppositions. Naturalism is not a default, *value neutral* worldview! The scientific method itself relies on numerous assumptions and presuppositions in order to be possible. As Nash states:

---

10. Geisler, *Big Book Christian Apologetics*, 593. According to Geisler: "Finite Godism. A finite god exists beyond and in the universe. Finite godism is like theism, only the god beyond the universe and active in it is limited in nature and power. Like deists, finite godists generally accept creation but deny miraculous intervention. Often God's inability to overcome evil is given as a reason for believing God is limited in power. John Stuart Mill, William James, and Peter Bertocci hold this worldview." Cf: Caputo, *The Weakness of God*, and Pinnock, *Openness of God*. Caputo's weak "God" and Pinnock's God of open theism may be considered as variants of finite godism.

11. Geisler, *Big Book Christian Apologetics*, 593–94.

12. Geisler, *Big Book Christian Apologetics*, 594.

Even scientists make important epistemological, metaphysical, and ethical assumptions. They assume, for example, that knowledge is possible and that sense experience is reliable (epistemology), that the universe is regular (metaphysics), and that scientists should be honest (ethics). Without these assumptions, which scientists cannot verify within the limits of their methodology, scientific inquiry would soon collapse.[13]

Christians should adopt a worldview concept in order for their faith to be rational and systemic. Fragmented Christianity lacks unity and consistency and is thus more prone to error and heresy. According to Nash: "Instead of thinking of Christianity as a collection of theological bits and pieces to be believed or debated, we should approach our faith as a conceptual system, as a total world-and-life view."[14] This is of particular importance to Christian apologetics/scholarship as apologists must understand the ideas of their adversaries as well. Nash concludes: "Once people understand that both Christianity and its adversaries in the world of ideas are worldviews, they will be in better position to judge the relative merits of the total Christian system."[15]

Christians and atheists alike must realize the important role which presuppositions play in the formation of their worldviews. As Nash states: "We all hold a number of beliefs that we presuppose or accept without support from other beliefs or arguments or evidence. Such presuppositions are necessary if we are to think at all. In the words of the Christian thinker Augustine (A.D. 354–430), we must believe something before we can know anything."[16] James W. Sire begins his seminal text on worldviews with this maxim: "For any of us to be fully conscious intellectually we should not only be able to detect the worldview of others but be aware of our own—why it is ours and why in the light of so many options we think it is true."[17] This is good advice for the Christian and the atheist alike.

These questions about worldviews are of extreme importance according to R. C. Sproul. Reflecting on the work of Etienne Gilson,[18] Sproul

---

13. Nash, *Worldviews in Conflict*, 23.
14. Nash, *Worldviews in Conflict*, 19–20.
15. Nash, *Worldviews in Conflict*, 19–20.
16. Nash, *Worldviews in Conflict*, 21.
17. Sire, *Universe Next Door*, 1.
18. Etienne Gilson (1884–1978) was a philosopher, historian of philosophy and a Thomistic scholar. He is widely credited for the revival of Thomism in the twentieth century. He viewed philosophy as a history of new movements countering skepticism, becoming corrupted and raised to the level of idealism; and then being salvaged by a

agrees that our choice is not: "Between Immanuel Kant and René Descartes or between G. W. F. Hegel and Søren Kierkegaard. We must choose instead between Kant and Thomas Aquinas. Gilson insists that all other positions are mere halfway houses on the road to either absolute religious agnosticism or the natural theology of Christian metaphysics."[19] So profound was the effect of Kant on our worldview that it destroyed the former synthesis between natural theology, special revelation in Scripture and general revelation in nature.[20] But Sproul believes that this can be overcome; we need to restore this classic Thomistic synthesis. Sproul concludes: "The thinking person could embrace nature without embracing naturalism. All of life, in its unity and diversity, could be lived *coram Deo*, before the face of God, under his authority and to his glory."[21]

In this section, I will examine worldviews as they relate specifically to this inquiry. Of key importance will be the differences between science and scientism; as well as the philosophical presuppositions which make the scientific method possible. Understanding these presuppositions and the limits of scientific inquiry will reveal that there is in fact no innate conflict between science and religion. In this book, issues of worldview are of primary importance. The New Atheists (e.g., Richard Dawkins, Christopher Hitchens and Steven Hawking) often claim that no educated person can believe in Scripture. "Richard Dawkins has claimed that the nineteenth century was the last time when it was possible for an educated person to admit to believing in miracles."[22] They are positing *a priori* a worldview which presupposes metaphysical naturalism and a conflict between science and faith. This worldview will be shown not only to be erroneous; but inconsistent with the limits and methodology of proper scientific inquiry. Additionally, not only does this supposed conflict not exist, it can be shown

---

new movement. The cycle repeats itself throughout the history of philosophy. Gilson saw a return to Thomistic philosophy as the answer to the problems of philosophy including the prevalence of various systems. He did not view Aquinas as a scholastic, but rather as a revolutionary against scholasticism. Gilson saw Thomism was a means of revolting against the modern systems and restoring humanity to their rightful place as children of God, not mere animals in nature. For further insights from Gilson see Gilson, *Unity of Philosophical Experience*; Gilson, *Philosophy of Thomas Aquinas*; and Gilson, *Thomist Realism*.

19. Sproul, *Consequences of Ideas*, loc. 2762–2769 of 3097.
20. Sproul, *Consequences of Ideas*, loc. 2762–2769 of 3097.
21. Sproul, *Consequences of Ideas*, loc. 2762–2769 of 3097.
22. Lennox, *Miracles*, 22.

that almost every major branch of science was in fact discovered by orthodox Christians. The following is a brief list:

1. Calculus—Isaac Newton
2. Chemistry—Robert Boyle
3. Computer Science—Charles Babbage
4. Electronics—John Fleming
5. Galactic Astronomy—William Herschel
6. Genetics—Gregor Mendel
7. Oceanography—Matthew Murray
8. Paleontology—John Woodward
9. Statistical Thermodynamics—James Maxwell
10. Systematic Biology—Carolus Linnaeus[23]

2.2.1 The Supposed Conflict between Religion and Science

Previous to the enlightenment, there existed no division between science and religion as the two were allowed to operate in their own spheres of inquiry. In fact, as shown above, many important scientists of the enlightenment were professed Christians. It was not until the twentieth century that the conflict between the two disciplines became manifest due to the naturalistic presuppositions contained within the philosophy of ontological naturalism (scientism). As Rodney Stark notes: "Of the fifty-two leading scientists in the seventeenth century Europe, 62% were devout believers, 34% were conventionally religious, and only two of them were skeptics."[24]

What is in conflict, are the two worldviews undergirding the debate on scientific epistemology: naturalism and theism. According to John Lennox, this debate has gone on since the ancient Greeks with philosophers such as the Greek Atomists Democritus and Leucippus embracing materialism and bottom up causation. Conversely, Plato, Socrates and Aristotle believed in transcendence (e.g., there was more than just the material world), and thus believed in top down causation.[25] This debate much like the nominalism/

---

23. Morris, *Men of Science*, loc. 177–306 of 1113.
24. Noll, *When God and Science Meet*, loc. 303–308 of 785.
25. Lennox, *Miracles*, 5–6.

realism debate has been occurring throughout the centuries, within the academy, in one form or another.

However, it is easy to see why the conflict over methods of scientific inquiry can easily spill over into metaphysical issues. As Sir Peter Medawar states: "It's so easy to see the limits of science. It cannot answer the questions of a child: Where am I coming from? What is the meaning of life? Where am I going to?" We need to go outside science for answers to such questions."[26] Scientists and atheists who embrace ontological naturalism will claim that there are no answers outside of science, or the material world, as nothing else exists. As Bertrand Russel once stated: "What Science cannot tell us, mankind cannot know."[27] This is the worldview which gave rise to the modern incarnation of reductionistic materialism known as scientism.[28]

2.2.2 Scientism

Positing metaphysical naturalism (cf. ontological/philosophical naturalism) when engaging in scientific inquiry is the defining characteristic of what is known today as scientism. Proponents of this philosophy, when engaging in scientific inquiry, eliminate the supernatural as a causal possibility *a priori*. In this worldview, all causes by necessity must be physical, material, and reducible.

Scientism is usually traced back to the nineteenth century atheistic philosopher Auguste Comte (1798–1857). Comte is also seen as the father of secular humanism; and a precursor to the logical positivists of the twentieth century. Restricting scientific inquiry to the observable with materialistic presuppositions, Comte redeveloped the ancient worldview of

---

26. Lennox, *Miracles*, 10.

27. Lennox, *Miracles*, 9.

28. Agnostic Paleontologist Steve J. Gould proposed the concept of *non-overlapping magisteria* as a solution to the supposed conflict between science and religion. Briefly stated this concept is that science and religion simply operate in different realms. Facts vs. values. Science attempts to explain the natural world through facts. Religion attempts to give meaning and values. The two are appropriate within their given realms and should not intersect or overlap. Thus, Gould's framework serves as a critique both for the atheist and the evidentialist positions. Another one of Gould's theories, *punctuated equilibrium*, while naturalistic in nature, is also a serious challenge to conventional understandings of Darwinian evolution promoted by various atheists. See Gould, *Rocks of Ages*.

atomism into the modern method of scientism.[29] There are two types of scientism (strong/weak); as well as what is labeled methodological naturalism:

1. Strong scientism—The view that some proposition or theory is true and/or rational to believe if and only if it is a scientific proposition or theory; that is, if and only if it is a well-established scientific proposition or theory that, in turn, depends on its having been successfully formed, tested and used according to appropriate scientific methodology. There are no truths apart from scientific truths, and even if there were, there would be no reason whatever to believe them.[30]

2. Weak scientism—Advocates of weak scientism allow for the existence of truths apart from science and are even willing to grant that they can have some minimal, positive rationality status without the support of science. But advocates of weak scientism still hold that science is the most valuable, most serious and most authoritative sector of human learning. Every other intellectual activity is inferior to science. Further, there are virtually no limits to science. There is no field into which scientific research cannot shed light. To the degree that some issue or belief outside science can be given scientific support or can be reduced to science, to that degree the issue or belief becomes rationally acceptable. Thus we have an intellectual and perhaps even a moral obligation to try to use science to solve problems in other fields that, heretofore, have been untouched by scientific methodology. For example, we should try to solve problems about the mind by the methods of neurophysiology and computer science.[31]

3. Methodological Naturalism—Weak scientism can also be labeled as methodological naturalism. While many trace methodological naturalism all the way back to Thales, it was Robert Pennock who first coined the term in 1984. Unlike strong scientism which posits no divine agency or supernatural realm *a priori* (i.e., ontological naturalism); "methodological naturalism does not deny but rather ignores the supernatural for methodological reasons."[32]

---

29. Geisler, *Big Book Christian Apologetics*, 522–23.
30. Craig and Moreland, *Philosophical Foundations*, 347.
31. Craig and Moreland, *Philosophical Foundations*, 347.
32. Platinga, *Where the Conflict Really Lies*, 169–70.

2.2.3 Science (Scientific Method)

The scientific method is considered to have originated with Galileo, Newton, Claude Bernard and others. The method was first fully developed by Bernard in his seminal text *An Introduction to the Study of Experimental Medicine* (1865). In his text Bernard delineates several methodological principles for the experimental method: 1. Known and unknown. 2. Authority vs. observation. 3. Induction and deduction. 4. Cause and effect. 5. Verification and disproof.[33]

Of importance in Bernard's methodology is the idea of authority versus observation. Bernard states that the observations of the experiment must remain supreme even when they contradict generally accepted theories or are supported by famous scientists.[34] This is of important as Bernard understands the fallibility of science, and that what is accepted as scientific knowledge changes over time.[35]

Today's Scientist, borrowing from this methodology, begin with a question which is currently unanswered by science and thus they intend to experiment into the unknown (step one). Next the scientist researches the available knowledge and formulates a hypothesis (step two). Then the scientist conducts experiments to either verify or reject this hypothesis (step three). Next, they analyze the results of the experiment using inductive and deductive logic (step four). Finally, they repeat the experiment numerous times to achieve greater degrees of confidence in their results (step five).

Additionally, while the scientific method may seem to be firmly rooted in common sense empiricism; there are actually numerous philosophical presuppositions which must be posited in order for the scientific method to be possible. These include:

> (1) The existence of a theory-independent, external world; (2) the orderly nature of the external world; (3) the knowability of the external world; (4) the existence of truth; (5) the laws of logic; (6) the reliability of our cognitive and sensory faculties to serve as truth gatherers and as a source of justified true beliefs in our intellectual

---

33. Bernard, *Experimental Medicine*.
34. Bernard, *Experimental Medicine*, loc. 1088 of 4759.
35. Bernard, *Experimental Medicine*, loc. 989–995 of 4759: Bernard states: "They are only partial and provisional truths which are necessary to us, as steps on which we rest, so as to go on with investigation; they embody only the present state of our knowledge, and consequently they must change with the growth of science, and all the more often when sciences are less advanced in their evolution."

environment; (7) the adequacy of language to describe the world; (8) the existence of values used in science (e.g., "test theories fairly and report test results honestly"); (9) the uniformity of nature and induction; (10) the existence of numbers. [36]

Finally, according to Craig: "There is no such thing as the scientific method, but rather there is a cluster of practices and issues that are used in a variety of contexts and can be loosely called scientific methodologies."[37] What many choose to label as the scientific method is merely a particular methodology known as inductivism.[38] To show this diversity and arbitrariness of scientific methodology Craig constructs an alternative which he labels the seven part eclectic model of the scientific method: "(1) the formation of scientific ideas, (2) the nature of scientific questions and problems, (3) the use of scientific ideas and scientific explanation, (4) the nature of scientific experiments, (5) the testing of scientific ideas (scientific confirmation), (6) the nature of scientific ideas (laws and theories) and (7) the aims and goals of scientific ideas."[39]

2.2.4 Critical Analysis

2.2.4.1 *Science Requires Faith*

An understanding of the distinctions between science and scientism are important for both this study, as well for modern Christian apologetics in general. When the New Atheists or other opponents of religion declare that they are men of reason and science, they are presupposing a particular worldview which is full of numerous ontological and epistemological presuppositions; which must be accepted by faith in the naturalist paradigm. Ian Hutchison muses that scientism is very much like the religion which its opponents claim to despise, as it takes so much of its methodology and various presuppositions by *faith alone* in naturalism.[40]

It is evident that the presuppositions necessary for the scientific method to be possible require an element of faith. Any one of the ten listed presuppositions necessary for the scientific method can be vigorously

---

36. Mooreland and Craig, *Philosophical Foundations*, 348.
37. Mooreland and Craig, *Philosophical Foundations*, 310.
38. Mooreland and Craig, *Philosophical Foundations*, 310.
39. Mooreland and Craig, *Philosophical Foundations*, 313.
40. See Hutchinson, *Monopolizing Knowledge*, loc. 104–112 of 5016.

challenged and there are many more ontological and epistemological issues at play.[41] As William Lane Craig noted when constructing his alternative methodology: "Finally, our investigation of these seven areas of scientific methodology revealed several ways that theological and philosophical issues can enter into the very fabric of scientific methodology."[42]

Ian Hutchinson summarizes the knowledge gained through science as being fallible and *a posteriori* (after the fact). Any knowledge gained requires that the "world has stable coherent characteristics that can be uncovered by a pursuit of reproducibility and clarity. This is a belief that science has validated only *a posteriori*. It finds its confirmation not from prior logical proof, but from the fact that it seems to work rather well."[43] Scientists operating within either theistic or open-minded worldviews are well aware of these presuppositions, as well as the limitations of science.

However, those embracing scientism seek to limit all knowledge to what can be discovered through the scientific method. As Hutchinson concludes: "Scientism's fault does not lie in the mere fact that it is based upon prior unproven commitments. Science and most other areas of endeavor are similarly based. It lies in the pretense that it has no prior commitments, and in the consequent arrogance that it can and will replace all the other subjective disciplines with an objective science."[44]

2.2.4.2 Certainty vs. Clarity

Another common misconception is that science and the scientific method offer certainty. Despite the belief amongst laymen about the absolutes of science, scientists know that little is certain with science: most of science

---

41. Polkinghorne brings up an important distinction between epistemology and ontology. This distinction is important as the scientific method often relies upon empiricism and sense data. Polkinghorne and Beale, *Questions of Truth*, 18: "The need for this choice results from an important philosophical distinction between epistemology and ontology. Epistemology is concerned with what we can know; ontology is concerned with what is actually the case. The two are not necessarily the same, and there is room for philosophical choice and argument about what kind of relationship shall be assumed. How things appear to us might be different from the way they actually are in their true selves. Quantum theory may look indeterministic, but this could be because of a necessary ignorance of all the factors involved rather than the presence of an absolute indeterminacy."

42. Craig and Moreland, *Philosophical Foundations*, 324.

43. Hutchinson, *Monopolizing Knowledge*, loc. 3842–3850 of 5016.

44. Hutchinson, *Monopolizing Knowledge*, loc. 3850–3857 of 5016.

Epistemological Concerns

is based upon probability.[45] Certainty is not even a goal of the scientific method, as it is rarely obtainable. Rather than *certainty*, science seeks to offer *clarity* and degrees of confidence (i.e., certainty) based upon past experimentation.[46] The mere acknowledgement of the presuppositions of the scientific method negate any possibility in certainty. According to Troy Van Voorhis:

> Only in pure mathematics is reason alone enough to produce absolute certainty. In the natural world, things rarely work out so neatly. If I have a hypothesis, there's typically going to be evidence that supports the hypothesis and evidence that goes against the hypothesis. As Richard Feynman once said, in science, "We have found it of paramount importance that in order to progress we must recognize . . . ignorance and leave room for doubt. Scientific knowledge is a body of statements of varying degrees of certainty—some most unsure, some nearly sure, none absolutely certain.[47]

However, varying degrees of certainty and probability are not worthless as they lack certainty. Rather, probability has become a valuable tool in philosophical epistemology, scientific inquiry, and in the philosophy of religion. In a following section on reliabilism, I will posit Robert Audi's *fallible foundationalism* as one such epistemic tool. By using Audi's fallible foundationalism, the evidences for Special Divine Action can be believed through probabilistic reasoning.

2.2.4.3 Correlation vs. Causation

One important concept is the distinction between correlation and causation. As previously shown, most scientific knowledge (and knowledge in general), is based upon probability. Despite the belief amongst laymen about the absolutes of science, scientists know that little is certain with science; most of science is based upon probability.[48] And the findings of science are open to interpretation; a fallible interpretation which is usually done under the prevalent scientific paradigm of the era.[49] This fallibility

---

45. Voorhis, *Certainty*, 4–5.
46. Voorhis, *Certainty*, 4.
47. Voorhis, *Certainty*, 4–5.
48. Voorhis, *Certainty*, 4–5.
49. Voorhis, *Certainty*, 4–5, Van Voorhis further argues: "Even for a theory with no known exceptions, in science one must always be wary—because there's always the

coupled with the necessity of interpretation, opens the door for various errors such as concluding causation when there is merely correlation. For instance, the past belief in spontaneous generation. As Troy Van Voorhis cites: "For example, take the issue of spontaneous generation—the idea that inanimate objects under the right conditions can spontaneously bring forth life. Think, for example, of maggots forming in a bowl of corn meal. For about two thousand years, the dominant scientific interpretation of this fact was that corn meal and air came together to spontaneously make maggots."[50]

This is a classic example of confusing correlation with causation. The scientists wrongly believed that the mixture of air and cornmeal caused maggots (causation). The truth was that there was only a *correlation* between cornmeal, air and maggots. The causal factor was the flies laying eggs in the cornmeal. It can reasonably be assumed that today, there are many similar scientific beliefs which are making the same error and will be disproven by future generations of scientists.

2.3 RELIABILISM

Paul Moser defines epistemology as: "An account of knowledge. Within the discipline of philosophy, epistemology is the study of the nature of knowledge and justification: in particular, the study of (a) the defining components, (b) the substantive conditions or sources, and (c) the limits of knowledge and justification."[51] According to Moser the debate has traditionally been over "the analysis of knowledge and justification, the sources of knowledge and justification (in the case, for instance, of rationalism vs. empiricism), and the status of skepticism about knowledge and justification."[52]

Given the preceding discussion on the conflict between science and scientism, it is of importance to know that philosophers rarely construct epistemologies seeking certainty. Rather, the discipline of epistemology

---

chance that when more data comes in, the model will turn out to be wrong. And classical mechanics will give way to quantum mechanics. Newton will be followed by Einstein. The reality is that science has made great contributions to human knowledge, but not any significant contributions to human certainty."

50. Voorhis, *Certainty*, 7.
51. Moser, *Oxford Handbook of Epistemology*, loc. 115 of 15522.
52. Moser, *Oxford Handbook of Epistemology*, loc. 115 of 15522.

seeks a reasonable degree of certainty; based upon probability. This is very similar to the current status of scientific inquiries as well. Foundational epistemologies seek to construct systems for checking the probability of beliefs based upon some form of foundational knowledge. Robert Audi develops such a system in his text: *Epistemology: A Contemporary Introduction to the Theory of Knowledge* (1998).

2.3.1 Robert Audi's Fallible Foundationalism

The problem of infinite regress in epistemology (e.g., *Agrippa's Trilemma*), is an important issue in the area of apologetics, as skepticism is one of the key tools used by opponents. Simply stated, every belief has to be justified by another belief so that when asked the question: "how do we know what is true," we can provide truth for our knowledge. Unfortunately, that proof can also be challenged *ad infinitum*; and thus, we have an infinite regress.[53] While such a line of inquiry may or may not be done in good faith, it is nevertheless something which Christian philosophers, theologians, and apologists must overcome.

Christian philosopher Robert Audi's answer to the problem of *epistemic regress*[54] is what he labels as *fallibilistic foundationalism*. Audi believes that we have four conclusions to the problem of regress:

1. Infinite regress.
2. Circularity.
3. Belief that is not knowledge.[55]
4. Belief that is knowledge (justified belief).

It is only in the fourth possibility (justified belief), that we can have knowledge. While the previous ones do not necessarily end in error; the results are not trustworthy or independent enough to rise to the level of justified

---

53. Fumerton, "Foundationalist Theories," lines 1–59.

54. Audi defines the problem of regress: "Could all my knowledge be inferential? Imagine that this is possible by virtue of an infinite epistemic regress—roughly, an infinite series of knowings, each based inferentially on the next" (Audi, "Contemporary Foundationalism," 5).

55. Audi, "Contemporary Foundationalism," 8, defines this as: "A belief which is not knowledge, has been at best rarely affirmed." This does not mean that the belief is false, but rather that the belief does not have enough confirmation to rise to the level of justified belied.

belief. Audi states: "The fourth possibility is that epistemic chains that originate with knowledge end in non-inferential knowledge: knowledge not inferentially based on further knowledge (or further justified belief). That knowledge, in turn, is apparently based in experience."[56]

Audi's fallible foundationalism allows for the possibility of error as it is ultimately based upon probability. This allowance for error is in contrast to the more classical foundationalisms such as those rooted in Cartesian reductionism. These foundationalisms seek to establish basic beliefs (undoubtable), and to build knowledge layer upon layer based upon these beliefs. For Audi, and other foundationalists, this means reliance upon the axiomatic argument (adoption of some presupposition as ontological bedrock).[57, 58] I will next examine and evaluate Audi's fallible foundationalism as a means of acquiring justifiable religious belief.

In modern philosophy, using some form of foundationalism, and applying it to metaphysical questions, places the philosopher in the minority. Decades, if not centuries, of skepticism have held claims of religious knowledge and belief to a higher standard than what is used for other types of knowledge. What is demanded of religious claims is *infallible proof*. Audi's foundationalism does not rise to this level, nor does he believe that it must, in order to have *justified religious belief*. Audi states:

> Infallibility may be a reasonable ideal for proof, conceived as decisively demonstrating a conclusion from rock-solid premises, such as self-evident truths or, on the empirical side, propositions about the believer's immediate consciousness. For one cannot decisively prove something—or demonstrate it, to use a term that sometimes has wider scope—from insecure premises, or by making merely inductive and hence fallible steps from even the most trustworthy premises. But why should proof be our standard of the kind of justification (or even for a kind of certainty) appropriate to knowledge?[59]

Thus, for Audi, knowledge does not have to rise to the level of inerrant in order to be knowledge. Later in the text, Audi will argue that even scientific

---

56. Audi, "Contemporary Foundationalism," 8–9: Audi gives as an example of intuitive knowledge the ability to know if person A appears to be shorter than person B. This knowledge is based ultimately upon experience.

57. Audi, "Contemporary Foundationalism," 1.

58. Audi, *Epistemology*, 206–13.

59. Audi, *Epistemology*, 386.

knowledge (often held in high regard by skeptics); is usually quite fallible. Audi's standards for where we get knowledge from are less pretentious than the high reason so often debated in the academy. Audi also believes that we can obtain knowledge from our senses, our memories, and the testimony of others. Audi states: "Once we have beliefs directly grounded in one of the five common sources of non-inferential knowledge and justification—perception, memory, consciousness, reason, and, secondarily but indispensably, testimony—we are in a position to extend whatever justification and knowledge we then have."[60]

Audi believes that we can use the empirical knowledge derived from our senses in combination with our reason to gain other knowledge through reason *a priori*. For instance, in chapter 5 he uses the analogy that we can deduce though reason *a priori* that if we can see three various trees, we can know their comparative heights through reason and experience. This usage of reason and experience in obtaining knowledge is very similar to Kant's *synthetic a priori*. Audi states:

> That if the spruce is taller than the maple and the maple is taller than the apple tree then the spruce is taller than the apple. This belief is as natural, and would be no less difficult to resist when I vividly consider its propositional content than my belief that there is something blue before me when I squarely see the spruce. Clearly, this a priori belief is also justified, and it constitutes knowledge.[61]

2.3.2 Scientific Knowledge (Probability)

For Audi, *justifiable religious belief* is epistemically very similar to scientific knowledge. Audi states:

> Commonly, what we call scientific knowledge is regarded by scientists as needing refinement and as possibly mistaken. Quite properly, their attitude is fallibilistic. If scientists accept fallibilism regarding scientific beliefs—the view that these beliefs may be mistaken and the accompanying rejection of dogmatic attitudes—they nonetheless tend to hold a kind of objectivism: the view that there is an objective method for ascertaining whether beliefs about the world are true, that is (roughly speaking), a method which can be used by any competent investigator and tends to yield the same

---

60. Audi, *Epistemology*, 381.
61. Audi, *Epistemology*, 380.

results when properly applied by different competent investigators to the same problem.[62]

However, sceptics have long held that those proposing religious knowledge should have to "prove" their beliefs. Thus, they hold theistic claims to a higher standard of proof than science itself![63] This sentiment is wrong on two accounts according to Audi:

1. Scientific knowledge is usually inductive and the scientists do not think they have "proven" anything, they accept fallibilism.[64]

2. Accepting something as true is not necessarily "proving" it as true.[65]

Most of us readily accept testimonial knowledge from others without having to prove every assertion as being true.

2.3.3 Justifiable Religious Belief

Once Audi has developed a fallible foundationalism (which allows for justified beliefs), he then applies his foundationalism to the issue of *justifiable religious belief*. Audi first summarizes the skeptical stance taken by many philosophers about proving the existence of God. Audi states: "And if, as many philosophers think, there are no cogent arguments for God's existence and, in addition, God is not directly knowable through the experiential or rational sources that ground knowledge, how can there be knowledge of God?"[66]

Audi strongly rejects the premises of this argument on several grounds. For instance, Audi does not see any incompatibility with his framework of knowledge and theistic questions.[67] Additionally, Audi believes that one need not adopt a foundationalist model as knowledge about God can be gained in the coherentist model of epistemology as well.[68]

Audi's foundationalism does reject the evidentialist position since it usually necessitates infallible proof based upon propositional knowledge. Audi believes that propositions cannot be stated either *a priori* or *a posteriori* inferring God's existence logically (e.g., classical apologetics); due

62. Audi, *Epistemology*, 303.

63. This is a very important point and is often the lynchpin of the atheist/theist debate: the level of proof and the burden of proof.

64 Audi, *Epistemology*, 385.

65. Audi, *Epistemology*, 388.

66. Audi, *Epistemology*, 384.

67. Audi, *Epistemology*, 319.

68. Audi, *Epistemology*, 319.

to the design of the universe.⁶⁹ He further argues against the evidentialist approach by stating that:

> If, however, it is even possible that there is an all-powerful (omnipotent) God, then that God could create such direct theistic knowledge. If there can be such knowledge, then one form of what is called evidentialism is mistaken, namely, evidentialism about theistic knowledge, the view that knowledge of God is impossible except on the basis of adequate (propositional) evidence.⁷⁰

This however does not mean that Audi rejects all evidentialist approaches, just those relying on propositional knowledge. As Audi later states: "One or another kind of religious experience might provide non-inferential grounds of justification, or of knowledge, or of both, somewhat in the way familiar kinds of perception do."⁷¹

While Audi's argument does carry considerable weight, I think that he is boxing in the evidentialist position too much. He should allow for arguments made for God's existence based upon fulfilled prophecies or modern miracles. Usually, such arguments do not ultimately conclude in infallible proofs, but rather in strong probabilities based upon evidences, methodological reasoning, and statistical inferencing. It is for this reason that I believe Audi's foundationalist system for justified religious belief can be adopted for this study.

2.4 EVIDENTIAL APOLOGETICS

There are numerous types of Christian apologetics including: classical, presuppositional, scientific and evidential. By far the most commonly known arguments come from classical apologetics (e.g., the ontological argument, the cosmological argument and the teleological argument). Lists of famous classical apologists include R. C. Sproul, William Lane Craig, and Norman Geisler. However, in recent years, there has been a resurgence in the area of evidential apologetics due to the popularity of Lee Strobel's *The Case for Christ* (1998) and Gary Habermas' *The Case for the Resurrection of Jesus* (2004).⁷²,⁷³

---

69. Audi, *Epistemology*, 319.
70. Audi, *Epistemology*, 320.
71. Audi, *Epistemology*, 385.
72. Habermas and Licona, *Resurrection of Jesus*.
73. Habermas's minimalist facts approach is unique as he is able to argue for the

Evidentialists have tended to be evangelical scholars leaning towards cessationism. Thus, they have based the bulk of their arguments on the Bible only. Lee Strobel, Josh McDowell and others have written numerous texts defending the biblical witness of Scripture. However, very little has been written from an evidential perspective about the ongoing signs and wonders throughout church history and being witnessed today. In short, an evidential Renewal apologetic is currently lacking; thus, the need for this book!

Norman Geisler argues that although there are numerous approaches to apologetics and numerous interrelated arguments, the whole of apologetics can be summarized in the following twelve propositions:

1. Truth about reality is knowable.
2. The opposite of true is false.
3. It is true that the theistic God exists.
4. If God exists then miracles are possible.
5. Miracles can be used to confirm a message from God.
6. The New Testament is historically reliable.
7. The New Testament says Jesus claimed to be God.
8. Jesus's claim to be God was miraculously confirmed by:
    A. his fulfillment of numerous prophecies about himself.
    B. his sinless and miraculous life.
    C. his prediction and accomplishment of his resurrection.
9. Therefore, Jesus is God.
10. Whatever Jesus (who is God) teaches is true.
11. Jesus taught that the Bible is the Word of God.
12. Therefore, it is true that the Bible is the Word of God and that anything opposed to it is false.[74]

Classical apologists often use a two-step approach in their arguments. They first argue for the existence of God based upon various philosophical arguments. Next, they argue for the truth claims of Christianity based upon the biblical texts. These truth claims help to form the Christian worldview.

---

truth of the Resurrection based only upon facts which are agreed upon by Christians and skeptics alike.

74. Geisler, *Christian Apologetics*, 293–94.

Finally, these arguments are used to show why Christianity is unique and the one true religion. Proponents of this approach see the two-step approach as vital to the Christian apologetic: "As Sproul, Gerstner, and Lindsley argue, "Miracles cannot prove God. God, as a matter of fact, alone can prove miracles. That is, only on the prior evidence that God exists is a miracle even possible."[75]

Conversely, evidential apologists argue based upon a one-step approach. They argue by citing the truth claims of miracles within the bible as evidences of God. As Steven Cowan summarizes:

> Miracles do not presuppose God's existence (as most contemporary classical apologists assert) but can serve as one sort of evidence for God. This method is fairly eclectic in its use of various positive evidences and negative critiques, utilizing both philosophical and historical arguments. Yet it tends to focus chiefly on the legitimacy of accumulating various historical and other inductive arguments for the truth of Christianity.[76]

2.4.1 Evidences for Special Divine Action

Throughout history, the overwhelming majority of people have believed in Special Divine Action (SDA). Today, the majority of people in the world, including the west, believe in SDA. It is only a small minority of people (mostly academics) who relegate belief in SDA to the realm of the ignorant and deluded. The prevalent worldview in western academia is one which has been greatly influenced by the enlightenment. Reductionistic thinking in addition to philosophical presuppositions such as secularism, naturalism, and cessationism are all obstacles which must be overcome in any scholarly discussions on SDA. However, the dismissal of claims of SDA in the third world by western scholars can easily denigrate into a form of Eurocentric elitism according to Keener.[77] The philosophical presuppositions which scholars posit must be understood and critically evaluated throughout any inquiry on SDA. This will help ensure that the testimonies of reliable witnesses are not discounted as mere tales by members of savage cultures as argued by Hume.

---

75. Cowan, *Five Views on Apologetics*, loc. 211–224 of 7207.
76. Cowan, *Five Views on Apologetics*, loc. 224–240 of 7207.
77. Keener, *Miracles*, 166.

For the good faith sceptic, the question remains: "what constitutes evidence for Special Divine Action?" For this study, the Vatican Criteria listed in chapter 1 will be used to evaluate modern claims of SDA. In the next two sections, I will broaden the argument to show both the reasoning behind such criteria, as well as some other philosophical issues which come into play in the evaluation of SDA claims.

2.4.2 Causation vs. Correlation (Odds Against Chance Alone)

Many cases of alleged SDA have to be dismissed since the cure could have been due to naturalistic causes. This does not mean that the healings were not supernatural in origin; rather, that plausible naturalistic explanations make them not of apologetical significance. It is by focusing only on untreatable illnesses or instantaneous healings that arguments of correlation and other naturalistic explanations are no longer valid. SDA can be seen as causal in the cases where there are no naturalistic explanations, and which include the element of prayer.

Claims of Special Divine Action (in healing miracles) are almost always accompanied by prayer. These prayers can come from the suffering person themselves, or from another Christian. The element of prayer is essential in judging if the claim is truly a case of SDA or merely a coincidental cure via natural causes. Healings without prayer can be dismissed more easily as being due to some unknown scientific explanation (God of the gaps objection). However, unexplainable healings which occur simultaneously with prayer more strongly suggest that the element of prayer was the causal factor for Special Divine Action. God is answering a prayer with a miracle.

2.4.3 Certainty vs. Probability (Supernatural Is Most Likely Explanation)

As shown in the previous sections on science vs. scientism; science is largely based upon probability, with certainty being an unobtainable ideal. Probability also factors heavily into the philosophy of religion as many arguments are based upon probability. For instance, Josh McDowell's argument from fulfilled prophecy in *Evidence that Demands a Verdict* (chapter 11), is based on eleven biblical prophecies about the destruction or refounding of ancient cities. McDowell shows the historical evidence that these

Epistemological Concerns

prophecies were fulfilled centuries after their pronouncement. Statisticians have concluded that the odds of such occurrences being fulfilled by chance alone are infinitesimal; thus, it is most reasonable to believe that they occurred by acts of God. As McDowell cites:

> Listing eight prophecies which we have considered and three by Stoner, the probabilities of their fulfillment are:
>
> Tyre 1 in 7.5×10 to the 7th power.
> Samaria 1 in 4×10 to the 4th power.
> Gaza and Ashkelon 1 in 1.2×10 to the 4th power.
> Jericho 1 in 2×10 to the 5th power.
> The Golden Gate 1 in 10 to the 3rd power.
> Zion Plowed 1 in 10 to the 2nd power.
> Jerusalem Enlarged 1 in 8×10 to the 10th power.
> Palestine 1 in 2×10 5th power.
> Moab and Ammon 1 in 10 to the 3rd power.
> Edom 1 in 10 to the 4th power.
> Babylon 1 in 5×10 to the 9th power.
>
> The probability of these 11 prophecies coming true, if written in human wisdom, is now found by multiplying all of these probabilities together, and the result is 1 in 5.76×10 to the 59th power.[78]

Such arguments can be challenged based upon their methodology and conclusions. However, what emerges, is that it is possible to make arguments for Special Divine Action based upon probability. If the conclusion is that SDA is more probable than not; then an apologetical argument has been formed![79] This methodology reflects a significant current trend in the philosophy of religion. According to Jake Chandler:

> Of the numerous approaches to the philosophy of rational belief, it is the probabilistic framework that has arguably proven to be the most fruitful to date and remains the dominate approach in contemporary philosophy of science and epistemology. In particular, a body of research carried out under the heading of Bayesian confirmation theory has, over the last 50 years or so, applied the tools of probability theory to deliver some extremely promising insights into the nature and logic of evidential support.[80]

---

78. McDowell, *Evidence Demands a Verdict*, 318–19.
79. This methodological principle is foundational for this study!
80. Chandler and Harrison, *Probability Philosophy of Religion*, 1.

2.5 OTHER CONCERNS

2.5.1 God of the Gaps

The phrase "God of the gaps" is a derisive phrase used to label theistic arguments which commit the logical fallacy of *appeal to ignorance*.[81] According to Eric Metaxas, the term was coined by the evangelist and scientist Henry Drummond in the nineteenth century.[82] These types of arguments see something unexplainable in nature and conclude that the explanation must be supernatural (i.e., God).[83] In the past, a large percentage of sicknesses and healings were attributed to the supernatural, as science lacked the ability to explain their causes.

Today, this phenomenon is far less pronounced as the vast majority of sicknesses and healings have verifiable, naturalistic causes. As natural science has advanced, there are less and less scientifically unexplainable natural phenomena. Thus, what was once a large area of unknowable science (left up to supernatural explanations), can now been seen as a much smaller area. It is for this reason, that many atheists and apologists alike, believe that God of the gaps arguments should not be used within apologetics. As Troy Van Voorhis states: "The key fallacy at work here is that God can only exist in those phenomena that science cannot explain, that the expansion of science necessarily squeezes God into smaller and smaller boxes. But the truth is that God is not just the God of the gaps, but the God of everything."[84]

Critics of *intelligent design*[85] often label it as a God of the gaps argument. However, such critics are themselves committing the exact same fallacy (appeal to ignorance) by assuming that all phenomena have naturalistic explanations. They are expanding empirical science outside of its natural limits and are instead engaging in metaphysics! Positing metaphysical naturalism as an *a priori* (as a means of filling the gaps in natural science);

---

81. The appeal to ignorance fallacy states that a proposition is either assumed to be true or false until proven otherwise. The main rhetorical purpose of this fallacy is to deceptively shift the burden of proof onto the other side within the debate.

82. Metaxas, *Miracles*, 32.

83. Ratzsch and Koperski, "Teleological Arguments," lines 16–23.

84. Voorhis, *Certainty*, 3.

85. Intelligent design is the argument that the universe is far too complex to not have a creator. Proponents often analogize that for the universe to have come into existence by mere chance would be like a tornado hitting a junk yard and creating a 747 jet airplane. For a more detailed explanation see Kennedy, *Why I Believe*, 45–60.

is just as much of an *appeal to ignorance* as it is to posit God! Rather than committing these fallacies, scientists and theologians must remain agnostic on the gaps within the natural sciences. Their conclusions on SDA should be based upon evidence, not speculation.

2.5.2 Confirmation Bias

Critics of Special Divine Action often allege that testimonials from Christians are merely examples of confirmation bias. The *God of the gaps* critique is largely an attack on this phenomenon. However, both proponents and sceptics of Special Divine Action need to be aware of confirmation biases in both scientific research as well as theological inquiry. Positing either metaphysical/ontological naturalism or even methodological naturalism will lead to examples of confirmation bias on the part of the sceptics. As Troy Van Voorhis notes: "The secret to being a good scientist is to recognize your biases and leave them outside the lab when you come in so that you can perform objective testing. And in this respect, atheism doesn't provide any particular advantage or disadvantage. It's just another bias you need to check at the door."[86, 87]

Proponents of SDA must be sure to follow a rigid methodology such as the Vatican Criteria when evaluating possible instances of SDA. Under such criteria the vast majority of possible occurrences of SDA are either eliminated as having plausible naturalistic explanations; or not being of apologetical significance.[88] However, following the criteria will ensure that they themselves are not guilty of confirmation bias. While confirmed acts of SDA will point towards a theistic conclusion, they are not absolute proof. As Polkinghorne states: "The Creator has not filled creation with items stamped "made by God." God's existence is not self-evident in some totally unambiguous and undeniable way."[89, 90]

---

86. Voorhis, *Certainty*, 3.

87. Atheists are very prone to this error as they tend to view scientism as being value neutral—a default worldview.

88. See Cranston, *A Protestant Looks at Lourdes*, loc. 168–175 of 385.

89. Polkinghorne and Beale, *Questions of Truth*, 11.

90. This is a key point. This is why the evidential apologetical arguments must be made based upon probabilities, not absolutes.

2.5.3 Open vs. Closed Universe

Within the enlightenment the tendency was to see the universe as closed and mechanistic. This led to a view of the universe as being essentially like a clock and reducible to its smallest components, atoms. R. C. Sproul states:

> Among the ideas that have shaped Western culture, one of the most significant is the idea of a closed, mechanistic universe. This view of the world has persisted for a couple of hundred years and has had tremendous influence in shaping how people understand the way life is lived out. I would argue that in the secular world, the dominant idea is that we live in a universe that is closed to any kind of intrusion from outside, a universe that runs purely by mechanical forces and causes. In a word, the issue for modern man is causality.[91]

Physicists such as Polkinghorne believe that the universe is more cloudlike than clock like as there is a lot of space within the material at the atomic and quantum levels. There is also a lot of indeterminacy at these levels. Today few scientist/physicists believe that the universe is a closed system, and most have adopted the open view. This adoption of the open-model universe is of importance to the discussion of Special Divine Action, as only within a closed universe model can actions from outside be totally discounted.[92] Instead, the universe is seen as essentially flat and expanding as expanding as astrophysicist and Christian apologist Hugh Ross notes:

> Few people yet realize that current cosmological research demonstrates a physical universe with no spatial center. All the matter and energy of the universe reside on the three-dimensional surface of the expanding four-dimensional universe. Just as all Earth's cities reside on the planet's two-dimensional surface and none can be identified as geographically central to all others, likewise none of the galaxies, stars, and planets hold the center position on the cosmic 3-D surface.[93]

Additionally, physicists have to admit that very little is known about many aspects of the universe. Current theories such as quantum mechanics and general relativity are at the moment beyond reconciliation. According to Polkinghorne:

---

91. Sproul, *Does God Control Everything*, 5.
92. Metaxas, *Miracles*, 27–28.
93. Ross, "Anthropic Principle," lines 61–66.

EPISTEMOLOGICAL CONCERNS

But the current understanding of cosmology is surely not the last word. It is now known that only 4% of the matter and energy in the universe is made of what we understand as matter, and most of the universe seems, on current understandings, to be "dark matter" (22%) and "dark energy" (74%) about which we know very little. In addition, no one knows how to reconcile quantum mechanics with general relativity. The string theory has certainly inspired some elegant and deep mathematics, but it looks increasingly unlikely that it will yield good new physics without some fundamental new insights, and many of the speculations that have emerged from it have a rather desperate feel.[94]

What physicists have long sought is a *Unified Theory of Everything*.[95] However, this may be impossible, in part, due to *Gödel's Incompleteness Theorem*. Gödel's Incompleteness Theorem is two parts. Part one states that within any given axiomatic mathematical system containing arithmetic, there will be certain problems which cannot be either proven or falsified. Part two states that the axiomatic/mathematical system itself cannot be used to prove the consistency of itself.[96] According to Panu Raatikainen, Gödel's incompleteness theorem has had a "great impact on the philosophy of mathematics and logic."[97]

Given this complication, most physicists including Stephen Hawking believe that a Unified Theory of Everything which explains everything as necessarily and not contingently true; is not possible given the limits of science and mathematics in light of Gödel's theorem.[98] In Hawking's text *The Grand Design* (2012), Hawking admits the futility of developing such a theory. Craig Callender summarizes the current impasse:

---

94. Polkinghorne and Beale, *Questions of Truth*, 40.

95. A "theory of everything" was extensively and unsuccessfully worked on by Albert Einstein. Stephen Hawking was initially optimistic stating that there was a 50% chance of having a unified "theory of everything" (e.g., M-Theory) by the year 2000. However, in recent years he is far less optimistic of the prospect. See Callender, "No Theory of Everything." Hawking' current version of M-Theory theory (which stretches the bounds of credulity) is that there are an infinite number of multi-universes existing parallel in time (which is not constant) and a reality which is "model dependent." Models which provide widows into an infinite number of realities which exist simultaneously in parallel; but are dependent on the perceiver See Hawking, *Grand Design*.

96. Raatikainen, "Gödel's Incompleteness Theorems," lines 1–7.

97. Raatikainen, "Gödel's Incompleteness Theorems, lines 7–8.

98. Polkinghorne, *Questions of Truth*, 51–52.

This multiplicity of distinct theories prompts the authors to declare that the only way to understand reality is to employ a philosophy called "model-dependent realism". Having declared that "philosophy is dead", the authors unwittingly develop a theory familiar to philosophers since the 1980s, namely "perspectivalism." This radical theory holds that there doesn't exist, even in principle, a single comprehensive theory of the universe. Instead, science offers many incomplete windows onto a common reality, one no more "true" than another. In the authors' hands this position bleeds into an alarming anti-realism: not only does science fail to provide a single description of reality, they say, there is no theory-independent reality at all. If either stance is correct, one shouldn't expect to find a final unifying theory like M-theory —only a bunch of separate and sometimes overlapping windows.[99]

Rather, as Nicholas Beale concludes: "A grand unified theory isn't really a "theory of everything" in the sense of predicting everything. Gödel certainly shows that there are limits to mathematical and scientific knowledge even within the domains in which you would expect them to apply. But no wise philosopher claims that science can fully explain everything."[100] This is the fundamental error of scientism and atheism!

2.5.4 Nominalism vs. Realism

The nominalism/realism debate has been ongoing since at least the time of the ancient Greek philosophers (e.g., 500 BC). Some theologians such as John MacArthur say that it has existed since the Garden of Eden. MacArthur labels the serpent as the world's first postmodernist; as he twisted the meaning of words to get Adam and Eve to eat the apple.[101] The sophists of ancient Greece can be seen as the ancient forerunners of today's postmodernists. When debating Socrates, the sophists were defending the nominalist position: that concepts such as justice, the good and other universals were man made and did not point towards anything universal or transcendent.[102] This of course is completely contrary to Christianity and the biblical witness.

99. Stenger, "Hawking and the Multiverse," lines 14–24.
100. Polkinghorne, *Questions of Truth*, 51–52.
101. See MacArthur, *The Truth War*.
102. For an in-depth treatment of sophistry, read the dialogues on justice contained in Plato's *Republic* wherein the sophists such as Thrasymachus proclaim the

The current manifestation of nominalism is usually seen in the form of postmodernism. While postmodernism is difficult to define, as proponents often eschew such labeling, there are nevertheless several key defining characteristics of postmodernism. For instance, Richard B. Davis defines postmodern theology as a rejection of: "(a) the correspondence theory of truth; (b) the referential use of language; and (c) a person's ability to access reality directly, unmediated by conceptual or linguistic schemes."[103, 104]

Theologians holding to a postmodern worldview can best fit the label of nominalists as they believe that the language, logic, and the very message of scripture are manmade artifices. Thus, there are no transcendent truths to be gleaned from scripture. There is no truth, only truths to be discovered "in community." Consequently, in this worldview, there is no normative truth; only truths of particularity.[105]

These distinctions are of importance to this book as it will be shown in later chapters that many of the proponents of non-literal interpretations of scripture (e.g., historical criticism), and the critics of Special Divine Action, presuppose a nominalist worldview. Many such as Hume are desists; and others such as Hawking and Dawkins are atheists.[106] Thus, an understanding of this debate is foundational for understanding the philosophical presuppositions held by sceptics of SDA.

---

nominalist position: "Justice is nothing else than the interest of the stronger." See Plato, *The Republic*, 11.

103. Davis, "Can There Be," 111.

104. J. P. Moreland gives a more specific definition of the four degrees of postmodernism. Moreland states: "In what follows, I shall distinguish four grades of postmodern involvement from most to least extreme. In order, those grades are ontic, alethic, epistemic, and axiological/religious (a.k.a. nonempirical) postmodernism. In speaking of 'grades of postmodern involvement' I am referring to what we might call 'degrees of ingression.' What I have in mind is this. The more deeply ingressed or strongly graded one's postmodernism is, the more pervasive is the impact of postmodern ideas throughout one's worldview. More specifically, with rare exceptions, ontic postmodernism entails the other three (if one is an ontic postmodernist, then if one is consistent, one will also be a postmodernist of the other sorts); alethic postmodernism entails epistemic and axiological/religious postmodernism; and epistemic postmodernism entails axiological/religious postmodernism" (Moreland, "Four Degrees," loc. 397–404 of 6393).

105. See Erickson et al., *Reclaiming the Center*.

106. One of Hume's lesser known arguments against miracles is contained in his essay "Natural History of Religion" (1757). Hume argues (within the deistic framework) that since God is like a clockmaker, it would be contradictory that he would intervene within creation to cause a miracle to occur.

Postmodernists (nominalists) will often mischaracterize anything which is not postmodern as a remnant of modernism (reductionistic). The *classical Christian worldview* rejects both postmodernism and modernism. It rejects the relativity and nihilism of postmodernism. It also rejects the materialism, secularism, and reductionism of modernism as well.

Traditional orthodox Christianity sees Scripture as a way of acquiring knowledge. The Christian worldview is closely aligned with what is called philosophical realism. Philosophical realism can be defined as the belief that actual reality can be known. This is of importance for this study as most scientists can be described as philosophical realists. According to Polkinghorne:

> The philosophical stance that seeks to align epistemology and ontology as closely as possible is called realism. Scientists are instinctively realists. They believe that what we know should be taken to be a reliable guide to what is the case. It is difficult to see why one should go to all the trouble involved in scientific research if one did not believe that it was telling us what the world is actually like.[107]

While the Christian worldview does believe that truth is ascertainable and is contained within Scripture, it also recognizes that there are beliefs which are ineffable (beyond language, logic, and reason). This truth is similar to Wittgenstein's ladder which is used and discarded once the limits of logic and truth are reached.[108] If the Christian worldview is to be defined most accurately within a philosophical system; it would be the *Via Antiqua* of Augustine, Aquinas and Anselm.[109] Seeing a timeless transcendence to the Christian faith which crosses all epochs and geographical boundaries is one of the implications of this worldview. Having some access to an actual reality which actually exists is another. Understanding that reason and logic have limits, that there are ineffable truths, but that these truths are not irrational, but rather are *suprarational,* would be a third implication.

---

107. Polkinghorne, *Questions of Truth*, 19.

108. Wittgenstein's final proposition (6.54) states: "My propositions are elucidatory in this way: he who understands me finally recognizes them as senseless, when he has climbed out through them, on them, over them. (He must so to speak throw away the ladder, after he has climbed up on it.) He must surmount these propositions; then he sees the world rightly. Whereof one cannot speak, thereof one must be silent" (Wittgenstein, *Philisophico Logicio Tractatus,* loc. 2640 of 2652).

109. For an in-depth discussion on this worldview, see Hahn and Wiker, *Politicizing the Bible.*

Within this worldview, reason and access to truth are presupposed. However, there is also that element of the universe which is ineffable; beyond reason. This is where the concepts of mystery, human finitude, and faith enter into the equation. The heart of the Via Antiqua is the usage of word analogies or "growing words." It is by the usage of these words that concepts such as matter and form become apparent via analogy.[110]

2.5.5 The Kantian Wall

According to R. C. Sproul, Immanuel Kant's *The Critique of Pure Reason*[111] (1781), is a watershed moment for philosophy. Kant's synthesis of rationalism and empiricism overcame the extreme skepticism of David Hume.[112] But, most importantly, Kant's categories of *noumena* (objects of thought) and *phenomena* (objects of sense perception) created a *wall of separation* which completely altered the function of philosophy until today. Previous to Kant, questions about metaphysics and epistemology dominated philosophical inquiry (noumenal realm). After Kant, questions about history, anthropology, and linguistic analysis have been the dominate focus (phenomenal realm).[113]

Kant was not an extreme sceptic, his motivations were not to destroy knowledge, but rather, to restore the use of reason as a means of acquiring knowledge. David Hume's extreme skepticism and empiricism is what Kant famously said: "awoke me from my dogmatic slumber."[114] Kant's primary accomplishment was the development of *synthetic a priori* knowledge. Simply stated, this is knowledge which can be known ahead of time, through reason, but based upon prior experience.

One common illustration of synthetic *a priori* knowledge is the second half of a football game. If one has watched other sports such as basketball and has also watched the first half of a football game; then they will be able to use reason to conclude that the second half of the game will follow the rules and conventions of the first half. This conclusion will be reached through reason, and experience, *a priori* (before the fact).

---

110. For a fuller discussion on the Via Antiqua and the Via Moderna, see Hahn and Wiker, *Politicizing the Bible*.
111. See Kant, *The Critique of Pure Reason*.
112. Sproul, *Consequences of Ideas*, loc. 1591–1595 of 3097.
113. Sproul, *Consequences of Ideas*, loc. 1812 of 3097.
114. Kant, *Prolegomena Future Metaphysics*, 4.

However, Kant limits synthetic *a priori* knowledge to the phenomenal realm; that which we can experience through our senses. In the noumenal realm (objects of thought), Kant places God, freedom, the soul, and the object (i.e., the thing in itself: *Ding an sich*). These are the very subjects of metaphysical inquiry. By placing God in the noumenal realm, Kant is declaring not that God does not exist, rather, that we cannot know of his existence through reason.[115]

Since the establishment of the Kantian wall, philosophers have abandoned many areas of philosophy as they see their inquiries as pointless; due to an inability to scale the Kantian wall and reach ontological bedrock. R. C. Sproul has stated that due to this dilemma, most philosophers no longer do philosophy, rather they merely examine the tools of philosophy.[116]

Kierkegaard and Schopenhauer are two philosophers who have attempted to overcome Kant's wall. Kierkegaard's solution is a "leap of faith" over the wall towards God. Schopenhauer's "will" (i.e., idealism and mysticism) calls for a plowing under the wall via mystical knowledge and insight. However, as Sproul mentions, it is the Bible and church tradition that gives the best answers to Kant's wall. Sproul states:

> Most important for Kant's role in the history of philosophy, he includes God in the noumenal realm. God, according to Kant, can never be perceived. He is not part of the sense manifold. The same limits that apply to our knowledge of things-in-themselves and our knowledge of the self apply to God. These are all part of the noumenal or metaphysical realm, about which knowledge is suspect. It is the phenomenal realm, not the noumenal realm, that is the arena of scientific inquiry. The idea that God cannot be known by direct sense experience is not a novel idea in either philosophy or theology. The classic debate between natural theology and Kantian skepticism relates to the question of whether God can be known mediately through the phenomenal world. Thomas Aquinas, for example, insists that God (the noumenal) is known by and through the phenomenal. Aquinas argues this point from the

---

115. By eliminating rational arguments for God's existence Kant is said to have made room for faith. See Sproul, *Consequences of Ideas*, loc. 1591–1595 of 3097. Additionally, Kant's argument in the *Critique of Practical Reason* (1788) is that a belief in God is necessary as a practical matter as there must be an ultimate judge and judgement for our ethics to have any basis. See Kant, *The Critique of Practical Reason*.

116. Sproul further states: "In one sense the rise of linguistic analysis, like the waving of white flags, signals philosophy's metaphysical surrender to defeat" (Sproul, *Consequences of Ideas*, loc. 2744 of 3097).

New Testament, citing a passage from Paul: "What may be known of God is manifest in them, for God has shown it to them. For since the creation of the world His invisible attributes are clearly seen, being understood by the things that are made, even His eternal power and Godhead" (Rom. 1:19-20). Paul argues that, although God is "invisible" or imperceivable, nevertheless he is "seen" and "known." Paul declares not that God is seen directly through sense perception but that he is perceived in and through the created order. For Paul the noumenal can be and is known through the phenomenal. If Kant is correct in his critique, then Paul is wrong. Conversely, if Paul is correct in his assertion, then Kant is wrong. Both cannot be right. [117, 118]

This discussion is of importance is it illustrates the reasons many philosophers and scientist have for being agnostic on issues of metaphysics and ontology. Even those not familiar with Kant are operating under philosophies and methodologies which have been developed in response to Kant.[119]

2.6 MICHAEL POLANYI ON EPISTEMOLOGY

"Any attempt rigorously to eliminate our human perspective from our picture of the world must lead to absurdity."[120]

—MICHAEL POLANYI

Michael Polanyi (1891–1976) was a chemist turned philosopher. In his text *Personal Knowledge: Towards a Post Critical Philosophy* (1958),[121] the idea of pure objective scientific observation is challenged. In doing so, he was attacking the core ideas of logical positivism, empiricism, and

---

117. Sproul, *Consequences of Ideas*, loc. 1680–1692 of 3097.

118. Both Paul and Aquinas argue for a natural theology: God can be known through creation. Additionally, although we cannot see God, we can perceive him both with the internal leading of the Holy Spirit, as well as externally by viewing creation.

119. Sproul states: "Immanuel Kant's revolutionary philosophy was, as we have seen, a watershed in the history of theoretical thought. In one respect or another virtually all schools of philosophy that have developed since Kant have relied on him (see fig. 10.1)." **Figure 10.1** Process Philosophy, Personalism, Pragmatism, Linguistic analysis, Phenomenology, Idealism, Marxism, Logical Positivism, and Existentialism. Sproul, *Consequences of Ideas*, 1808–1811 of 3097.

120. Polanyi, *Personal Knowledge*, 1.

121. Polanyi, *Personal Knowledge*, 1.

materialism. Furthermore, Polanyi used words such as "belief" and "conversion" to describe paradigm shifts within science. Usage of this language drew harsh criticism from fellow scientists who viewed their work as being "objective."[122] As Polanyi scholar Mary Jo Nye states:

> "Belief," which is a keyword in Polanyi's philosophy of science, carried the common connotation in the 1950s of ideology, religion, or opinion. "Belief" triggered skepticism or outrage in formal philosophy unless explained rationally, for example by degree of probability. "Conversion" was an even more objectionable word to philosophers of science, since it was tinged with psychological or religious meaning.[123]

Polanyi began his career as a chemist, and thus was a scientific insider. He knew that much of the knowledge in science was passed down from mentor to student. The key element of "trust" was important element in this process as the student eventually became an independent researcher in their own right; and a member of a community of scientists sharing similar beliefs. In many ways, this process can be described as similar to religious conversion, instruction, and membership.[124]

While engaging in science (within a given paradigm), the scientist is often forced to make many subjective decisions. Many of these decisions are decided due to *a priori* presuppositions. For instance, previous to the discovery of Neptune, scientists were puzzled why the gravitational interactions between the planets did not occur as they should. For sixty years they dismissed their findings as anomalies, as they were operating within a paradigm which did not include the planet Neptune. Their faith was in Newtonian gravity, and anything which contradicted this paradigm had to be rejected. Polanyi states:

> There is an even wider area of personal judgment in every verification of a scientific theory. Contrary to current opinion, it is not the case that a proven discrepancy between theoretical predictions and observed data suffices in itself to invalidate a theory. Such discrepancies may often be classed as anomalies. The perturbations of the planetary motions that were observed during sixty years preceding the discovery of Neptune, and which could not be explained by the mutual interaction of the planets, were rightly set

---

122. Polanyi, *Personal Knowledge*, 1.
123. Polanyi, *Personal Knowledge*, 19.
124. Polanyi, *Personal Knowledge*, 19.

aside at the time as anomalies by most astronomers, in the hope that something might eventually turn up to account for them without impairing—or at least not essentially impairing—Newtonian gravitation.[125]

However, as in the case of the discovery of Neptune, eventually there is a paradigm shift, or what Thomas Kuhn calls a *Scientific Revolution*.[126] Eventually there are enough anomalies to generate a "crisis," where the current paradigm must be rejected for a new one. Once the scientist(s) accomplish this they in turn must lead others into this new framework in order to achieve a new consensus.[127] Kuhn further argued that scientific progress is not continuous, but rather is: "Punctuated by violent intellectual revolutions that overturn long periods of conservative puzzle-solving. Periods of so-called 'normal' science are characterized less by independent and objective research than by adherence to agreed assumptions and expected outcomes."[128] Polanyi and Kuhn agreed to this framework assessment (paradigm) in opposition to Karl Popper's belief that scientist should be "eternally skeptical" about their theories and abandon them if anomalies occur.[129]

2.6.1 Types of Knowledge

According to Nye:

> "Tacit knowledge" and "personal knowledge" are perhaps the two most important keywords that Polanyi coins, and he ties their meanings to other keywords that he marshals in order to explain how science works: articulate and inarticulate knowledge, commitment, connoisseurship, conviviality, fiduciary mode, framework, indwelling, logical gap, passion, skill, subsidiary and focal knowledge, unspecifiability, wholes, and particulars.[130]

---

125. Michael Polanyi, *Personal Knowledge*, 19.
126. See Kuhn, *Structure of Scientific Revolutions*.
127. Polanyi, *Personal Knowledge*, foreword.
128. Stokes, *Philosophy 100 Essential Thinkers*, loc. 3532–3536 of 3634.
129. Polanyi, *Personal Knowledge*, foreword.
130. Polanyi, *Personal Knowledge*, foreword.

2.6.1.1 Tacit Knowledge

According to Polanyi, tacit knowledge is knowledge which we have which is beyond description; it is ineffable. However, Polanyi does not mean some type of mystical knowledge. Rather, he means the type of knowledge which defies description. Such as how one knows a beautiful painting.

2.6.1.2 Personal Knowledge

Polanyi labels personal knowledge as knowledge which includes a personal appraisal but is attempting to apply universal standards towards this appraisal. In this way, the person attempts to go from mere subjectivity towards objectivity. This is the process used in the development of all factual knowledge.[131]

2.6.1.3 Naive Objectivism

According to Polanyi, knowledge gained through our senses is highly suspect due to our own personal subjectivity. Therefore, knowledge based upon intellectual theory should be seen as of more value and as more objective than knowledge based upon our sensory experience. When we encounter readings, which go against established theory we must constantly scan for the possibility of personal bias.[132] Often, this personal bias is hidden as science and epistemology in general are based upon probabilities. When an anomaly occurs, the researcher operating under a probability statement will usually dismiss the anomaly as being "too improbable to be entertained as true."[133]

2.6.2 Heisenberg Uncertainty Principle

This theory arising from the area of physics (Werner Heisenberg, 1925) closely aligns with Polanyi's assessment that the human perspective necessarily taints any scientific experimentation; and, that true objectivity is impossible. The researcher participates and affects their own research. For instance, when looking at atoms, one can look at the electrons or the protons; but not both at the same time. And, if one looks at either element

---

131. Polanyi, *Personal Knowledge*, 16.
132. Polanyi, *Personal Knowledge*, 19.
133. Polanyi, *Personal Knowledge*, 23.

first, the second element will change by the time it is observed. What is of importance here, is that the researcher (i.e., scientist), cannot possibly remain completely objective as they themselves are a part of the experiment; if, for no other reason than the phenomena they choose to examine during the experiment itself.[134]

Thus, in Polanyi's work, we see a rejection of the naive enlightenment ideas of reason being entirely objective and neutral; and of a mechanistic universe which can be known purely by deductive reason. Rather, the universe is far more complex, and whatever theories are currently held by scientist reflect a tentative, agreed upon consensus in light of incomplete evidences and knowledge.

2.7 CONCLUSION

"Reason is the greatest enemy that faith has; it never comes to the aid of spiritual things, but—more frequently than not—struggles against the divine Word, treating with contempt all that emanates from God."
—MARTIN LUTHER, TABLE TALKS (1569)

In this chapter, I have sought to lay the ground work for several areas which will be addressed in the coming chapters. First, I have differentiated between the discipline of science and scientism. I have summarized the various philosophical presuppositions necessary in order for the scientific method to be possible. I have shown the errors of scientism as they posit ontological naturalism and thus draw scientific inquiry into other spheres where in it is incapable of acquiring knowledge. Second, I have explicated Robert Audi's fallible foundationalism as an appropriate framework to use in this inquiry. Finally, I have given a brief overview of Christian apologetics in general, and a more detailed summary of evidential apologetics in particular.

In conclusion, as scholars of Special Divine Action such as Craig Keener will readily admit; there will be no level of proof which will satisfy the ardent sceptic who is clinging to naturalism as a religion; thus, this group is not the target audience for this inquiry. While any Christian apologetic must be defensible against various attacks made by atheists, sceptics,

---

134. For a more in-depth discussion, see Hilgevoord and Uffink, "The Uncertainty Principle."

and various other scholars, they are not and should not be the focus of an apologetic. The hearts and minds of hardened skeptics are often too closed to fairly consider anything which contradicts their worldview. Rather, the target of any apologetical work must remain the *good faith sceptic* (defined in chapter 1), who will follow the evidence wherever it leads, rather than stubbornly clinging to naturalistic presuppositions.

Chapter 3

Overview of Special Divine Action Scholarship: Confronting Hume

3.1 INTRODUCTION

"Therefore, when a person refuses to come to Christ it is never just because of a lack of evidence or because of intellectual difficulties: at root, he refuses to come because he willingly ignores and rejects the drawing of God's Spirit on his heart. No one in the final analysis fails to become a Christian because of a lack of arguments; he fails to become a Christian because he loves darkness rather than light and wants nothing to do with God."
— WILLIAM LANE CRAIG

The era of the enlightenment saw two developments which were at odds with the traditional belief in Special Divine Action. First, many enlightenment philosophers were proponents of deism and viewed God as the great clockmaker of the universe who did not interact with his creation. The naturalistic presuppositions held by the deists made belief in either contemporary SDA or biblical signs and wonders impossible. The second obstacle for belief in contemporary SDA was a theological one (largely caused by the Protestant Reformation), the doctrine of cessationism. Cessationism is the belief that signs and wonders ceased at the end of the apostolic era (100 AD), as the sole purpose of these signs and wonders was to authenticate the gospel message. This belief was developed by post-Calvin reformers, largely as a polemic against the ongoing SDA in the Roman Catholic Church. In essence, the argument was that any alleged SDAs still occurring within Catholicism were either the result of deception or demonic activity as all true signs and wonders had ceased after the death of the last apostles. This doctrine of cessationism was to hold large sway within mainstream Protestantism for the next 300 years.[1]

Conversely, during this era, in England, Christian apologists such as Joseph Butler and Charles Babbage were using the argument from miracles as a foundation for Christian belief. They argued that a belief in signs and wonders was common sense given the mountain of evidence for their occurrence. According to Ruthven, apologists such as Butler and Babbage held to a: "Closed cosmology resting on the three pillars of causality, continuity and objectifiability. Whereas for these apologists, miracles, as divine irruptions into his natural order, provided an empirically observable event demonstrating God's presence, later skeptics either subsumed these events under natural (versus divine) causality or attributed them to enthusiastic imaginations."[2]

It was into this *Great Debate* that Hume formulated his extreme skeptical empiricism. Hume sought to take the cessationist position of the Reformers a step further and to declare the abolition of all miracles.[3] Hume believed that his argument against the miraculous would be timeless and would be useful "As long as the world endures."[4] Today, skeptics of SDA still cite the four arguments made by Hume in one form or another. It can be said that the *New Atheists* (Richard Dawkins, Daniel Dennett, Sam Harris and Christopher Hitchens), have contributed nothing new and of significance to Hume, and thus, are simply reframing his essential arguments. As Craig Keener states: "Hume is generally regarded today as the starting point for modern discussion of miracles. Hume provided the basis for most Enlightenment arguments against apologetic use of miracle reports, and many modern arguments simply restate Hume's earlier claims."[5] Thus, overcoming Hume, becomes a key focal point for any Christian apologist or believer in SDA.

1. Stafford, *Miracles*, 127–28.
2. Ruthven, *Cessation of the Charismata*, 25–26.
3.. Ruthven, *Cessation of the Charismata*, 25–26.
4. Hume, *Inquiry Concerning Human Understanding*, 50.
5. Keener, *Miracles*, 119–20.

3.2 DAVID HUME'S ARGUMENT

In order to understand Hume's extreme skepticism, one must first understand Hume's problem with induction. Briefly stated, Hume believes that we have no good reason to believe that past events will be replicated by future events, since there is no uniformity to nature. Just because a pool ball moves when hit by another ball today, does not mean that it will do so tomorrow. Tomorrow, it could explode, or turn into a frog, or an infinite number of other possibilities. Thus, according to Hume, our beliefs and faith in the scientific method are ultimately based upon probability and convention.[6]

Hume believes a philosopher is engaged in a fool's errand when they engage in metaphysics; as metaphysical systems are so prone to error. He analogizes metaphysical systems to the intricate workings of a grandfather clock; wherein, it takes but one grain of sand to stop the clock from working. According to Hume, the philosopher engaged in metaphysics is very often like a marathon runner running in the wrong direction, the faster he runs, and the harder he tries, the more off course he goes.[7] Thus, we see that Hume's skepticism is foundationally rooted in his epistemology. His overall argument against SDA is consistent with both his skepticism and empiricism.

Hume's most well-known text is *An Enquiry Concerning Human Understanding* (1748). This text is a summary of the much larger and lesser known text *A Treatise of Human Nature* (1739). Being an extreme sceptic and an empiricist; Hume believed that there was only a small body of knowledge which could be gained through reason. This included self-evident propositions such as a triangle has three sides, or a bachelor is an unmarried man. The rest of our knowledge, the overwhelming amount, was gained empirically through the experience of sense data.

Hume's greatest objection to SDA is that we cannot have any definitive knowledge through our empiricism; rather, our empiricism leads us towards having a knowledge based upon probabilities. Therefore, almost all of our knowledge is rooted in probabilistic assumptions (e.g., this has always happened this way before therefore it probably will happen the same way again). Reliance upon these probabilistic assumptions is for Hume the strongest objection to the occurrence of SDA. Since all of our scientific knowledge

---

6. Hume, *Inquiry Concerning Human Understanding*, 19.
7. Hume, *Inquiry Concerning Human Understanding*, 42.

is based upon probabilities, then when there is an unexpected outcome, it must be seen as an anomaly, not something supernatural, according to Hume. Hume's skepticism of SDA is a byproduct of his overall skepticism on the limits of empirical knowledge. Hume believes that our conceptions of the world, the appearances of causal relationships, or even seeing future events as being predictable based upon past events, is not something which is empirically verifiable, and thus is cannot be definitively known.[8]

Hume's work is of considerable interest as he is perhaps the most cited sceptic of Special Divine Action. He gives a strong philosophical challenge to any account of the supernatural, based upon the limits of human knowledge. In essence, Hume is stating that an apparent supernatural event cannot be labeled as such since the laws of nature are merely based upon probabilities. The apparent causality of the laws of nature is just an inference based upon past events. Therefore, we can have no knowledge about the future laws of nature, nor causality. Thus, there are no events which could ever appropriately be labeled as miraculous.

Hume's three primary arguments against miracles will be covered in the following sections. Geisler summarizes these arguments as philosophical, historical, and religious. Geisler states:

> Hume laid out three arguments against miracles: philosophical, historical, and religious. The first argument is an argument in principle, based on the incredibility of claiming natural laws are ever contravened. The second is an argument in practice, which challenges whether miracles have ever had credible witnesses. The last is from the self-canceling nature of similar miracle claims that abound in all religions.[9]

3.2.1 Miracles Are a Violation of a Law of Nature

Hume begins his argument by defining a miracle as: "A transgression of a law of nature by a particular volition of the deity, or by the interposition of

---

[8]. Many scientists who are skeptics of the miraculous would be surprised if they studied the philosophy of science and saw all of the presuppositions (leaps of faith) necessary in order for the scientific method to be possible. Having said this, Hume's skepticism seems to go too far in disallowing causality as though it might not be 100% predictable of future causality it has worked since the discovery of the scientific method at least and should fit any standard definition and criteria for knowledge.

[9]. Geisler, *Big Book Christian Apologetics*, 324–25.

Overview of Special Divine Action Scholarship

some invisible agent."[10] And, it is by this very definition that he attempts to define miracles out of existence; by arguing that miracles are impossible as they are a violation of a law of nature:

> For first, there is not to be found, in all history, any miracle attested by a sufficient number of men, of such unquestioned good-sense, education, and learning, as to secure us against all delusion in themselves; of such undoubted integrity, as to place them beyond all suspicion of any design to deceive others; of such credit and reputation in the eyes of mankind, as to have a great deal to lose in case of their being detected in any falsehood; and at the same time, attesting facts performed in such a public manner and in so celebrated a part of the world, as to render the detection unavoidable: All which circumstances are requisite to give us a full assurance in the testimony of men.[11]

Here Hume asserts an argument against the credulity of the eye witnesses of miracles. Hume believes that those who have witnessed them are either delusional, lack integrity, or are liars. Hume bases this upon his presupposition that men of education have not seen miracles first hand.

3.2.2 The Laws of Nature Are Based on Very High Probabilities

> Secondly. We may observe in human nature a principle which, if strictly examined, will be found to diminish extremely the assurance, which we might, from human testimony, have, in any kind of prodigy. The maxim, by which we commonly conduct ourselves in our reasonings, is, that the objects, of which we have no experience, resembles those, of which we have; that what we have found to be most usual is always most probable; and that where there is an opposition of arguments, we ought to give the preference to such as are founded on the greatest number of past observations. But though, in proceeding by this rule, we readily reject any fact which is unusual and incredible in an ordinary degree; yet in advancing farther, the mind observes not always the same rule; but when anything is affirmed utterly absurd and miraculous, it rather the more readily admits of such a fact, upon account of that very circumstance, which ought to destroy all its authority.[12]

10. Hume, *Inquiry Concerning Human Understanding*, 51.
11. Hume, *Inquiry Concerning Human Understanding*, 53.
12. Hume, *Inquiry Concerning Human Understanding*, 53.

In this argument Hume is asserting that the testimony of the laws of nature remains much stronger than any testimony to the contrary (e.g., the witnessing of a miracle). Thus, Hume is concluding that miracles (as a violation of a law of nature), are extremely improbable.

3.2.3 Lack Credible Witnesses

> Thirdly. It forms a strong presumption against all supernatural and miraculous relations, that they are observed chiefly to abound among ignorant and barbarous nations; or if a civilized people has ever given admission to any of them, that people will be found to have received them from ignorant and barbarous ancestors, who transmitted them with that inviolable sanction and authority, which always attend received opinions.[13]

Hume's final argument is that enlightened people from "civilized countries" such as England do not witness miracles as they are the domain of the ignorant and barbarous. Likewise, Hume elsewhere includes the first century witnesses to the New Testament miracles in this grouping of unreliable witnesses. The importance of the first century witnesses is central to the Christian faith as John Lennox notes: "C.S. Lewis reminds us that the first fact of the history of Christendom is the number of people who say they've seen the resurrection. If they died without making anyone else believe this Gospel, no gospels would ever have been written."[14]

3.3 REBUTTALS TO HUME: (SWINBURNE/POLKINGHORNE/LENNOX)

3.3.1 Swinburne—Special One-Time Events (God Is Not Restricted)

Oxford philosopher Richard Swinburne provides a strong rebuttal to Hume. Swinburne's work has been primarily in the philosophy of religion, and the philosophy of science. His Christian apologetical material includes the seminal text *The Existence of God* (1979). Swinburne's work largely attacks the Humean tradition by showing the progress of science since Hume, as

---

13. Hume, *Inquiry Concerning Human Understanding*, 54.
14. Lennox, *Miracles*, 22.

well as showing Hume's logical inconsistencies. Swinburne's essential argument against Hume is twofold:

1. Miracles do not violate the laws of nature.
2. We should believe testimony unless we have a good reason not to.

3.3.1.1 Miracles and the Law of Nature

Swinburne believes that Hume had a crude view of induction and the scientific method. For Hume, induction was a generalization from an observation. Previous to the nineteenth century, all of science was science of the observable. Today, we practice science at the subatomic level, via quantum theory. Today, postulating unobservable things as the best explanation of observable things is often done by scientists. Quantum theory itself shows that there is indeterminism in nature.[15]

Swinburne also believes that Hume's philosophy is both mistaken and full of contradiction when it comes to the laws of nature. Hume's views on induction do not fit with his views about miracles. Hume holds the "laws of nature" as being absolute and invaluable, yet he does not believe in inductive reasoning nor the scientific method! Rather than positing the laws of nature as absolute and inviolable; Swinburne proposes that miracles be defined as a "non-repeatable counter instance to a law of nature."[16] Timothy McGrew summarizes Swinburne's position:

> If a putative law has broad scope, great explanatory power, and appealing simplicity, it may be more reasonable, Swinburne argues, to retain the law (defined as a regularity that virtually invariably holds) and to accept that the event in question is a non-repeatable counter-instance of that law than to throw out the law and create a vastly more complex law that accommodates the event.[17]

Since Swinburne rejects the monism of Polkinghorne, he believes that God must inject a special one-time exception into the physical world. There is no violation of the laws of nature as:

1. God created the laws of nature and is not bound to them.

---

15. Swinburne, *Existence of God*, loc. 3825 of 5297.
16. McGrew, "Miracles," lines 32–33.
17. McGrew, "Miracles," lines 33–35.

2. The universe is not a closed system so an interaction from beyond is in keeping with currently held scientific models.[18]

Swinburne does not believe that miracles are pervasive rather they are used by God to respond to prayer or to confirm the doctrine of a prophet. Thus, miracles occur at specific times in clusters according to Swinburne: "...and if communities go too far astray and people forget about God."[19]

3.3.1.2 Acceptance of Testimony

Contrary to Hume, Swinburne asserts that we must have two guiding principles when accessing religious experience:

1. The principle of credulity—accept what you see as true unless you have a good reason not to.
2. The principle of testimony—accept what eyewitnesses/others say as true unless you have a good reason not to.[20]

Thus, Hume and Swinburne begin with competing *a priori* presuppositions about the value of testimony. Hume believes that since the limited testimony of miracles contradicts the copious testimony for naturalism, the testimony on miracles must be rejected. Hume's contention is puzzling as the very definition of miracle implies something which is rare and unusual. Conversely, while Swinburne believes that miracles are very rare, he does not see them as overthrowing *the laws of nature*; rather, he sees them as a means by which the creator of the laws of nature (God), is able to function within a system which he himself created.[21]

3.3.2 Polkinghorne

A second major rebuttal to Hume comes from Cambridge physicist/Christian apologist John Polkinghorne. Like Swinburne, Polkinghorne argues that Hume's views of the laws of nature and science are both inconsistent and incomplete; a product of a bygone era. However, Polkinghorne takes

---

18. Swinburne, *Existence of God*, loc. 3830–3835 of 5297.
19. Swinburne, Existence of God, 3742 of 5297.
20. Swinburne, *Existence of God*, loc. 4113 to 4444 of 5297.
21. Swinburne, *Existence of God*, loc. 3698 to 3979 of 5297.

his critique a step further and argues that Hume's conception of the universe is also a byproduct of an enlightenment view of the universe.

Polkinghorne is a monist and believes that the universe is more cloudlike than clocklike. This rejection of mechanistic materialism allows for the interaction of the divine to occur not as a force from outside of nature, but rather as a part of nature. Polkinghorne self identifies as a *critical realist*: meaning that we can have knowledge of things, but this knowledge is always incomplete. These beliefs serve as the foundation for his attack on Hume, and Polkinghorne's belief in Special Divine Action.[22]

3.3.2.1. Rejection of Mechanistic View of the Universe

Since Polkinghorne believes that the universe is cloudlike, not clocklike as Hume and others believed during the enlightenment; this cloudlike state allows for "higher level causation." Higher level causation (downward causation), is usually defined as causation from high levels within a system down to the low levels within a system. It is believed that there are less laws and rules within these higher levels, and thus, it is not possible to be reductionistic in applying rules and laws from the bottom upward. However, Polkinghorne has a unique perspective which is bottom up wherein "active information" at the quantum level of indeterminacy/unpredictability is where God's Special Divine Action (i.e., miracles) occurs.[23]

3.3.2.2 God = Quantum Vacuum
(The Space of Nothing between Particles)

Highly related to Polkinghorne's monistic, cloudlike view of the universe is Polkinghorne's view that God operates within the quantum vacuum (the space of nothing between particles). Polkinghorne states:

> I shall suggest that recent advances in science point to an openness and flexibility within physical process—not only at the microscopic level of quantum theory but also at the macroscopic level of large systems—that begin to offer hope of some understanding of how both we ourselves, and also God, can exercise our wills in the physical world.[24]

22. Polkinghorne, *Science and Providence*, 58.
23. See also: Winters, *Christian Theology of Nature*.
24. Polkinghorne, *Science and Providence*, 17.

3.3.2.3. Hume's Inconsistency on Miracles: Induction and the Laws of Nature

Polkinghorne, along with Swinburne and Lennox, criticize the inconsistencies in Hume's argument. Hume does not believe that "knowledge" is possible through induction and thus believes that the scientific method is also incapable of producing knowledge. Yet Hume uses both as a means of arguing against the miraculous. As Polkinghorne states: "It is rather touching to find the stern critic of induction placing such firm faith in the unalterable character of nature's laws. The idea that they are totally known, and totally inflexible in their consequence, has been sufficiently rebutted in what has gone before for us to be able to pass on immediately to the four arguments which Hume alleges against there ever having been a miracle."[25]

Finally, Polkinghorne's interpretation of the miraculous is of importance. Polkinghorne believes that not only can one prove the existence of miracles and overcome Hume; but, that this is not even the biggest challenge for scholars of the miraculous. Polkinghorne believes that the interpretation of miracles remains the largest problem for scholars.[26] I will address this concern in-depth in chapters 6 and 7. While seeing interpretation as the greatest difficulty for the Christian scholar, Polkinghorne does agree with C. S. Lewis' view that: "God does not shake miracles at Nature at random as if from a pepper-castor. They come on great occasions: they are found at the great ganglia of history—not of political or social history, but of that spiritual history which cannot be fully known by men. . .Miracles and martyrdoms tend to bunch together about the same areas of history."[27]

3.3.3 John Lennox

John Lennox is an Oxford mathematics professor, as well as a philosopher of science and Christian apologetics. He is able to draw from these diverse disciplines when he analyzes the arguments of Hume. Lennox believes that miracles are not normal, but that they do occur. Lennox argues that one must weigh the evidence for and against a miracle before they have judged if one has occurred. In short, belief must be proportional to the evidence. This is something which Hume is unwilling to do according to Lennox.

---

25. Polkinghorne, *Science and Providence*, 63.
26. Polkinghorne, *Science and Providence*, 62.
27. Polkinghorne, *Science and Providence*, 62.

3.3.3.1 *Laws of Nature*

In analyzing Hume's methodology, Lennox also finds many logical inconsistencies and errors. For instance, Hume argues that the laws of nature are uniform and are thus inviolable. However, Hume in other passages states his problems with both the laws of nature and induction. Lennox states:

> He famously argues that, just because the sun has been observed to rise in the morning for thousands of years, it does not mean that we can be sure that it will rise tomorrow. This is an example of the Problem of Induction: on the basis of past experience you cannot predict the future, says Hume. But if that were true, let us see what it implies in particular. Suppose Hume is right, and no dead man has ever risen up from the grave through the whole of earth's history so far; by his own argument he still cannot be sure that a dead man will not rise up tomorrow. That being so, he cannot rule out miracle. What has become now of Hume's insistence on the laws of nature, and its uniformity? He has destroyed the very basis on which he tries to deny the possibility of miracles.[28]

3.3.3.2 *Evidence of Testimony*

Hume argues that those who believe in miracles tend to come from barbarous nations or from prescientific times such as first century Israel; thus, the accounts of miracles given by such people are to be entirely discounted. Hume further argues that one must always weigh the testimony of a miracle against the uniform testimony against. In this way Hume is in essence defining miracles out of existence *a priori*.

Lennox of course objects to this argument on a number of grounds. For instance, he states that it is obvious that an event such as a resurrection would be against the uniform experience of humanity. But to argue that this cancels out the belief that a resurrection has occurred is to *beg the question*. The very reason why a resurrection is a miracle is precisely because it goes against the uniformity of human experience![29]

---

28. Lennox, *Gunning for God*, 169.
29. Lennox, *God's Undertaker*, 194–95.

3.3.3.3 *The Universe is not a Closed System*

A final critical mistake made by Hume is that he assumes that the universe is a closed system and thus fails to understand the arguments made by Christians in favor of miracles. As Lennox notes in regard to the miracle of the resurrection: "What Christians are claiming about the resurrection of Jesus is not that he rose by some natural processes; that would violate the laws of nature. No. Christians claim that Jesus rose because God injected enormous power and energy from outside the system. Now, unless you have evidence that the system is totally closed, you cannot argue against the possibility of miracles."[30] This is a very important point for the entire discussion and debate on Special Divine Action!

In Lennox's critique of Hume, we find the logical inconsistencies of Hume's arguments. He appeals to the uniformity of the laws of nature; while not believing that nature's uniformity can be proven. Hume's problem with induction prohibits him from believing in both cause and effect as well as the scientific method. Thus, Hume's critique of miracles lacks both internal and external consistency.

3.4 C.S. LEWIS AND BERTRAND RUSSELL

C.S. Lewis (1898–1963) is widely considered one of the most important Christian authors of the twentieth century. His trilogy of Christian apologetics texts: *The Problem of Pain* (1940),[31] *Miracles: A Preliminary Study* (1947),[32] and *Mere Christianity* (1952),[33] were foundational in the development of twentieth century apologetics. His 1947 text *Miracles: A Preliminary Study* is a book length refutation of Hume's arguments against miracles.

3.4.1 C.S. Lewis's Position

In *Miracles: A Preliminary Study*, Lewis tackles Hume's four main arguments against miracles. In addition, Lewis also argues against one of Hume's lesser known arguments; the argument from deism. In Hume's

---

30. Lennox, *Miracles*, 25.
31. See Lewis, *Problem of Pain*.
32. See Lewis, *Miracles*.
33. See Lewis, *Mere Christianity*.

essay *The Natural History of Religion* (1757), Hume argues from the deistic worldview against miracles that:

1. An omnipotent, omniscient, and morally perfect God would never make mistakes.
2. If (1), then such a God would never perform miracles.
3. Therefore, an omnipotent, omniscient, and morally perfect God would never perform miracles.[34]

Lewis rejects Hume's argument from deism by stating that there are other reasons besides error which would cause God to perform miracles. In Lewis' chapter on natural law (chapter 8), he states that miracles do not violate the laws of nature, and are consistent with nature. He believes that miracles are consistent with nature but go beyond the ordinary functioning of natural law. Lewis concludes: "If Nature brings forth miracles then doubtless it is as 'natural' for her to do so when impregnated by the masculine force beyond her as it is for a woman to bear children to a man. In calling them miracles we do not mean that they are contradictions or outrages; we mean that, left to her own resources, she could never produce them."[35, 36]

3.4.2 Russell's Position

Bertrand Russell (1872–1970) was a mathematician, logician, and philosopher. He is considered to be one of the founders of analytic philosophy, a movement which is closely associated with logical positivism. Importantly, he was also the mentor for Ludwig Wittgenstein. Wittgenstein's *Philisophico Logicio Tractatus* (1920) is considered one of the seminal works of the twentieth century as it defined the limits of reason, logic, and language.[37]

Bertrand Russell's works: *Why I am not a Christian* (1957),[38] *Human Knowledge: Its Scope and Limits* (1967),[39] et al., served as a foundation for

---

34. Wielenberg, *God and the Reach of Reason*, 124.
35. Lewis, *Miracles*, 98.
36. This is a very good analogy for understanding God's interaction with the physical universe.
37. In the Tractatus, Wittgenstein concludes that there is something else there, outside the bounds of reason and logic. See Wittgenstein, *Philisophico Logicio Tractatus*.
38. See Russell, *Not a Christian*.
39. See Russell, *Human Knowledge*.

many critics of Christianity during the twentieth century. Russell's arguments are in general anti-metaphysical, although he does also argue specifically against Christianity and miracles. Russell argues that religion is based upon emotion and a fear of the unknown. Thus, he believes Christianity is at best irrational and cowardly; at worst, it is immoral and has stood in the way of the progress of civilization. Russell states:

> You find as you look around the world that every single bit of progress in humane feeling, every improvement in the criminal law, every step toward the diminution of war, every step toward better treatment of the colored races, or every mitigation of slavery, every moral progress that there has been in the world, has been consistently opposed by the organized churches of the world. I say quite deliberately that the Christian religion, as organized in its churches, has been and still is the principle enemy of moral progress in the world.[40]

3.4.3 Civility in Debate

While Russell and Lewis vehemently disagreed with one another, they did manage to enjoy each other's company and keep a level of civility in their exchanges. Unlike the modern debate with the New Atheists, the debate in the mid-twentieth century was more intellectual and less rhetorical. Russell is to be commended for trying to formulate philosophical arguments against theism which rose above mere rhetoric and insult. In contrast, Erik J. Wielenberg has described the current debate with the New Atheists as "shrill and vapid."[41]

Wielenberg is not alone in this assessment. When Richard Dawkins refused to debate William Lane Craig in 2011, Daniel Came, bemoaned the lack of substance and civility displayed by the New Atheists:

> What is new is the belittling posture toward religious believers and the fury of the polemics. The New Atheism is certainly a far cry from the model of civilized interlocution between "old atheist" Bertrand Russell and Father Copleston that took place and was broadcast on BBC Radio in 1948. The New Atheists could learn a lot from the likes of Russell, whose altogether more powerful approach was at once respectful and a model of philosophical precision.[42]

---

40. Russell, *Not a Christian*, loc. 231–232 of 1266.
41. Wielenberg, *God and the Reach of Reason*, i.
42. Came, "Dawkins's Refusal to Debate," lines 35–41.

Daniel Came is himself a sceptic, but he disagrees with the tactics of Dawkins and the other New Atheists as being: "fundamentally ignoble and potentially harmful to public intellectual life."[43] Came finds their tactics not only insulting to the theists that they debate, but to the audiences of their debates as well. Came states:

> For there is something cynical, ominously patronizing, and anti-intellectualist in their modus operandi, with its implicit assumption that hurling insults is an effective way to influence people's beliefs about religion. The presumption is that their largely non-academic readership doesn't care about, or is incapable of, thinking things through; that passion prevails over reason. On the contrary, people's attitudes towards religious belief can and should be shaped by reason, not bile and invective.[44]

Likewise, Ravi Zacharias has stated that:

> The hallmark of the so-called "new atheists" is the anger and ridicule that is hurled toward anyone's belief in the sacred. Need I add, not all atheists have the same disposition. In fact, many find the hostility of the new atheists an embarrassment. I have met many a cordial conversationalist who is atheistic in his or her belief, and we've had the best of conversations. Many have remarked that they have been able to take only so much of Dawkins and his followers and then stopped even reading them.[45]

3.4.4 Lewis' Civility

"Whatever worldview we espouse, dialogue and debate should take place with civility and courteous listening."[46]

—RAVI ZACHARIAS

According to Michael Ward, C.S. Lewis had numerous personality and intellectual traits which facilitated discussions/debates with atheists and sceptics of the Christian faith. Lewis often engaged in rigorous debate with his colleagues as he believed that the truth would always win out in the

43. Came, "Dawkins's Refusal to Debate," lines 65–66.
44. Came, "Dawkins's Refusal to Debate," lines 66–72.
45. Zacharias and Vitale, *Jesus Among Secular Gods*, 3–4.
46. Zacharias and Vitale, *Jesus Among Secular Gods*, 4.

end. He also believed that the process of intellectual debate helped him to sharpen and clarify his own work. Lewis possessed several character qualities which helped him in debating atheists in a cordial way including pugnacity, magnanimity, and corrigibility.[47]

3.4.4.1 Pugnacity

Lewis enjoyed debate. He sought out colleagues and students who disagreed with him on a daily basis to debate his ideas about God, government, and philosophy. He did not care that they were in disagreement, he only sought to sharpen the debating skills of himself and his students.[48]

3.4.4.2 Magnanimity

Lewis never allowed his debates to become personal; he separated the individual from their ideas. It was this quality which allowed him to debate atheists like Gilbert Ryle and Bertrand Russell without it damaging their friendships. In *The Personal Heresy* (1939), Lewis publicly attacked E.M.W. Tillyard's work without attacking him personally. In *An Experiment in Criticism* (1961), Lewis attacked the work of F.R. Leavis in a strong and forceful manner. However, Leavis was not named directly, rather, Lewis used a pseudonym to avoid any public animosity.[49]

3.4.4.3 Corrigibility

The earlier Lewis was not always magnanimous, but he learned from his mistakes. He came to view his younger self as a bit of a bully who would shout down others during debate. However, overtime he learned to be more cordial and magnanimous in his debates. As Ward concludes: "So Lewis went from pugnacity to magnanimity by way of corrigibility."[50]

Perhaps this ideal set by Lewis is unobtainable in twenty-first century debate; largely due to the nearly monolithic collapse of classical liberalism

---

47. Ward, "C. S. Lewis and Disagreement."
48. Ward, "C. S. Lewis and Disagreement," lines 17–22.
49. Lewis, *An Experiment in Criticism*.
50. Ward, "C. S. Lewis and Disagreement," line 70.

in favor of progressivism?[51] Regardless, apologists and atheist debaters can improve their argumentation by studying the positions of their opponents and interacting within debates.[52]

3.5 JOSEPH BUTLER'S PROBABILISTIC ARGUMENT

Joseph Butler's *The Analogy of Religion* was written in 1736. Butler's text was seen in its era as a strong refutation to Hume's argument against miracles. Today, it remains a foundational text for evidential apologetics due to its argument from miracles and fulfilled prophecy. Hume himself stated that he had "castrated" *The Treatise of Human Nature* (1739) due to the strength of Butler's argument. Charles Babbage concluded that Hume had no good answer to Butler. And finally, Cardinal John Henry Newman (a former sceptic), became a Christian due to the strength of Butler's argument.

Butler's argument is very simple: he argues that miracles and fulfilled prophecy are the most direct and fundamental proofs of Christianity (evidences). Butler reasons that miracles can be proven and are thus proof of God; as he alone can work miracles. Butler bases his argument for miracles upon probability: the probability that they did occur is more likely than the probability that the witnesses are liars. Butler's argument is based on two premises:

1. The strength of the collective whole of Christian evidences.
2. The connection the witnessing of miracles had on the spread of Christianity.

---

51. Classical liberalism promoted discussions on ideas. Progressivism which has now become more dominant in academia promotes censorship of ideas which are in disagreement with the academic establishment. For a classical liberal viewpoint see Mill, *On Liberty*.

52. One caveat rings true in the area of apologetics as in any area of intellectual inquiry, the possibility of spiritual warfare. Just as only the most well-grounded of priest are chosen for the rigors of exorcism and the spiritual warfare which it entails; so too should be the academy, especially in the area of apologetics. We are told in scripture that the devil is far more powerful than we are. Peter is warned that the devil could sift him as wheat if not for the protection of God (Luke 22:31). Exorcists are warned not to engage the devil in intellectual debate or curiosity during an exorcism, but rather to rebuke him in the name of Jesus Christ. The key principle is that apologetics is often a supernatural as well as an intellectual battle. See also: Burton, *Traditional Catholic Rites*.

3.5.1 Testimony (Christianity vs. Islam)

Butler argues that true miracles are unique to Christianity. He makes a comparison between Christianity and Islam to exemplify. Christianity had the signs and wonders of Christ and the apostles. This is the method by which Christianity was spread. For the apostles, their signs and wonders served as an authentication of their authority and the gospel message itself. For Jesus, signs and wonders confirmed that he was the messiah, sent by God. Christianity spread due to the witnessing of signs and wonders. This stands in stark contrast to Hume's assertion that there were no credible witnesses to miracles. Rather, the witnessing of signs and wonders was the very reason why Christianity spread!

Other religions lacked signs and wonders. For instance, Butler cites the case of Islam. Muhamad lacked the ability to perform signs and wonders. Butler reasons, that first generation Jews and gentiles alike witnessed the healings performed by Jesus and the apostles and became converts to the Christian faith. By contrast, since Muhammad was devoid of miracles, he resorted to the sword instead.[53]

3.5.2 Totality of Evidence

Butler argued that although any given miracle or prophecy could be doubted; as a collective whole, they were far more probable than not. This is why critics of Christianity and sceptics of the miraculous always attack individual miracles; but choose to ignore the collective whole body of evidence of miracles and fulfilled prophecy. As later shown by William Paley, Josh McDowell, and Hugh Ross: there are over 2000 cases of fulfilled biblical prophecy.[54] Likewise, the historical record shows an enormous amount of credible eyewitness testimony for miracles, including the very spreading of Christianity. Butler argues that even if several miracles were challenged, it would do nothing to the collective whole of the argument as the body of evidence is so strong. Butler states:

> The truth of our religion, like the truth of common matters, is to be judged of by all the evidence taken together. And unless the whole series of things which may be alleged in this argument, and every

---

53. Butler, *Analogy of Religion*, loc. 3644 of 4648.

54. See Ross, "Fulfilled Prophecy"; McDowell, *Evidence that Demands a Verdict*; and Paley, *Evidences of Christianity*.

particular thing in it, can reasonably be supposed to have been by accident (for here the stress of the argument for Christianity lies); then is the truth of it proved: in like manner, as if in any common case, numerous events acknowledged, were to be alleged in proof of any other event disputed; the truth of the disputed event would be proved, not only if any one of the acknowledged ones did of itself clearly imply it but, though no one of them singly did so, if the whole of the acknowledged events taken together could not in reason be supposed to have happened, unless the disputed one were true.[55]

3.5.3 Probability

Butler's argument for miracles is ultimately tied to his collective whole argument and is finally based upon the general truthfulness of credible witnesses. Butler contended that the sheer number of credible witnesses testifying to miracles makes their occurrence far more probable than not. Given the large number of these miracles, the argument from miracles, along with fulfilled prophecy, serve as the strongest evidence for the Christian faith.

In 1837, Charles Babbage concluded that Hume had no good answer to Butler. Babbage's reasoning was due to the general truthfulness of testimony. Babbage argued that since it is possible to find credible, independent, witnesses to miracles; then the argument that they occur cannot be overcome. This is because it can always be argued that it is more likely that credible people are telling the truth than lying. This argument is very similar to Swinburne's principles of testimony and credulity given in section 3.3.

3.6 CONCLUSION

3.6.1 Analysis

Hume once stated that he had developed a timeless argument against miracles.[56] To the extent that sceptics of the miraculous (e.g., New Atheists) continue to base their arguments in Hume's critique; his statement has been

---

55. Butler, *Analogy of Religion*, loc. 4073 of 4648.

56. It is amazing that Hume had such foresight to make such a bold claim. His claim has proven true as nothing essential has been added to his position of skepticism nearly four centuries later.

proven correct. However, Hume's critique is fundamentally flawed in both its presuppositions and its views on the limits of science as an epistemological tool. The idea that somehow presupposing ontological naturalism is more *scientific* is erroneous. As concluded in chapter 2, a scholar must know the uses and limitations of science so as to not engage in scientism.

Also, as Craig Keener states, there are literally millions of testimonies about miraculous healings throughout the world. Keener's text highlights over a hundred modern medical miracles which have occurred in America with documentation. Some of these miracles involve such things as the immediate disappearance of cataracts or the resuscitation of someone after forty minutes with no heat beat. It is because of cases like these that 55% of American doctors believe that they have witnessed a miracle. To dismiss the numerous testimonies of such expert witnesses based upon holding to a rigid naturalism, as done by Hume, is to not objective nor scientific according to Keener.[57]

3.6.2 Probability

Craig Keener readily admits that modern miracles do not and cannot meet the highest criteria of the sceptics. Hume argues that extraordinary claims require extraordinary evidences.[58] There is no logical reason to hold a belief in the supernatural to higher standard than any other scientific or epistemological/ontological claim. The *burden of proof* should not be greater for the theistic position than for the naturalistic position![59]

This point is key. Since the majority of our knowledge is fallible and is based upon probabilities, and not absolutes, then arguments such as Butler's totality of the evidence must be allowed. In Butler's case, the instances of fulfilled prophecies and miracles as more probable than not. In Keener's argument, the fact that hundreds of millions of people claim to have witnessed a modern miracle is given credence due to the quality of the witnesses. These witnesses include people from all cultures and class levels. Keener's acceptance of their testimony is more reasonable than Hume's belief that "all" the witnesses to miracles are either lying or delusional.

57. Keener, *Miracles*, 108.

58. This actually is a modern paraphrase of Hume which shortens his longer statement. Nevertheless, this is the essential argument made by modern skeptics placing the burden of proof on the Christian apologist.

59. This is a very important point in any apologetical debate.

I would concur with Joseph Butler's Probability argument that modern miracles are the more likely possibility when compared to the less plausible naturalistic explanations. Butler's argument is the most reasonable in that individual miracles can be doubted, but the collective whole cannot be overcome. He does not argue that they obtain an extremely high degree of proof. Rather, that belief in miracles is simply more probable than not. This is the very way in which scientific inferencing is done.

3.6.3 Further Obstacles

There are still many obstacles for Christian apologists who might seek to make an evidential argument based upon miracles. These include: possible naturalistic causes, lack of medical documentation, and reliance upon testimonies. However, as has been shown, there are countless claims of miracles which meet the criteria established by sceptics such as Hume. Craig Keener presents over 100 such miracles which have occurred in modern America with medical documentation. The Vatican's *Consulta Medica* has applied its rigid criteria to authenticate sixty-nine such miracles to have occurred in Lourdes France during the past century.

However, even if miracles can be proven to occur, the question remains "why?" Why would God intervene in such a way as to violate laws which he himself set up? Perhaps equally important, is the question why God does not usually intervene with a miracle? Why does he allow most to suffer? While these questions will be addressed in-depth in chapters 6 and 7, I can briefly state that the answers about the meaning of miracles are of primary importance to the Christian message. Miracles reveal not only God's character but also his special relationship with his people as well.

Chapter 4

History of Signs and Wonders

4.1 INTRODUCTION

"Although it is true God doesn't overwhelm us with his presence, he does at times show himself through the gift of miracles. From Moses to Jesus, and throughout the history of the Church, God has been manifesting himself through wondrous deeds."[1]

—Karlo Broussard

"Even though the Bible was written for us, it wasn't written to us. When we take our Western, modern culture and impose it on the text, we're putting in meaning that wasn't there, and we're missing the meaning that the text has."[2]

—Dr. John H. Walton

During the twentieth century, many strains of Christianity became more open to the ongoing work of the Holy Spirit. This was most evident in the practicing of the *gifts of the Spirit*[3] within the Renewal movement. While

---

1. Broussard, *20 Answers*, loc. 33–36 of 778.
2. Walton and Keener, *NIV Cultural Backgrounds Study Bible*, loc. 712–715 of 350904.
3. A partial list of spiritual gifts is given in 1 Corinthians 12:8–10: wisdom, knowledge, faith, healing, miracles, prophecy, discerning of spirits, speaking in tongues, interpretation of tongues.

signs and wonders have been part of Christian witness from the beginning, the prominence given to them within the Renewal movement is unprecedented since the apostolic age. Beginning with the Welsh Revival (1904–1905) then spreading to Azusa Street in 1906, and continuing worldwide during the twentieth century.

While Catholicism has always held to some form of *continuationism*, many Protestant denominations post-Calvin embraced various forms of *cessationism*.[4] In doing so, the message and power of the gospel, and the biblical text, was compromised as a *truncated* gospel was preached.[5] However, in the beginning of the twenty-first century cessationism is a doctrine largely in retreat in the west, and has always been extremely rare in the developing world. This chapter will show the signs and wonders which have occurred in both the biblical and church eras. Additionally, some of the underlying theological and exegetical issues will be examined as the various types of signs and wonders are explicated.

Before giving specific examples of signs and wonders, it is first necessary to understand the differences in worldview between modern readers and the ancient and first century Jewish authors. As Tremper Longman III notes: "The occurrence of supernatural events. This immediately brings the role of the interpreter's presuppositions to the fore."[6] That is, those holding to a classical Christian worldview versus a naturalistic worldview will immediately have different interpretations. Thus, the tendency of critical scholars following the lead of Rudolf Bultmann, is to look past the alleged miracle and for some deeper hidden meaning for the miracle. The kernel of truth of the kerygma. Although Bultmann originally coined the term *demythologizing* in 1941, similar methods have been practiced in liberal/critical circles for over three hundred years (e.g., Spinoza).[7]

Conversely, conservative scholars such as Longman and Raymond Dillard will read the text in a literal, *prima facie* way, not disbelieving the literal occurrence of signs and wonders due to the enlightenment presuppositions held by critical scholars. The text will be interpreted using the historical grammatical method. This method allows for analysis due to

---

4. Continuationism is the theological position that the sign gifts of the Holy Spirit did not cease after the apostolic age. Cessationism is the view that the sign gifts of the Holy Spirit did cease after the apostolic age. For a full discussion of the major views see Grudem, *Miraculous Gifts*.

5. Ruthven, *Cessation of the Charismata*, xxiv.

6. Longman and Dillard, *Introduction Old Testament*, 20.

7. See Bultmann, *New Testament and Mythology*.

metaphor, genres and context. However, the occurrence of signs and wonders will not be dismissed due to a priori presuppositions.[8] As Longmann summarizes:

> In the Old Testament one reads of a bush that burns but is not destroyed, a donkey that speaks, dead people who live again, seas that part, the sun's stopping in mid-sky, and more. If an interpreter approaches the Old Testament as he would any other book—that is, if he perceives it as written from a human vantage point, about human affairs—skepticism is warranted. However, a second interpreter; who admits the reality of God and who believes that God is the ultimate and guiding voice of the Bible, will not have difficulty accepting the supernatural events of the bible.[9]

However, most modern scholars (including conservatives), will still have a worldview difference with the biblical authors, as there is a tendency today to separate the natural from the supernatural world. No such division existed in the minds of the ancient Jews who saw everything as being from God, and thus as supernatural. According to Walton:

> Today we are inclined to separate our understanding of events and phenomena into the categories of "natural" or "supernatural," the former of these two being the result of natural laws and explainable as natural cause and effect; the latter being acts of God beyond scientific explanation. In the ancient world there was no such classification system. Nothing would have been considered purely natural with God/the gods uninvolved.[10]

Rather, what today we would label as miracles or supernatural occurrences would be referred to by the ancients as "signs and wonders." Yes, these signs and wonders were "manifestations of God's power;" however, they pointed towards a deeper reality believed by the ancients.[11] This deeper reality was

---

8. Longman, while believing in miracles and literal readings, does state that conservatives need to not "overhistoricize" the bible. As "Legitimate genre questions genre questions must be addressed in the interpretation of certain books. Why are there differences between the narration of the same events in Samuel—Kings over against Chronicles? What is the historical kernel of the Job story? Is Jonah history or parable?" (Longman and Dillard, *Introduction to the Old Testament*, 20–21).

9. Longman and Dillard, *Introduction Old Testament*, 20.

10. Walton and Keener, *NIV Cultural Backgrounds Study Bible*, loc. 2358–2363 of 350904.

11. Walton and Keener, *NIV Cultural Backgrounds Study Bible*, loc. 2358–2363 of 350904.

that human events were but a small part of reality, what really mattered was the actions of the divine. What today we call myth was not only real to them, but was more real and more important than human events and history. This worldview was not unique to the Jews, but rather, was shared throughout the ancient world.[12] As Walton concludes: "Even though the Bible was written for us, it wasn't written to us. When we take our Western, modern culture and impose it on the text, we're putting in meaning that wasn't there, and we're missing the meaning that the text has."[13]

4.1.1 Trial by Ordeal (*Judicium Dei*—Judgment of God)

One topic which exemplifies the ancient/premodern worldview about the regularity of Special Divine Action, is the occurrence of *trial by ordeal*. In the mind of the ancient world, up through the Middle Ages, and continuing in the nonwestern world today, the expectation that God would directly intervene to save an innocent person from death, was common. Thus, in this mindset, Special Divine Action is not something rare and miraculous, rather, it is something normal and to be expected.

For instance, in the Old Testament book of Numbers chapter 5, the test for adultery is given as a trial by ordeal. The priest puts a curse upon dirt and ink etc.; all of which would ordinarily cause the woman to become sick and eventually die. However, since there was also a supernatural element to the ritual (the curse of the priest); the accused person would die instantly if they were guilty. However, if they were innocent, then God would not only cause them to be saved from the poisonous mixture and curses, but they also would be blessed for having undergone such an ordeal. In Adam Clarke's commentary on Numbers 5:31, he states:

> This woman shall bear her iniquity—That is, her belly shall swell, and her thigh shall rot; (see Numbers 5:22). But if not guilty after such a trial, she had great honor, and, according to the rabbins, became strong, healthy, and fruitful; for if she was before barren, she now began to bear children; if before she had only daughters, she now began to have sons; if before she had hard travail, she now had easy; in a word, she was blessed in her body, her soul, and her

---

12. Walton and Keener, *NIV Cultural Backgrounds Study Bible*, loc. 2358–2363 of 350904.

13. Walton and Keener, *NIV Cultural Backgrounds Study Bible*, loc. 712–715 of 350904.

substance: so shall it be done unto the holy and faithful woman, for such the Lord delighteth to honor; (see 1 Timothy 2:15).[14]

The trial by ordeal is seen both in the Old Testament (e.g., Numbers 5) as well as in the New Testament (e.g., 1 Peter 4:12). It is also found in the *Code of Hammurabi*. Eventually, the trial by ordeal was condemned by the Lantern Council in 1250. However, the practice did continue throughout the middle ages in Europe; most notably in the trials of witches and heretics. The *Malleus Maleficarum* (The Hammer of Witches) was written in 1486, and contains many possible methods and trials to be used to conclude if the accused were a witch or not.[15] Despite the condemnation of trial by ordeal in 1250, the text was written in response to the Pope Innocent VIII's papal bull: *Summis desiderantes affectibus* in 1284. One passage from the *Malleus Maleficarum* states: "So, when a person has been loaded with insults and injuries by any community, he can clear himself of any criminal or civil charge by means of a trial by ordeal. Also, since less hurt is caused to the hands by the red-hot iron than is the loss of life in a duel, if a duel is permitted where such things are customary, much more should the trial by red-hot iron be allowed."[16]

Of importance to this study, are both the worldview and biblical endorsement of the trial by ordeal. It was believed that God would intervene and perform a miracle in order to save the innocent from punishment. This shows the strength of the belief in Special Divine Action and divine imminence by Christians up until the enlightenment. The Oneness Pentecostals today who engage in such activities as snake handling and ingestion of various poisons could also be said to be engaged in a form of trial by ordeal. They are relying upon God to save them from what would otherwise make them sick or kill them. Theologically, they are taking a *wooden literal* interpretation of passages such as Mark 16:18 and Luke 10:19. However, these practices are erroneous and must be also interpreted in light of Christ's words to Satan of not putting God to the test

---

14. Clarke, *Commentary on the Bible*, loc. 26008–26017 of 219647.

15. Kramer and Sprenger, *Malleus Maleficarum*. The Malleus Maleficarum was written in 1486 by the German clergymen Heinrich Kramer Institoris and Jacob Sprenger and was used extensively in Europe during the middle ages as well as in colonial America. Some of the various forms of trial by ordeal included in the text are torture and intense interrogation in an attempt to produce tears. It was believed that witches were incapable of crying.

16. Kramer and Sprenger, *Malleus Maleficarum*, 237–38.

(Luke 4:12; Matthew 4:7; Deuteronomy 6:16);[17] and, not turning sings and wonders into a mere spectacle.

4.2 OLD TESTAMENT SIGNS AND WONDERS

"With that said, let's address the skepticism that often surrounds Old Testament miracles. If someone doubts the Old Testament accounts of miracles just because he thinks miracles are too fantastical, like the splitting of the Red Sea (Exod. 14:21), then his issue is not historical but philosophical."[18]

—KARLO BROUSSARD

The occurrence of signs and wonders in the Old Testament causes many interpretive issues for modern scholars. As previously mentioned, the ancient Israelites had a vastly different worldview which did not divide the natural and supernatural; as all was from God. The covenant relationship between God and the Israelites is foundational in understanding many of the signs and wonders contained in the Old Testament. Additionally, an interpretive framework of the ancient texts is needed; one which allows for divine inspiration, but understands the various literary forms and genres used by the authors. Finally, the entirety of Scripture and the signs and wonders contained within, need to be viewed and interpreted in light of one another. There must be a *unity of the Bible*.

Unity of the Bible necessitates the development of a *biblical theology*: a theology which can trace various motifs and patterns throughout scripture. In today's scholarship, a heavier emphasis is often placed on the New Testament. Christian apologists are far more likely to use New Testament signs and wonders in defense of the faith than ones from the Old Testament. Critical scholars at times can be more accepting of the New Testament narratives than those from the Old Testament. This is a mistake as Wood argues: "Some liberal treatments of the question of miracles draw a marked distinction between the miracles of the New Testament, particularly those of our Lord himself, and those of the Old Testament. Both more radical and

---

17. Wooden literal interpretation is the most literal form in that it denies the usage of metaphors entirely and interprets scripture in its *prima facie* meaning. This stands in contrast to the more popular method of historical grammatical interpretation which allows for the usage of metaphor in interpretation.

18. Broussard, *20 Answers*, loc. 258–260 of 778.

more conservative critics have pointed out that in principle the narratives stand or fall together."[19]

According to Dan O Via: "The purpose of biblical theology is to mediate between biblical religion and dogmatic theology. Its subject matter is the former, but its method is theological, a systematizing of the teachings of biblical religion."[20] In order to facilitate this, the bible must be interpreted correctly using the *historical grammatical method*. This method has been attacked consistently by critical scholars, but is now also undermined by conservatives who allow for various postmodern errors to infect their methodologies.

According to Kaiser the "single meaning hermeneutic" is foundational to the entire enterprise:

> No definition of the process of interpreting the Bible can be more fundamental than this: to interpret we must in every case reproduce the sense the scriptural writer intended for his own words.1 The first object in the interpretive process must be to link those ideas with the author's language 2. That he first connected with them. 3. Then we may proceed to express those same ideas understandably for our own day.[21]

While conservative interpreters and biblical theologians agree to this foundational premise, many have inadvertently violated this rule by adopting false methodologies. They have allowed postmodern approaches to seep into their interpretive process. Kaiser believes that by affirming any of the following statements, scholars violate the single meaning hermeneutic:

> (1) It is often possible to extend the authorial intention and world beyond the human author by means of the canonical context. (2) The New Testament writers read new meanings into the Old Testament. (3) "The meaning of the Bible is not static and locked up in the past, but is something living and active." (4) "An author may intend to convey multiple meanings or levels of meaning." Evaluations of the interpretive process such as these tend to introduce a whole new set of rules into the way biblical texts have been interpreted for centuries.[22]

However, according to R. C. Sproul, not all the tools of criticism need to be eliminated from the conservative interpreter's tool box. Sproul states:

19. Wood, *New Bible Dictionary*, 771.
20. Via, *What Is New Testament Theology?* loc. 25–27 of 1533.
21. Kaiser, *Recovering the Unity of the Bible*, loc. 4112–4116 of 4925.
22. Kaiser, *Recovering the Unity of the Bible*, loc. 4117–4125 of 4925.

In the history of biblical studies, we have seen in the last two centuries the rise of so-called "higher criticism." So much of higher criticism is fueled by skepticism with respect to the reliability of the biblical texts. Since orthodox Christians stand opposed to many of the arguments of higher critics, they sometimes overlook valuable insights that can be gained through critical analysis of the text. Some of these analyses can be very helpful to our endeavor of seeking an accurate understanding of the Bible.[23]

One such exception would be source criticism. For instance, Sproul believes that source criticism can help scholars to understand the methodology of the synoptic gospels in relation to the Q hypothesis.[24]

4.2.1 Dating of the Book of Isaiah

Overall, critical scholarship has been largely in retreat in recent years due to various archeological discoveries and the increasing prominence of biblical theology. These discoveries are providing evidence for Old Testament signs and wonders such as the destruction of Sodom and Gomorrah, and the prophecies in Isaiah about King Cyrus of Persia. Traditionally, scholars have dismissed the prophecies found in Isaiah as being *ex post facto* prophetic fulfillments.

One example of the conflict between conservative and critical scholarship is the dating of the Book of Isaiah. According to J. Harold Thomas, the authorship and dating of Isaiah was not seriously challenged for the first 1700 years of church history.[25] However, with the development of historical criticism, and the rejection of the supernatural elements of scripture during the enlightenment, the authorship of Isaiah and the pre-exilic dating came under heavy attack. This is due in large part to the predictive prophecies contained in Isaiah. As Hugh Ross states:

> The prophet Isaiah foretold that a conqueror named Cyrus would destroy seemingly impregnable Babylon and subdue Egypt along with most of the rest of the known world. This same man, said Isaiah, would decide to let the Jewish exiles in his territory go free without any payment of ransom (Isaiah 44:28; 45:1; and 45:13). Isaiah made this prophecy 150 years before Cyrus was born, 180

---

23. Sproul, "Witness of Matthew," lines 1–6.
24. Sproul, "Witness of Matthew," lines 18–27.
25. Thomas, "Authorship of Isaiah," 55.

> years before Cyrus performed any of these feats (and he did, eventually, perform them all), and 80 years before the Jews were taken into exile. (Probability of chance fulfillment = 1 in 10 to the 15th power.)[26]

A prophecy so unlikely would have to be interpreted as a supernatural act. However, since critical scholars presupposed a naturalist worldview (which disallowed Special Divine Action), they began to develop alternate theories including later datings and redactors (e.g., Deutero-Isaiah and Trito-Isaiah). As Thomas states: "The naming of Cyrus by Isaiah ben Amoz as the servant of God in the returning of the captives in the minds of the critical scholars is particularly incredible. They regard prediction of this nature as impossible and they reject every instance of it to be found in the Bible as spurious."[27]

By the mid-twentieth century the scholarly consensus was nearly complete. Christopher Seitz stated that: "the division of the book of Isaiah into two or three Isaiahs is "in many ways the greatest historical consensus of the modern period."[28] The three main reasons which caused critical scholars to give a exilic or post exilic dating to at least Isaiah 40–66 (or the entire book) were: "(1) The references to Judah as ruined and deserted with the temple destroyed (e.g., 44:26b; 58:12; 61:4; 63:18; 64:10f), (2) The difference of language and style between chapters 1–39 and 40–66, (3) The advanced theological ideas in chapters 40–66, and (4) the occurrence of the name Cyrus (Is. 44:28; 45:1)."[29] Regardless of the particulars, the underlying purpose was to deny the occurrence of signs and wonders (e.g., fulfilled prophecy) which occurred in Isaiah as plausible or even possible.

However, during the later twentieth century, developments in the conservative position had begun to sway many of the more critical scholars back to an earlier dating (700–800 BC) and authentic authorship of Isaiah 40–66. There were numerous reasons for this including:

> (1) The references to the widespread practice of idolatry (which was eradicated in the exilic and post-exilic period), (2) The apparent Palestinian setting of the geographical and topographical references (44:14; 41:19), (3) The unlikelihood that the esteemed author of chapters 40–66 would forever remain anonymous, and

---

26. Ross, "Fulfilled Prophecy," lines 66–73.
27. Thomas, "Authorship of Isaiah," 46–55.
28. Rooker, "Dating Isaiah 40–66," 303.
29. Rooker, "Dating Isaiah 40–66," 303.

(4) New Testament passages that explicitly refer to texts from Isaiah 40–66 as coming from the prophet Isaiah.[30]]

But perhaps the strongest evidence during the twentieth century came from the area of diachronic linguistic analysis. This method was pioneered by the work of Arno Kropat in the early twentieth century.[31] Rooker's analysis of various Hebrew words and their lack of evolution led him to conclude on a pre-exilic dating of Isaiah. Rooker concludes:

> But it should be emphasized that where diachronic comparison can be made, based on the present state of diachronic research, Ezekiel, from the exilic period as well as post-exilic Hebrew literature always indicates later linguistic features than those we find in Isaiah 40–66. Thus, if critical scholars continue to insist that Isaiah should be dated in the exilic or post-exilic period, they must do so in the face of contrary evidence from diachronic analysis.[32, 33]

What can be concluded by the example of Isaiah, is that critical scholars, by presupposing an anti-supernatural worldview, have sought to explain away the prophecies in Isaiah as *ex-post facto* fulfillments. However, due to developments in archeology and linguistic analysis, this thesis was no longer plausible. This leaves critical scholars in a bit of a quandary as they must now either admit a prophecy so remote as the naming of Cyrus occurred by chance alone (one in a quadrillion), or admit that a legitimate act of Special Divine Action occurred!

In the following sections I will give a brief overview of the signs and wonders contained in the Old Testament. The purpose in the following sections is not to be exhaustive, but rather to accurately represent the signs and wonders contained in Scripture so that they can serve as a background for modern examples of Special Divine Action. Due to space limitations, these sections will necessarily be brief with the knowledge that whole books

---

30. Rooker, "Dating Isaiah 40–66," 303.
31. Rooker, "Dating Isaiah 40–66," 304.
32. Rooker, "Dating Isaiah 40–66," 312.

33. In 1967 when the critical views on Isaiah were nearly ubiquitous, Thomas nevertheless stated: "But this is a plea not to yield to the consensus of the modernistic school without due consideration of the arguments of the defenders of Isaiah's authorship of the whole book. A position that was not seriously challenged for the first 1700 years of Christian history discloses solid merit. The views of those who have rejected it are far from unanimous. They are divided as to the nameless author to whom they credit various portions and radically in their dating of them. This discloses that the logic of their appeals, even among themselves, is far from unassailable" (Thomas, "Authorship of Isaiah," 55).

could be written on the instances of signs and wonders from any one of these eras.

There are at least two hundred and fifty occurrences of signs and wonders as well as over two thousand examples of fulfilled prophecy contained in scripture.[34] These signs and wonders and prophecies occur throughout both the Old Testament and New Testament texts. Despite this, some authors such as John McArthur have embraced a form of cessationism when viewing the Old Testament.[35] The argument is that throughout the two millennia B.C., there were only a few periods of miracles. As Stafford summarizes: "The exodus, the early prophets, and the time of Jesus produced the vast majority of the miracles. Together they cover approximately 140 years—perhaps 7 percent of the two-thousand-year total."[36] However, as there are many miracles described or alluded to throughout each of the other periods of the Old Testament; MacArthur's thesis does not withstand scriptural scrutiny.[37] Rather, what is seen in the Old Testament is the power of God acting to bring about his purposes: establishing and protecting his people, chastising evil and fulfilling his promise of salvation in the promised messiah.

Before analyzing particular types of signs and wonders which occur in the Old Testament, I will first briefly analyze some of the Hebrew words and phrases used. According to TR McNeal:

> The two Hebrew words most frequently used for "miracle" are translated "sign" (*oth*) and "wonder" (*mopheth*). They are synonyms and often occur together in the same text (Exodus 7:3; Deuteronomy 4:34; Deuteronomy 6:22; Deuteronomy 7:19; Deuteronomy 13:1; Deuteronomy 26:8; Deuteronomy 28:46; Deuteronomy 34:11; Nehemiah 9:10; Psalm 105:27; Isaiah 8:18; Jeremiah 32:20; Daniel 6:27). "Sign" may be an object or daily activity as well as an unexpected divine action (Genesis 1:14; Exodus 12:13, RSV; Joshua 4:6 Ezekiel 24:24. The basic nature of a sign is that it points people to God. "Wonders" describe God's supernatural activity, a special manifestation of His power (Exodus 7:3), but false prophets can perform actions people perceive as signs and wonders. (Deuteronomy 13:1–3). Wonders can serve as a sign of a future event. Signs seek to bring belief (Exodus 4:5; compare Exodus 10:2), but they do not compel a person to believe (Exodus 4:9).

---

34. McDowell, *Evidence that Demands a Verdict*, 267–320.
35. For a full view and refutation of this position see Graves, *Strangers to Fire*.
36. Stafford, *Miracles*, 82.
37. See Graves, *Strangers to Fire*.

> At times God invites people to ask for signs (Isaiah 7:11). The signs He has done should make all peoples on earth stand in awe (Psalm 65:8). They should join the Psalmist in confessing that the God of Israel "alone works wonders" (Psalm 72:18).[38]

McNeal additionally states that modern interpreters have a harder time understanding the meaning the scriptures had in antiquity due to the effect of the enlightenment. Previous to the enlightenment, the worldview was theistic, not naturalistic. There was no division between the natural and the supernatural, all was controlled by God. As McNeal states: "In the "natural" event the Bible views God as working providentially; whereas, in the miraculous, God works in striking ways to call attention to Himself or His purposes."[39] But, according to Walton and Keener, the Hebrew word for wonder: ". . .does not necessarily designate something supernatural as opposed to natural (i.e., a "miracle"). In the ancient world, people did not consider anything truly "natural"—God was involved in everything and therefore "miracle" was a meaningless designation."[40] This worldview was held not only by the authors of the Old Testament and the New Testament; but by the pre-enlightenment church as well. As McNeal Concludes:

> One's view of the miraculous is related to one's view of the universe. A mechanistic perspective believes the world is controlled by unalterable natural laws and cannot allow for the possibility of miracles. Christians in every century have refused to have their universe so limited. They have affirmed the continuing miraculous work of God in the universe He created, continues to care for, uses to reveal Himself, and has promised to redeem.[41]

4.2.2 Old Testament Motifs

4.2.2.1 *God—Creator*

The Old Testament begins in Genesis with the story of creation. In this book God is established as the creator of the universe and mankind (Genesis 1–2). As Elwell notes: "Therefore, nature herself was a miracle (Job 5:9–10;

---

38. McNeal, "Miracles, Signs, Wonders," lines 6–18.

39. McNeal, "Miracles, Signs, Wonders," lines 48–49.

40. Walton and Keener, *NIV Cultural Backgrounds Study Bible*, loc. 124199–124201 of 350904.

41. McNeal, "Miracles, Signs, Wonders," lines 56–60.

Pss 89:6; 106:2), and an act of kindness or victory over one's enemies is so described (Gen 24:12–27; 1 Sam 14:23). The natural order is totally under Yahweh's control, so a miracle was observable not because of its supernatural nature but because of its character as part of the divine revelation."[42]

Despite living an existence which could be described as paradise, man quickly fell into sin, and evil entered the world (Genesis 3). Soon God saw that the entirety of mankind had become evil and decided to cleanse the planet and start over (Noah's Ark and the flood: Genesis 6–8). Even after the flood, mankind persisted in their rebellion and thus were scattered by God at the *Tower of Babel* (Genesis 11). Throughout the narrative God's *providence* and role as creator and judge of the world is exemplified in these supernatural acts. The acts and motifs of Genesis will be echoed throughout the rest of Scripture. As William MacDonald summarizes:

> The twin themes of blessing and cursing are carefully woven throughout the fabric of Genesis, and indeed, the whole word of God. Obedience brings enrichment of blessing, and disobedience the opposite. The great curses are the penalties of the fall, the universal Flood, and the confusion of tongues at Babel. The great blessings are the promise of a Redeemer, the salvation of a remnant through the Flood, and the choice of a special nation to be a channel of God's grace, Israel.[43]

4.2.2.2 God—Father (Covenant Relationship)

"The Lord had said to Abram, "Leave your native country, your relatives, and your father's family, and go to the land that I will show you. I will make you into a great nation. I will bless you and make you famous, and you will be a blessing to others. I will bless those who bless you and curse those who treat you with contempt. All the families on earth will be blessed through you."

GENESIS 12:1–3

If there is one overarching motif in the Old Testament signs and wonders, it is the providence of God. Not willing to give up on mankind, God chose Abraham, a pagan man, to be the father of his people (Genesis

---

42. Elwell and Comfort, "Miracles," 900.
43. MacDonald, *Bible Believer's Commentary*, 16.

12). While Abraham himself is not known to have performed signs and wonders, we see God working signs and wonders all around him. For instance, Abraham's wife Sarah becomes pregnant with Isaac, despite being ninety years old (Genesis 17:17). God punishes the Egyptian pharaoh with plagues for placing Sarah in his household (Genesis 12). Finally, God shows his approval of Abraham both with the act of consuming his sacrifice with fire (Genesis 15:7), as well as by blessing him with enormous wealth (Genesis 24:35). God does all of these signs and wonders because of his covenant relationship with Israel.

According to MacDonald: "Our word "covenant" translates the Hebrew word berîth. In the NT covenant and testament both translate the same Greek word (diathēkē). In the title of the Scriptures the meaning "covenant" seems definitely preferable because the Book constitutes a pact, alliance, or covenant between God and His people."[44] While many modern Christians place a far heavier emphasis on the *new covenant* and neglect to study the Old Testament, this is a mistake. MacDonald states: "The relationship between the OT and the NT was nicely expressed by Augustine: The New is in the Old concealed; The Old is in the New revealed."[45]

This covenant relationship with God as the father of the Israelites continues throughout the Old Testament with many more signs and wonders occurring. For instance, the various victories over the Canaanites and other pagan tribes who were to be purged from the Promised Land. In the case of Joshua, God intervened several times to grant him victory. First, God caused giant hail to fall on the enemies of Israel in battle (Jos 10:11). Next God caused the sun to stop so that the Israelites could achieve victory (Jos 10:12–13). Finally, God caused the walls of Jericho to fall and allow the Israelites to conquer the city (Jos 6:20).[46]

4.2.2.3 *Prophets—Confirm their Mandate*

"The LORD brought us out of Egypt with a mighty hand and an outstretched arm, with a terrifying display of power, and with signs and wonders."

DEUTERONOMY 26:8

---

44. MacDonald, *Bible Believer's Commentary*, 1.
45. MacDonald, *Bible Believer's Commentary*, 1.
46. Stafford, *Miracles*, 88–89.

Renewal Apologetics

Prophets in the Old Testament used signs and wonders to confirm their divine mandate; this is similar to what occurs later in the New Testament with the apostles. Beginning with Moses, and continuing with Elijah, Elisha, Daniel and others, God empowered his prophets to cause signs and wonders to show that their messages and authority were divinely ordained. As Elwell notes: "This connection with salvation history is crucial, for Israel at all times tried to guard against a desire for the spectacular. Deuteronomy 13:1–4 warns against accepting a wonder as authenticating a prophet; rather, the authentication must come from the fact that he worships Yahweh."[47]

For example, in the case of Moses, God used signs and wonders to both convince, and punish Pharaoh for keeping the Israelites in bondage. Moses was able to turn his staff into a snake, turn water into blood, and to foretell the various plagues which would befall Egypt. After convincing Pharaoh to release the Israelites, God hardened Pharaoh's heart leading to the killing of the Egyptian army at the Red Sea. Some of these miracles were done by God through Moses; others such as the plagues and the hardening of Pharaoh's heart were done directly by the hand of God. The common thread throughout, was God using a prophet to facilitate his judgement on those who were enemies of his people. Elwell states that there are two themes to the signs and wonders in Exodus:

> The miracles of the exodus account have two foci: The plagues represent the absolute power of Yahweh over the gods of Egypt, and the miracles of the wilderness show God's absolute care and protection of his people. The plagues are particularly interesting because each one is directed at one of the gods of Egypt and reveals Yahweh as the only potentate. The basic theme is found in Exodus 7:5 and is repeated throughout the account (cf. 7:17; 8:6, 18; 9:14–16, 29; 12:12): "When I show the Egyptians my power and force them to let the Israelites go, they will realize that I am the Lord." In this regard they were directed not only at the Egyptians but also to the Israelites, who needed to know that their God would vindicate them against the Egyptians. This is borne out in the major miracle, the crossing of the Red Sea. The plagues themselves show a gradual increase in severity.[48]

The prophetic period is another era of scripture which contains a high frequency of signs and wonders. In particular, the time of Elijah and Elisha

---

47. Elwell and Comfort, "Miracles," 900.
48. Elwell and Comfort, "Miracles," 900.

presented a crisis point in Jewish history as many of the people had fallen into Baal worship. It was then that God reasserted his power through signs and wonders, and showed the weakness of Baal, thus restoring many Israelites to their faith. As Elwell notes:

> Here the wondrous nature of the miracles is more evident than anywhere else in the OT. There are conscious allusions to the exodus miracles, perhaps looking to Elijah as a new Moses reinstituting the true worship of Yahweh. Parallels are seen in the challenge to the priests of Baal (1 Kgs 18; cf. Ex 7); the revelation of God on Mt Horeb with the wind, earthquake, and fire (1 Kgs 19; cf. Ex 19); and the parting of the Jordan (2 Kgs 2:10–14; cf. Ex 14). Many of the miracles were intended to demonstrate the impotence of Baal, such as the drought, the contest on Mt Carmel, and the miraculous sustenance supplied by God. Again, God's actions within history were part of his self-revelation, the vindication of his messengers, and the punishment of his enemies.[49]

In the rest of the Old Testament, God continued to use his prophets to act as his spokesmen to his people. They warned of the coming consequences for rebellion (Amos 3; Jer 33:26), warned foreign leaders of their impending punishment (Dan 5), and foretold the coming of the messiah (Isa 7:14; Isa 53). While signs and wonders did occur with greater frequency during the times of Moses, Elijah and Elisha, they were nevertheless omnipresent in the entirety of the Old Testament.[50]

4.3 NEW TESTAMENT SIGNS AND WONDERS

"The most important point to be made about the miracles of the New Testament in particular is that they are all signs of things beyond themselves."[51]

—ERIC METAXAS

---

49. Elwell and Comfort, "Miracles," 900.

50. The three periods of signs and wonders argument given by McArthur and other cessationists is erroneous as it fails to see the persistent occurrence of signs and wonders throughout every period of history in ancient Israel. Yes, some periods had more signs and wonders than others, but there was never a period where signs and wonders ceased. For more on the cessationist position See McArthur, *Charismatic Chaos*, McArthur, *Strange Fire*, and Warfield, *Counterfeit Miracles*. For a thorough refutation of this position see Ruthven, *Cessation of the Charismata*, and Graves, *Strangers to Fire*.

51. Metaxas, *Miracles*, 75.

The largest cluster of signs and wonders per year occurs during the New Testament era. In the three-year period of Jesus' ministry, dozens of miracles occurred. The time of the messiah and the New Covenant had been foretold since the fall in Genesis when God promised to crush the devil (Gen 3:14–15). The central focal point of the New Testament is in the miracle of the *Resurrection of Christ*. Signs and wonders are not something ancillary to Christianity; rather, the Christian faith is based upon signs and wonders!

In the New Testament, we see signs and wonders serving numerous functions. Jesus used them as object lessons to show how faith and repentance could be rewarded with miraculous healings. And perhaps, most importantly, he used signs and wonders to authenticate himself as the messiah by showing his power over the kingdom of darkness. Likewise, the apostles authenticated their divine mandate by preforming numerous miraculous healings. Following the example of Christ, the apostles refused to let their signs and wonders become a sideshow and used the power of the Holy Spirit to achieve the greater glory of God.

There are four Greek words used to describe Special Divine Action in the New Testament and these words are translated as "signs and wonders" in several passages:"(Matthew 24:24; Mark 13:22; John 4:48; Acts 2:43; Acts 4:30; Acts 5:12; Acts 6:8; Acts 7:36; Acts 14:3; Acts 15:12; Romans 15:19; 2 Corinthians 12:12; 2 Thessalonians 2:9; Hebrews 2:4)."[52] The four Greek words are:

1. "Sign" (*semeion*) in the New Testament is used of miracles taken as evidence of divine authority. Sometimes it is translated as "miracle" (Luke 23:8 NIV; Acts 4:16, Acts 4:16, 4:22 NAS, NIV). John was particularly fond of using "sign" to denote miraculous activity (see John 2:11, John 2:11,2:18, John 2:18,2:23; John 3:2; John 4:54; John 6:2, John 6:2, 6:14; John 6:14,6:26; John 7:31; John 9:16; John 10:41; John 11:47; John 12:18; John 37:1; John 20:30; Revelation 12:1, Revelation 12:1,12: 3; Revelation 13:13–14; Revelation 15:1; Revelation 16:14; Revelation 19:20).

2. "Wonders" (*teras*) translates a Greek word from which the word *terror* comes. It denotes something unusual that causes the beholder to marvel. Although it usually follows "signs," it sometimes precedes it (Acts 2:22, Acts 2:22, 2:43; Acts 6:8) or occurs alone (as in Acts 2:19). Whereas a sign appeals to the understanding, a wonder appeals to the imagination. "Wonders" are usually presented as God's activity (Acts 2:19; Acts 4:30; Acts 5:12; Acts 6:8; Acts 7:36; Acts 14:3; Acts 15:12), though sometimes

---

52. McNeal, "Miracles, Signs, Wonders," lines 19–22.

they refer to the work of Satan through human instruments (Matthew 24:24; Mark 13:22; 2 Thessalonians 2:9; Revelation 13:11–13).

3. New Testament writers also used *dunamis*, power or inherent ability, to refer to activity of supernatural origin or character (Mark 6:2; Acts 8:13; Acts 19:11; Romans 15:19; 1Corinthians 12:10, 1 Corinthians 12:28–29; Galatians 3:5; 2 Thessalonians 2:9; Hebrews 2:4).

4. "Work" (*ergon*) is also employed in the New Testament in the sense of "miracle." John the Baptist heard of the "works" of Jesus while he was in prison (Matthew 11:2). The apostle John used the term frequently (Matthew 5:20, Matthew 5:20, 5:36; Matthew 7:3; Matthew 10:38; Matthew 14:11–12; Matthew 15:24)."[53]

4.3.1 Jesus—Confirm as Messiah/Teach Lessons

"Like every miracle that ever was, it is a sign from beyond this world, pointing us to the God beyond this world, to the God who came into this world to lead us back to himself and who is himself the way back."[54]

—ERIC METAXAS

"The Kingdom of God is at hand; the kingdom of evil is being destroyed" forms the basic teaching of Christianity. As John the Evangelist wrote, "The reason the Son of God appeared was to destroy the devil's work" (1 John 3: 8). In all of these confrontations we cannot miss seeing Jesus' fierce determination to heal the sick."[55]

—FRANCIS MACNUTT

Jesus used signs and wonders to confirm that he was the messiah. As God incarnate, Jesus had the ability to perform signs and wonders at will. However, Jesus also knew that his ministry had a specific timeframe and initially chose to hide the fact that he was the messiah (John 2:4; Matthew 6:20). However, in time, Jesus began to use his miraculous power to confirm his messiahship to the multitudes. Jesus preformed many signs

---

53. McNeal, "Miracles, Signs, Wonders," lines 23–41.
54. Metaxas, *Miracles*, 87.
55. MacNutt, *Healing Reawakening*, 51.

and wonders in this regard, and this led to him achieving a wide following (John 6:2; Mt 8:1).

Nevertheless, just as in the case of many modern skeptics, no amount of proof would suffice with his opponents! The Pharisees, for instance, immediately seized on the fact that he performed signs and wonders on the Sabbath (Matthew 12:10; Mark 3:2; John 9:14–16). They told the Romans that he was causing unrest and needed to be executed (Luke 23:2; Matthew 27:25). They even accused him of performing signs and wonders by the power of the devil (Matthew 12:24–25)! According to Michael Rydelnik the Pharisees failed to see the signs and wonders performed before them as "signs of the messianic times" (Moody Commentary on Matthew 16:1).[56] Rather, as Rydelnik notes:

> His earlier miracles led the Pharisees to accuse Jesus of working with the Devil, yet they wanted more miracles. Sign means "an unusual act with special meaning," and here carries the nuance of a miraculous act. The scribes and Pharisees were looking for such an astounding display of power that all reservations about Jesus could be dismissed. Perhaps if Ursa Major (the Big Bear constellation) would run across the sky and bite Orion's belt—then they could believe (Moody Commentary on Matthew 12:38–45).[57]

Jesus combined signs and wonders with his ministry to show his authority. He knew that his claims of messiahship and power over evil would require signs and wonders to authenticate. As Bock states: "Jesus deals with spiritual forces we otherwise cannot see. Claims with words are often cheap and empty, but actions can raise questions and show things words can only attempt to describe. So, Jesus does not appeal primarily or merely with words; rather, he acts and explains. In this way, those around him can see he has acted with unusual force and authority."[58]

So, while the words of Jesus's ministry were vital; it was through his healings and exorcisms that Jesus displayed his power and messiahship.[59]

---

56. Rydelnik and Vanlaningham, *Moody Bible Commentary*, loc. 59133–59136 of 93487.

57. Rydelnik and Vanlaningham, *Moody Bible Commentary*, loc. 58850–58855 of 93487.

58. Bock, *Who Is Jesus*, 91–92.

59. Bock, *Who Is Jesus*, 80: Bock further notes: "Exorcisms and the battle with cosmic forces are part of a worldview associated with Jewish eschatological and apocalyptic hope. Central to this way of seeing the world is a belief in the struggle between spiritual forces of good and evil, not just social and political concerns. Among the Jews, Sadducees

Jesus knew that the Pharisees had hardened hearts; this is why he often refused to perform signs and wonders in their presence (Matthew 12:38–39). Rather, Jesus used his signs and wonders to teach the pure in heart, and to heal those who were repentant (Mark 10:52). In this way, the signs and wonders of Christ are very different from the magic of the pagans of his era, and the counterfeit miracles in the age to come (Matthew 24:24; 2 Thessalonians 2:9). Christ's signs and wonders were performed for specific purposes which ultimately served to glorify God.

Finally, while Christ's signs and wonders were powerful, they still needed to be correctly interpreted by faith. If the people lacked faith, Jesus often refused to provide a sign (Matthew 13:58) (Mark 8:11–12).[60] Perhaps his strongest condemnation against those who lack faith occurs in his references to the towns of Chorazin and Bethsaida:

> Woe to you, Chorazin! Woe to you, Bethsaida! For if the miracles that were performed in you had been performed in Tyre and Sidon, they would have repented long ago in sackcloth and ashes. But I tell you, it will be more bearable for Tyre and Sidon on the Day of Judgment than for you. And you, Capernaum, v will you be lifted to the heavens? No, you will go down to Hades, for if the miracles that were performed in you had been performed in Sodom, it would have remained to this day. But I tell you that it will be more bearable for Sodom on the Day of Judgment than for you." (Luke 10:13–15)

4.3.2 The Resurrection
(Matthew 28; Mark 16; Luke 24; and John 20)

"The resurrection can be doubted on philosophical grounds, but it is a historical certainty that the first disciples of Jesus believed He had actually risen from the dead (1 Co 15). Such belief cannot be accounted for merely by hallucination, wishful thinking, or conspiracy to commit fraud."[61]

—*Ted Cabal*

---

did not hold to this way of seeing the world, but many of those in other groups did, especially among the Essenes and Pharisees."

60. Elwell and Comfort, "Miracles," 901.
61. Cabal, *Apologetics Study Bible*, loc. 86544–86546 of 93255.

The central sign and wonder of Christianity, the central event of Scripture, is the Resurrection of Jesus Christ. In the Resurrection of Jesus Christ, we see sin and death being conquered by God. Jesus served as a substitution for us, and fulfilled the requirements of the Old Covenant and established a New Covenant based upon faith. This theological linchpin is best summarized by the apostle Paul:

> Now if Christ be preached that he rose from the dead, how say some among you that there is no resurrection of the dead? But if there be no resurrection of the dead, then is Christ not risen: And if Christ be not risen, then is our preaching vain, and your faith is also vain. Yea, and we are found false witnesses of God; because we have testified of God that he raised up Christ: whom he raised not up, if so be that the dead rise not. For if the dead rise not, then is not Christ raised: And if Christ be not raised, your faith is vain; you are yet in your sins. Then they also who are fallen asleep in Christ have perished. If in this life only we have hope in Christ, we are of all men most to be pitied (1 Cor 15:12–19).

The apostle concludes: "For as in Adam all die, even so in Christ shall all be made alive" (1 Corinthians 15:22). So, it is in Christ's Resurrection that we have new life and that sin is conquered in the new covenant relationship.

D. R. Wood summarizes that salvation is necessarily connected with the Resurrection, without the Resurrection there can be no assurance of our salvation. Wood states: "The point is that Christianity is a gospel, it is good news about how God sent his Son to be our Savior. But if Christ did not really rise, then we have no assurance that our salvation has been accomplished. The reality of the Resurrection of Christ is thus of deep significance." Citing the apostle Paul, Wood argues that since Christ died for our sins and rose for our justification (Romans 4:25), that the "Resurrection of Christ is the central act whereby we are saved. Salvation is not something that takes place apart from the Resurrection."[62]

Not all scholars believe in a literal Resurrection. Many critical scholars take the view that the Resurrection was a metaphor and that it should be interpreted as Christ living on in the hearts of his followers.[63] Others, have argued that the apostles themselves stole the body and that the resurrection was a fraud. Neither of these two objections can withstand historical scrutiny because of the lives lived by the apostles after the death and resurrection

---

62. Wood, "Resurrection," 1012.
63. Nash, *Worldviews in Conflict*, 156.

of Christ. The ministry and eventual martyrdom of the apostles does not necessarily mean that the resurrection occurred; but rather, it proves that the apostles believed that it occurred. They had enough belief that they had seen the risen lord, that they were willing to die for this belief.[64]

Like any sign and wonder, the Resurrection has its critics within Christian scholarship who believed that it did not really occur. According to Maas, the four main theories are:

1. The Swoon theory—Christ did not actually die on the cross, but rather temporarily lost consciousness. This theory was originally promoted by Paulus (See "Exegetisches Handbuch"1842). But the theory lacked credibility and was even later criticized by Strauss.

2. The Imposition Theory—The disciples of Jesus stole his body from the tomb. This feat was accomplished by bribing the guards placed at his tomb. This theory was originally promoted by Celsus (See Origen, Against Celsus II.56).

3. The Vision Theory—Mary Magdalen first hallucinated/lied that she had seen the risen Christ. Then the rest of his followers began to have mass hallucinations that they too had seen the risen Christ.

4. The Modernist View—The resurrection is not provable as it is not empirically verifiable (See Loisy "Autour d'un petit livre").[65]

Eric Metaxas challenges each of these views head on. He states of the *swoon theory*:

> Although this is generally now—because of medical science and other evidence—thought risible, we should compose ourselves to consider it, because it still makes its appearance in books every few years.[66] The theory was first composed about 200 years ago when modern science was still in its infancy. Today it is well known that the amount of injuries inflicted on Jesus and others who were crucified meant certain death.[67]

64 Nash, *Worldviews in Conflict*, 156.
65. Maas, "Resurrection of Jesus Christ," lines 63–154.
66. Metaxas, *Miracles*, 106.
67. Metaxas, *Miracles*, 106: Metaxas notes that Jesus was whipped with a flagellum (this was not done to most crucifixion victims). According to Metaxas: "The flagellum had a number of cords, at the end of each of which was affixed a piece of bone or metal, which would hook and tear the flesh of the person scourged. The third-century historian Eusebius tells us that the "veins were laid bare, and . . . the very muscles, sinew, and bowels of the victim were open to exposure."

Metaxas also discounts the imposition or theft theory as highly implausible for numerous reasons. To begin with, the disciples or anyone else would have had to overcome sixteen Roman soldiers in order to steal the body from the tomb.[68] The bribery theory does not hold water either, as any Roman soldier caught accepting a bribe would themselves be crucified or burned alive in their own clothing according to Metaxas.[69]

Rather, what Metaxas correctly sees in the critical objections to both biblical miracles in general and the Resurrection in particular, is an unwillingness to get past the material world. Because of these presuppositions, the critical scholar is often trapped using the most implausible of scenarios in order to defend their naturalistic/materialistic worldview.[70] As Metaxas concludes:

> So how can scholars say such things? It is no great mystery. From where they are, they have no choice. They are materialists who have dismissed the very idea of a literal resurrection, and with it every other kind of bona fide miracle. But in overemphasizing the materialistic world and dismissing the idea of anything supernatural, they ironically inflate metaphor beyond the bursting point. They say that this cannot happen literally, because all there is, is the natural, materialistic world.[71]

Most Christian scholars now agree that the evidence for a literal view of the Resurrection of Christ is overwhelming. According to Nash, the Resurrection is supported by the "strongest possible eyewitness testimony (1 Corinthians 15:5–8). For the apostle Paul, the historicity of the resurrection is a necessary condition for the truth of Christianity and for the validity of Christian belief (1 Corinthians 15:12–19). Paul writes, ". . .if Christ has not been raised, your faith is futile; you are still in your sins. Then those also who have fallen asleep in Christ are lost. If only for this life we have hope in Christ, we are to be pitied more than all men" (1 Corinthians 15:17–19)."[72]

Nash further argues that although denying a literal Resurrection is "fashionable" with many scholars, this view is not supported by any evidence. The mere existence of the church disproves this theory. Nash concludes: "So long as we are not controlled by naturalistic presuppositions, we are able

---

68. Metaxas, *Miracles*, 101.
69. Metaxas, *Miracles*, 101.
70. Metaxas, *Miracles*, 97.
71. Metaxas, *Miracles*, 97.
72. Nash, *Worldviews in Conflict*, 155.

to accept the possibility of miracles; indeed, the miracle of the Resurrection is possible. But when our attention turns to the issue of its actuality, we need to look at the evidence and what that evidence says with regard to the plausibility of alternative explanations."[73] Nash rightly concludes that these alternative explanations run contrary to a mountain of evidence.

4.3.3 Apostles—Confirm Their Mandate/Work of the Holy Spirit (Pentecost)(Acts 2:1–4)

"The disciples went out and preached everywhere, and the Lord worked with them and confirmed his word by the signs that accompanied it."
MARK 16:20

"God also bearing them witness, both with signs and wonders, and with various miracles, and gifts of the Holy Spirit, according to his own will?"
HEBREWS 2:4

The signs and wonders of the apostles served as an authentication of their message. During the life of Christ, the apostles were empowered to perform signs and wonders. In many instances, they went out and healed the sick and expelled demons as they preached the gospel (Mark 3:15) (Mark 16:20) (Hebrews 2:4).[74] However, it was not until Pentecost when they were filled with the Holy Spirit that they fully were empowered to perform signs and wonders as a means of spreading the gospel (Acts 2). According to MacDonald: "Gifts of the Holy Spirit were special enablements given to men to speak and act in a manner that was completely beyond their natural abilities. The purpose of all these miracles was to attest to the truth of the gospel, especially to the Jewish people, who traditionally asked for some sign before they would believe."[75, 76]

---

73. Nash, *Worldviews in Conflict*, 156.

74. According to Bock: "Another passage from Q is part of the instruction for the mission of the disciples in Matthew 10: 7– 8 = Luke 9: 1– 2, where Jesus gives this authority to the disciples. This text also has a variation of a summary in Mark 6: 7–13" (Bock, *Who Is Jesus*, 81).

75. MacDonald, *Bible Believer's Commentary*, loc. 2147 of 87060.

76. This is of importance as it reflects the worldview still held by most today in the global south. As many missionaries report, the people will not follow anyone incapable of performing signs and wonders.

After the death of Christ, the apostles were in hiding. Having lost their leader, and being in fear for their lives, they huddled in a room in Jerusalem. It was in this room that they were given the power of the Holy Spirit during Pentecost. After Pentecost, several things changed. For instance, the apostles were no longer afraid, and most of them eventually died as martyrs. The apostles also had more insight into divine righteousness and at times possessed limited omniscience (Acts 5:1–11).[77] As Elwell states:

> Paul in 2 Corinthians 12:12 and Romans 15:18–19 considered them as "sign-gifts," which authenticated the divine authority of the "true apostle." He listed healing and miracles as specific "gifts of the Spirit" in 1 Corinthians 12:9–10. In Galatians 3:5 he considered them evidence for the presence of the Spirit. The author of the letter to the Hebrews in 2:4 said "God bore witness" to the true message of salvation via miracles. Therefore, in the apostolic age the miracles of God's servants were seen more directly as authenticating signs of God's action in his messengers.[78]

However, these signs and wonders were not to be limited to the apostles; rather we are told that signs and wonders are the very sign of all believers. In the Great Commission, Jesus tells us that not only do all believers have the ability to perform signs and wonders, but that the performance of signs and wonders is a necessary sign of a believer (Mark 16: 17–18).

4.4 CHURCH HISTORY MIRACLES

"Historical memory, like all memory, is selective, and there are many claimants to the telling of Christianity's early history. The Christian Church has a long and crowded past, and whether by design, forgetfulness, or ignorance, its history will be remembered in different ways. Our knowledge of the past is not objective but personal and participatory."[79]
—Robert Louis Wilkens

Proponents of cessationism argue that signs and wonders ceased after the apostolic age; as their sole purpose was to authenticate the gospel

---

77. See Acts 5 for the story of Ananias and Sapphira wherein Peter knows by divine revelation the deception the two had sought to commit within the church.
78. Elwell and Comfort, "Miracles," 902.
79. Wilken, *First Thousand Years*, 1.

message being preached by the first century apostles. However, this view does not withstand historical scrutiny. Even a cursory examination of the writings of the early church fathers will show that not only did signs and wonders continue to occur, but they remained a significant part of how the gospel was spread.[80] What is true however, is that at various times, different factions within the church have embraced the theology of cessationism. This phenomenon occurred in its fullest form within Protestantism (post-Calvin); and caused a dearth in signs and wonders. This happened as proponents of cessationism no longer believed that signs and wonders occurred; thus, they no longer prayed for them or attempted to perform them.

4.4.1 100 AD–1500 AD (The Age of Christendom)

"At least in the Western church what Confirmation is supposed to do is precisely release the power of the Holy Spirit in the Catholic's life. So we should all become charismatics when we're confirmed!"[81]

—PETER KREEFT

"Hence Gibbon says, "The Christian Church, from the time of the Apostles and their disciples, has claimed an uninterrupted succession of miraculous powers, the gift of tongues, of visions and of prophecy, the power of expelling demons, of healing the sick and of raising the dead" (Decline and Fall, I, pp. 264, 288), thus miracles are so interwoven with our religion, so connected with its origin, its promulgation its progress and whole history, that it is impossible to separate them from it."[82]

—JOHN DRISCOLL

By the time of Saint Augustine of Hippo (354–430 AD), the prominence of signs and wonders within Christendom had lessened. This is not because they were no longer occurring, but rather was due to the isolation of many towns and the lack of an authentication structure. As Stafford notes, signs and wonders continued to occur but were no longer

---

80. See Ruthven, *Cessation of the Charismata*.
81. Kreeft and Nevins, *Charisms*, 149–54.
82. Driscoll, "Miracle," loc. 437439–437443 of 700382.

publicized. Often signs and wonders would occur, and even people within the same town were unaware.[83]

In this climate, the early Augustine felt that the signs and wonders which were still occurring did not rise to the level of the biblical signs and wonders; this is why they were not written about as much as the former. However, over time Augustine came to witness numerous signs and wonders. In chapter 22 of *The City of God*, Augustine alludes to over seventy miracles which he knows to have occurred within his vicinity.[84] Augustine bemoans the lack of knowledge of these miracles:

> Even now, therefore, many miracles are wrought, the same God who wrought those we read of still performing them, by whom He will and as He will; but they are not as well known, nor are they beaten into the memory, like gravel, by frequent reading, so that they cannot fall out of mind. For even where, as is now done among ourselves, care is taken that the pamphlets of those who receive benefit be read publicly, yet those who are present hear the narrative but once, and many are absent; and so it comes to pass that even those who are present forget in a few days what they heard, and scarcely one of them can be found who will tell what he heard to one who he knows was not present.[85]

4.4.1.1 *Francis MacNutt (Gradual Cessationism)*

Francis MacNutt in his text *The Healing Awakening: Reclaiming Our Lost Inheritance* (2006),[86] argues that signs and wonders were very common amongst the church fathers and amid the Roman persecution. He states: "Spirit baptism, together with healing and exorcism, flourished in those early years following Pentecost. From those ancient times, long before the printing press, we have only a few records of how the poor, uneducated, ordinary Christians lived, but we have enough to know that they expected to be filled with and led by the Spirit."[87]

However, after Christianity became acceptable, and the Christians left the catacombs, a gradual dissipation in signs and wonders occurred. This

---

83. Stafford, *Miracles*, 120.
84. Augustine, *City of God*, 749–99.
85. Augustine, *City of God*, 765–66.
86. See MacNutt, *Healing Reawakening*.
87. MacNutt, *Healing Reawakening*, 79.

History of Signs and Wonders

dissipation was over the course of several centuries and was not complete, so it largely went unnoticed. MacNutt states:

> To destroy a belief as central to Christianity as healing was, the change had to take place so gradually that Christians didn't even realize that they had lost anything. In Part 2 we saw how, for the first three centuries of Christianity, healing prayer was an ordinary practice; any and every Christian had the confidence to pray for the sick. How ironic then that just when Christianity emerged from the catacombs victorious, following the vicious persecutions, healing and deliverance prayer started sliding down the slope into insignificance.[88]

This lack of signs and wonders occurred for numerous reasons and cannot be traced to one single cause. MacNutt gives several different reasons including: a lack of a charismatic view of the sacraments,[89,90] the adoption of Platonism (causing an embrace of suffering), view that only "heroic Christians" were capable of performing miracles, and the lack of an expectation of miracles.

4.4.1.1.1. Sacraments

According to MacNutt, the sacraments of baptism and confirmation were viewed as a means of spirit baptism by the early church. As MacNutt notes: "In the early Church, adults who were baptized expected, at the same time, to be baptized in the Spirit; they regarded the two experiences as the same event."[91] However, overtime infant baptism became the norm

---

88. MacNutt, *Healing Reawakening*, 103.

89. MacNutt, *Healing Reawakening*, 91–92: MacNutt recalls a woman he baptized trembling as if deeply touched by the Holy Spirit. She was subsequently able to pray in tongues for the first time. MacNutt believes that this is how sacraments such as baptism are supposed to occur.

90. MacNutt, *Healing Reawakening*, 93: MacNutt states: "Now, I personally believe that something does happen at baptism and confirmation. I met one Roman Catholic bishop who remembers seeing tongues of fire descend on all the other young people who were being confirmed with him. And yet, when he started to share this experience, he found, to his disappointment, that no one else had seen the fire. So he learned not to talk about this marvelous event, for fear of being seen as a fanatic."

91. MacNutt, *Healing Reawakening*, 62.

and by the eighth century baptism was no longer viewed as a "Pentecost experience." This view has unfortunately persisted until today.[92]

4.4.1.1.2. Platonism/Embracing Suffering

Originally the church viewed disease and suffering as something to be overcome. The witness of Christ was that they were caused by the kingdom of darkness and could be overcome by the kingdom of God. However, overtime, Christian theology was influenced by Platonism and began to instead embrace suffering. According to MacNutt: "Plato saw the body as a prison from which the soul needed to escape. This devaluing of the body was absorbed into Christianity."[93] As this view began to hold sway, the kingdom of God began to be identified with the next world. Suffering was embraced as a means of purification: "A cross in this life—a crown in the next. The body was to be "mortified"—which literally means to be "put to death"—for the soul's sake."[94]

4.4.1.1.3. Heroic Christians

Over time, the charismata were viewed as the sole providence of the Saints and holy men. Augustine himself did not initially believe he was capable of performing a healing miracle.[95] "In the early apostolic Church, manifestations of the presence of the Holy Spirit—tongues, joyfulness, prophetic words, visions—were regarded as normal."[96] Overtime the connection between healing and sainthood became so strong that even the desert fathers such as Saint Anthony refused to pray for the sick as: "They did not want to appear proud, as if they felt themselves worthy of sainthood."[97]

---

92. MacNutt, *Healing Reawakening*, 92.
93. MacNutt, *Healing Reawakening*, 107.
94. MacNutt, *Healing Reawakening*, 107.
95. MacNutt, *Healing Reawakening*, 116: MacNutt further cites an example wherein Augustine himself had healed a person by laying hands on them and praying for them. Thus three years before his death Augustine wrote a book called *Revisions* where he corrected some of his earlier theology including his initial belief in cessationism. See Also: Augustine, *Revisions*.
96. MacNutt, *Healing Reawakening*, 91–92.
97. MacNutt, *Healing Reawakening*, 91–92.

4.4.1.1.4. Lack of Expectation

In the early church, the examples of Jesus and Paul were used as the primary method of evangelism. Signs and wonders not only occurred, they were expected. Instead of arguing with words and reason alone, they demonstrated their power to heal and cast out demons as the means of demonstrating the power of God. As MacNutt notes:

> In the early Church—as in the Third World today—people not only believed in evil spirits but actively experienced demonic power firsthand. To proclaim the Kingdom of God was not just to get into a persuasive argument about the truth of Christianity; it meant casting out evil spirits and demonstrating God's power. As Paul claimed: "I came among you in weakness, in fear and great trembling and what I spoke and proclaimed was not meant to convince by philosophical argument, but to demonstrate the convincing power of the Spirit, so that your faith should depend not on human wisdom but on the power of God (1 Cor 2: 3-4).[98]

However, MacNutt agrees that a belief in signs and wonders persisted despite these obstacles, even if somewhat diminished. He states: "As late as the thirteenth century Thomas Aquinas explained this passage (1 Corinthians 2:3-4) as meaning that Paul confirmed the truth of his teaching by the power of the Holy Spirit—namely, by demonstrations of healing and transformed lives rather than by logic and philosophy."[99]

Despite this general trend away from the charismata and towards cessationism, miracles continued throughout the middle ages. For example, in the case of Bernard of Clairvaux (1090–1153). Stafford states: "Miracles gave tremendous prestige to the Catholic Church in the Middle Ages. Many, many miracles were recorded, sometimes in a form that seems almost modern in its historical detail. Bernard of Clairvaux, for example, healed hundreds of people as he traveled about Germany, and these healings are well documented, with times, places, and the names of witnesses recorded."[100]

---

98. MacNutt, *Healing Reawakening*, 86.
99. MacNutt, *Healing Reawakening*, 86.
100. Stafford, *Miracles*, 125–26.

4.4.2 Reformation Era (The Catholic Argument)

"The Protestant View of Miracle. The Protestant view changed little from that of Aquinas, except that it became a tool to attack the authority of the Roman Catholic Church, based on claims of miracles among their saints and shrines."[101]

—WILLIAM DYRNESS

The Reformation brought many changes to how post biblical signs and wonders were viewed. The original Reformers such as Martin Luther (1483–1546) and John Calvin (1509–1564) held to concentric cessationism (i.e., the belief that miracles still occurred in unevangelized areas to aid in the spread of the gospel).[102] However, in time the various denominations founded in the Reformation came to embrace full blown cessationism. This occurrence was largely to facilitate an attack on the authority and ongoing signs and wonders still occurring in the Roman Catholic Church.[103] The miracles still occurring within the Catholic Church according to Calvin were satanic in nature:

> You can't establish the truth simply by pointing to miracles, he said, because not all miracles come from God. "We must remember that Satan has his miracles, too," Calvin wrote. (For example, Pharaoh's magicians did miracles [Exodus 7: 11– 12]; the slave girl in Acts 16: 16 could predict the future by a spirit that possessed her; and Jesus warned in Matthew 7: 22– 23 that many people in the Last Judgment would protest that they did many miracles, only to be told by Jesus, "I never knew you!") Miracles associated with relics and shrines, Calvin asserted, linked to a false gospel of superstition and human attempts to please God by our own efforts. They were false miracles accrediting a false gospel. Furthermore, Calvin said, the Reformation churches did have accrediting miracles: Jesus' miracles and the apostles' miracles. Those were enough. They had accredited the true gospel of the Protestant churches—the gospel found in the Scriptures.[104]

Additionally, according to Jon Ruthven, the reformers emphasis on *sola scriptura* caused them to deny revelatory spiritual gifts (e.g., prophecy) as well

---

101. Dyrness and Karkkainen, *Global Dictionary of Theology*, 547.

102. Ruthven, *Cessation of the Charismata*, 22–24.

103. For a fuller discussion of this see Ruthven, *Protestant Theology* and Ruthven, *Cessation of the Charismata*.

104. Stafford, *Miracles*, 125–26.

as the ongoing miracles within Catholicism and the *Radical Reformation*.[105] This denial gave birth to *Protestant Scholasticism*.[106] This caused the authority claimed by the church, and the role of tradition and creeds, to be seen as irrelevant to biblical interpretation. Ruthven summarizes:

> We've now seen how the doctrine of cessationism was resurrected by Protestants—I say "resurrected," because this doctrine was invented a few centuries before by pagan Greeks and Jews who hassled each other and especially Christians over reports of miracles among them. This doctrine of cessationism paradoxically co-existed with all kinds of reports of miracles and prophecies throughout church history up to the reformation era. Why? Well, if you are defending your doctrines, the last thing you want to do is concede miracle-working among your opponents. It makes you look bad. This happened over and over again when some Christians took the New Testament seriously and started praying for sick people or started receiving revelatory dreams or messages; jealous church officials typically banned the practice. Or if they did it themselves it was cool. Saints Augustine, Gregory VI, and even some writers of the Westminster Confession both denied and affirmed revelation and miracles! (Sigh! More sausage).[107]

Within Catholicism, ongoing miracles were used as an apologetic and a polemic to attack the Reformation. The Catholics argued that since no miracles were occurring within the Protestant church, that the church lacked God's *stamp of approval*.[108] Due to the Reformation, the church did begin a more formalized process to both authenticate miracles as well the *Canonization of Saints*. The process of miracle authentication relied first on the three-degree classification system which had existed since the early middle ages:

1. First degree: Miracles against nature (e.g., Moses parting the Red sea).
2. Second degree: Miracles exercised over nature (e.g., Jesus resurrecting Lazarus).
3. Third degree: Miracles beyond nature (e.g., Jesus healing the blind).[109]

---

105. The Radical Reformation was a sixteenth century movement which began in Switzerland. Specific groups included the Anabaptists and Mennonites. Adherents rejected the ecclesiastical authority of the Catholic and Lutheran churches. Heavy emphasis was placed upon the invisible church of believers.

106. Ruthven, *Protestant Theology*, 3.

107. Ruthven, *Protestant Theology*, 23.

108. Stafford, *Miracles*, 125–26.

109. Parigi, *Rationalization of Miracles*, 37–38.

The Canonization process consisted of a series of seventeen trials covering the life, work and possible miracles of each candidate.[110] The paths towards sainthood were different depending upon the era of the saint. The lowest status (venerable), could be awarded simply by the petition of local authorities. However, to move to the next statuses (blessed or saint), required two miracles performed in front of eyewitnesses, three if there were no witnesses, and four if the case was not contemporary.[111]

Previous to this process, there were many local saints whose miracles lacked Vatican authentication. This however does not necessarily mean that their miracles did not occur, rather that the Vatican chose to remain silent on the matter due to a lack of evidence. While miracles and saints did help to bolster the faith of many Catholics, the church remained very guarded against false claims of miracles, and miracles which lacked authentication. As Parigi notes:

> Because of the pressures that local communities exerted on the Congregatio, particularly before 1642, few cases moved through all the steps in either process. Of the 348 cases that the Congregatio considered in the period from 1588 to 1751, almost 43 percent remain venerable today, that is, they sit at the lowest rung of the Congregatio's holy ladder (ASV Fondo Processi, 1147). More interestingly, 96 percent of all cases during this period moved less than one step. Besides the 108 cases that were made venerable and remain so to this day, there were also eleven contemporary candidates who were declared saints "on the spot."[112]

4.4.2.1 Scott Hahn: The Political Roots of Historical Criticism

"The constant misuse of historical criticism is sterile. It doesn't reproduce itself, and so it's dying. It's also parasitical, though, so we've got to be mindful of how it preys upon Catholic students who aren't formed adequately in philosophy."[113]

—Scott Hahn

---

110. Parigi, *Rationalization of Miracles*, 34.
111. Parigi, *Rationalization of Miracles*, 36.
112. Parigi, *Rationalization of Miracles*, 37.
113. Keating, "Scott Hahn," lines 442–444.

History of Signs and Wonders

Important to this discussion is the development of historical criticism. According to Scott Hahn, it was the historical critical method which first began to undermine confidence in scripture within Christendom. While undermining Scripture was the primary goal, an attack on miracles and God's interaction in the world was a necessary consequence as well. While most scholars trace historical criticism back to the eighteenth century; Hahn sees the roots of criticism going all of the way back to William of Occam (1285–1348) and Averroes (1126–1198). Tracing the lineage through the ages Hahn suggests that Benedict Spinoza, Richard Simon and Thomas Hobbes were the three founding fathers of historical criticism; with Spinoza being the most important. All three men were either excommunicated or condemned as heretics by their denominations.[114]

4.4.2.1.1 Political Motivations

Hahn believes that the methods of historical criticism (the analytical tools), are in and of themselves, value neutral. However, since their inception, these tools have been used for ulterior political and secular motivations. As Hahn states: "Because, at root historical criticism is grounded in a hermeneutic of suspicion—a basic distrust of tradition—and this was self-conscious on the part of those who developed the methods and of the early practitioners of them in Germany and England and throughout the world."[115]

What the practitioners of historical criticism were attempting to do was to shift authority from the priesthood, and the church, over to the secular. Hahn states: "In regard to political liberalism, as we recall, a common feature running from Marsillius through Hobbes, Spinoza, and Tolland was the denigration of the priesthood because the primacy of the priesthood implied a primacy of the sacred over the secular, the priest over the king."[116] This motivation however was not shared by the original reformers such as Luther and Calvin who actually desired to reform the Catholic Church, not splinter from it. As Hahn notes: "Luther and Calvin despite all their zeal, and for all of their concern for reform in the church and for all of their pride, didn't really believe that what they were doing was going to represent a permanent fragmentation of Christendom."[117]

---

114. Keating, "Scott Hahn," lines 45–49.
115. Keating, "Scott Hahn," lines 21–23.
116. Hahn and Wiker, *Politicizing the Bible*, 562.
117. Keating, "Scott Hahn," lines 28–31.

4.4.2.1.2 Philosophical Presuppositions

It is the misuse of the historical critical method which has caused many scholars and the laity to lose their faith in the authority of scripture, the role of tradition, and to ultimately adopt a secular worldview. Despite the claims of scholars such as Wellhausen, the historical critical method always preceded from various philosophical underpinnings.[118] Almost always the methods were abused for secular and political purposes.[119]

Hahn's analysis is of importance as Hume's critique is rooted in the same philosophical tradition of the enlightenment; which gave rise to the fullest expression of the historical critical method. Many Christian scholars who became proponents of historical criticism adopted deistic and anti-supernatural worldviews. Subsequently, these scholars also became sceptics of Special Divine Action. This phenomenon continues today and many scholars who do not hold to historical critical "orthodoxy" find themselves marginalized and blackballed. Karl Keating states: "Cutting-edge scholars who question these things are marginalized. Their books don't get reviewed, they don't get promoted, and the centers of this scholarship—certain universities—invite onto their staff only people who already agree with the majority opinion. It seems as if they're more concerned with maintaining this dike against leaks than in seeing whether there's some substance."[120]

Hahn's analysis of the contention between critical and conservative scholars is similar to Karl Keating's. Hahn states:

> This phenomenon is especially prevalent in American Catholic scholarly circles. But you seem to find many more Jewish and Protestant scholars doing what Cardinal Ratzinger called for in his 1988 Erasmus Lecture, that is, a "criticism of the critics"—and their misuse of historical-critical methods. And you don't need to look very far to find their vested interests and ulterior motives, their hidden agendas beyond their hypothetical reconstructions, and why these tenuous theories catch fire and become the rage of the day. But in Catholic circles you don't find the same sort of thing, at least in North America. Yet Ratzinger's lecture was a clarion call to do precisely this, to recognize the real but limited value of historical criticism: limited uses, but almost unlimited abuses.[121]

---

118. Hahn and Wiker, *Politicizing the Bible*, 8–9.
119. Hahn and Wiker, *Politicizing the Bible*, 8–9.
120. Keating, "Scott Hahn," lines 169–73.
121. Keating, "Scott Hahn," lines 174–83.

4.4.2.1.3 Hahn's Conclusion

The adoption of the historical critical method, over the biblical worldview, by many biblical scholars, amounts to a subornation of divine revelation to philosophy and reason. This began with Spinoza according to Hahn:

> He tried to create a natural civil religion by subordinating theological method and religious truth claims to the categories of philosophy. It wasn't simply the elevation of reason over revelation. It was a pitting of reason *against* faith. This marriage which has endured for many centuries throughout Europe—the marriage of reason and faith based upon divine revelation—was split, seemingly forever.[122]

And while proponents of this worldview believe it to be value neutral; this is far from the truth, as seen in my discussion on the philosophy of science and scientific naturalism in chapter 2. Adoption of a secular worldview requires numerous philosophical presuppositions. As Hahn notes: "If our own lengthy analysis has established anything, it is that philosophy did precede biblical criticism."[123] And, this worldview is at odds with what we are told in scripture. The solutions for these dilemmas according to Hahn are twofold:

1. Not to completely discard the entire artifice of historical criticism; rather: "...significantly more politicizing aspects of nineteenth-century scriptural scholarship are called for, and only such studies can hope to disentangle the legitimate tools of the historical critical method from the various political and secular aims."[124]

2. In terms of worldview, Christians should return to the classical Christian worldview which is largely exemplified in the *Via Antiqua* (e.g., Augustine, Aquinas, pre-modernism). In a word, this worldview could be described as philosophical *realism*. Seeing a timeless transcendence to the Christian faith; which crosses all epochs and geographical boundaries is one of the implications of this worldview. Having some access to an actual reality, which actually exists is another. Understanding that reason and logic have limits, that there are ineffable truths, but that these truths are not irrational, but rather are *suprarational*, would be a third implication. As Hahn concludes:

---

122. Keating, "The Bible Politicized," lines 61–65.
123. Hahn and Wiker, *Politicizing the Bible*, 561.
124. Hahn and Wiker, *Politicizing the Bible*, 566.

It is hard to define, but what I mean by "historical criticism" needs to be understood in two ways. First, the methods are analytical tools, and in and of themselves can be considered neutral. They can be used positively, and they can be used negatively. Second, the actual circumstances in which these tools were developed gives us another and a clearer understanding of what historical criticism is, because at root historical criticism is grounded in a hermeneutic of suspicion—a basic distrust of tradition—and this was self-conscious on the part of those who developed the methods and of the early practitioners of them in Germany and England and throughout the world.[125]

4.4.3 Modern day (Twentieth/Twenty-First Century)

"Jesus' teaching was demonstrated by His action: He had the authority to back it up. This is the basic teaching of the Gospel, which we have largely lost: The Kingdom of God is here; the kingdom of Satan is being destroyed."[126]

-FRANCIS MACNUTT

The enlightenment view against of Special Divine Action still holds sway today in many areas of the academy, including some more liberal streams of theological and biblical studies which still embrace historical criticism. This is especially true in western academia. As Dyrness states: "The topic of miracle shows a clash of cultures between traditional Christian theology and human experience worldwide. This is especially true for most non-Western societies, but increasingly, in the postmodern Western world as well, where, for example, 89% of Americans believe that even today, God performs miracles by his power."[127] The belief and occurrences of Special Divine Action is even stronger outside the west. According to Walton and Keener, millions of the conversions which have occurred in China, are the result of healing experiences. In India, one survey showed that more than 10% of non-Christians claimed to be cured by Christians praying for them in the name of Jesus.[128]

125. Keating, "Scott Hahn," lines 16–23.
126. MacNutt, *Healing*, 56.
127. Dyrness and Karkkainen, *Global Dictionary of Theology*, 546–47.
128. Walton and Keener, *NIV Cultural Backgrounds Study Bible*, loc. 215398–215402 of 350904.

While Catholics continued to believe in miracles and the ongoing work of the Holy Spirit after the Reformation, it can be argued that the influence of Thomistic theology did encourage a lesser form of continuationism. This is because Aquinas relegated miracles as gifts of the Holy Spirit only given to believers of great sanctity.[129] This belief made miracles outside the reach of the ordinary laity and priesthood. It was not until the *Catholic Charismatic Revival* began in the late 1960s that a large segment of Catholics began to operate in the special gifts of the Holy Spirit, and engage in miraculous healings. Spirit baptism was now seen as a mechanism available to all believers, not just to those of great sanctity and the saints. This overthrew the theology of Aquinas, which had been the dominant view for centuries. As Ruthven states:

> According to Aquinas, the central function of miracles was to serve as a signum sensibile, a testimonium to guarantee the divine source and truth of Christian doctrines, particularly the deity of Christ. To explain the lack of visible miracles in his day, Aquinas asserted that Christ and his disciples had worked miracles sufficient to prove the faith once and for all; this having been done, no further miraculous proof of doctrines could be required. In a number of other places, however, he vitiates this position by maintaining that miracles can recur if they aid in confirmation of preaching and bringing mankind to salvation. But even beyond this, Aquinas suggested that believers of great sanctity may exhibit miraculous gifts of the Spirit, a doctrine that strengthened the veneration of shrines and canonization of saints via miracles. A widespread belief in these last two exceptions, which essentially contradicted cessationism, resulted in the excesses surrounding miracles which precipitated the Reformation.[130]

Beginning in the early twentieth century, many miracles began to occur at various Protestant revivals. While initially mainstream Protestants and fundamentalists continued to hold to cessationism, by the end of the twentieth century various forms of continuationism had become dominant. Today cessationism is largely seen as a theology in retreat.[131] According to Grudem, the largest group of evangelicals do not fit within either

---

129. Ruthven, *Cessation of the Charismata*, 21–22.

130. Ruthven, *Cessation of the Charismata*, 21–22.

131. Grudem provides an in-depth discussion about the various views. He labels the "open but cautious" position as the largest group amongst evangelicals in America today. See Grudem, *Miraculous Gifts for Today*, 13.

cessationist or continuationist camps, but rather can be described as "open but cautious."[132] Due to this openness towards miracles, there are now hundreds of millions of testimonies of miracles within Protestantism.[133]

4.5 CONCLUSION

"Unless we share in Jesus' ministry of healing the sick and casting out evil spirits, our preaching about the Kingdom of God being here among us is simply an empty promise."[134]

— *Francis MacNutt*

While it is debatable if charismatic gifts and miraculous healings were less frequent in previous eras; it is beyond debate that we are living in a time of great healing worldwide. The last century has simultaneously (and not coincidentally) seen both the birth of the global Pentecostal revival and the Charismatic Renewal Movement; as well as the spread of the gospel into more unevangelized areas than in any previous era.

Previous to the Renewal movement, the Reformation overall had a negative effect on the frequency of Special Divine Action due to the belief in cessationism by many Protestant denominations.[135] Meanwhile, within Catholicism, there was an undeniable belief in Special Divine Action as a special grace, accomplished either via intercessory prayer or directly by God. However, the Catholic Charismatic Revival took the frequency of Special Divine Action to another level with its rejection of Thomistic theology.

This historical summary of the miraculous will help to serve as a foundation for the examination in chapter 6 of modern medically documented miracles. This chapter has shown that healing miracles have existed throughout both biblical and church history. The healing miracles occurring today are no different than ones which have occurred throughout history. What is different today is that medicine and science have advanced to a stage where they are better able to either authenticate healings as miraculous, or dismiss them to naturalistic causes. Thus, we are living in an unprecedented time for the evaluation of miracles.

---

132. Grudem, *Miraculous Gifts*, 13.
133. Keener, *Miracles*, 762.
134. MacNutt, *Healing Reawakening*, 56.
135. See Ruthven, *Cessation of the Charismata*.

Chapter 5

Documented Cases of Modern Special Divine Action

5.1 INTRODUCTION

Given the preceding discussion of Hume's skepticism, and the various ways of overcoming it, I will now focus on the available documentation of modern medical miracles. Unfortunately, the bulk of literature available on modern miracles is largely testimonial, and is thus lacking in scientific verification and rigor. This does not mean that these testimonies do not describe possible miraculous occurrences, but rather, the lack of documentation does not make them of apologetical value.

According to Candy Gunther Brown, it was the sceptics of the miraculous who first attempted to use medical records in an effort to discredit the claims of miraculous healings in the early twentieth century. However, by the 1960s it was the Pentecostals/Charismatics who were using *before-and-after medical documentation* of attested healings.[1] This enterprise has waned since the 1990s due both to an increasing emphasis on personal testimony, and the adoption of postmodern values. But, there remains today a large body of evidence pointing towards numerous instances of *medically surprising recoveries* including audio/visual impairments and metastasized cancers.[2]

---

1. Brown, *Testing Prayer*, 279.
2. Brown, *Testing Prayer*, 279.

However, such surprising recoveries do not constitute absolute proof for sceptics of the miraculous. Sceptics usually use the term *spontaneous remission* when referring to such occurrences, and have doubt about the long-term cure of the conditions. For instance, many cancers will go into remission for years only to later resurface. An additional complication is that the vast majority of cases lack enough medical documentation. Lacking this documentation, doctors are usually hesitant to label the occurrence a spontaneous remission. More often, doctors will simply doubt the initial diagnosis and testing.[3] This however does not preclude the existence of numerous well documented cases which defy any medical explanation. The fact that these cases are accompanied by prayer makes them of strong apologetical significance.

In this chapter, I will examine three documented medical miracles from three separate sources: Craig Keener, Jacalyn Duffin, and the Lourdes Medical Bureau. While each source has numerous documented modern miracles, I have chosen ones which I believe are of the most value apologetically. These cases have strong medical/scientific evidence, a strong causal linkage to prayer, and are lacking in plausible naturalistic explanations.

5.2 CRAIG KEENER

Craig Keener's text *Miracles: The Credibility of the New Testament Accounts* (2011), serves as a compendium on the topic of miracles. While the bulk of the material addresses biblical miracles, the topic of modern miracles is covered in-depth as well. Keener is a former atheist turned biblical scholar. He believes that he still has an initial bias in favor of naturalistic explanations of the miraculous.[4] However, Keener also concludes that the evidence of modern medical miracles is overwhelming. As will be shown, Keener's position in favor of the miraculous does not result from mere fideism, but rather, is based upon evidence, and reasoned deductions/conclusions.

5.2.1 Wealth of Testimonies

According to Keener, there are hundreds of millions of testimonies of the miraculous both in the west and in the third world.[5] Perhaps most

3. Brown, *Testing Prayer*, 153–54.
4. Keener, *Miracles*, 766.
5. Keener, *Miracles*, 212.

important is the fact that 55% of medical doctors in the west believe that they have witnessed a medical miracle.[6] While some of these miracles can be dismissed by sceptics as being psychosomatic or having other naturalistic causes; many cannot. As Keener notes, many of these miracles have occurred in the presence of doctors and numerous other witnesses, and involve healings which cannot be explained by naturalistic causes. For example, broken bones healed and undamaged as confirmed by x-rays, or the instant healing of cataracts.[7] As Keener summarizes:

> When we have not an isolated instance but a pattern of a number of highly extraordinary events accompanying prayer that do not normally occur without it, it may seem logical to explore prayer as a factor in the anomalous events. I think of circumstances like a number of persons apparently dead for hours abruptly recovering; cataracts immediately disappearing; long-term impaired hearing becoming normal; or the more unusual of the nature miracles I have mentioned. Some of these cases are strongly attested to by reliable eyewitnesses.[8, 9]

Keener readily acknowledges that the majority of miraculous testimonies come from the third world, and thus lack appropriate medical documentation. However, he was able to catalogue over one hundred modern medical miracles which have occurred in America, with strong medical documentation. The following miracle is one of the best examples as it involves a healing with no naturalistic explanation (resurrection); and occurred in front of numerous American medical professionals.[10]

5.2.2 Cardiologist's Testimony: Man Dead for Forty Minutes

This case involves the testimony of Dr. Chauncey Crandall, an American cardiologist with world class credentials.[11] As Keener summarizes:

6. Keener, *Miracles*, 721.

7. Keener, *Miracles*, 722, 762.

8. Keener, *Miracles*, 762.

9. Keener's contention that these types of healings usually do not occur without prayer is of the utmost importance!

10. In addition to Keener, the recent text: Rotbart, *Miracles We Have Seen*, has examples of over fifty medical miracles witnessed and described by American doctors. These miracles include resuscitations after more than thirty minutes, instant cures of terminal diseases and patients awakening from comas after being declared brain dead.

11. Keener, *Miracles*, 577.

> On Friday October 20, 2006, fifty-three-year-old auto mechanic Jeff Markin checked himself into the hospital in West Palm Beach, Florida, and died of a heart attack there. Emergency room personnel labored for nearly forty minutes to revive him, unsuccessfully shocking the flat lined man seven times. Crandall was called in to certify the obvious: there was no point in continuing attempts to revive the man. Crandall recounts that Markin was not merely dead but unusually obviously dead: his face, toes, and fingers had already turned black.[12]

Markin was subsequently declared dead and Crandall wrote up his assessment and went to return to his other patients. However, just then, he felt the Holy Spirit compelling him to return and to attempt resuscitation one more time. Crandall began with a prayer over the corpse: "Father, God, I cry out for the soul of this man. If he does not know you as his Lord and Savior, please raise him from the dead right now in Jesus's name."[13] After being shocked, Markin's heart immediately began beating again after more than forty minutes. Just as amazingly, Markin had no brain damage or other ill effects from the forty plus minutes without circulation.[14]

This was all witnessed by a full team of doctors and nurses. This case is of considerable apologetical value due to the credibility of the witnesses; as well as the implausibility of naturalistic explanations. Dr. Crandall's belief that medicine and God often work together and are not mutually exclusive was proven right, as Markin was resuscitated by a combination of both prayer and medicine.[15]

5.2.3 The Element of Prayer

The element of prayer is what gives the various testimonies cited by Keener apologetical value. Had these occurrences simply occurred at random then there would be more plausibility towards labeling them as mere gaps within our current understanding of science. The fact that they occurred due to prayers to God (within Christian contexts), and very rarely occur without

---

12. Keener, *Miracles*, 577.
13. Keener, *Miracles*, 577.
14. Lack of oxygen for more than six minutes usually causes severe brain damage and death.
15. Keener, *Miracles*, 577–78.

prayers,[16] suggests something more is at play, and shows a strong causal linkage between prayer and miracles.[17]

Craig Keener believes that God chooses to act as a loving father at times and to provide miracles for his children who ask. He also believes that miracles occur most where they are needed most (e.g., the third world). Since those in the third world are often lacking the necessary medicine to treat their conditions, there are more miracles occurring there. Additionally, people in the third world are less secular, and have a stronger belief in miracles, and thus they are more likely to pray for a miraculous healing. As Keener concludes:

> Since too many of the examples above seem implausible to me as pure coincidence, particularly cumulatively, I prefer a different hypothesis: a personal God ready and able to heal, but one who also often allows created nature to take its own course and who is not manipulated by formulas, as perhaps an impersonal or merely psychological force could be. Although miracles are consistent with the character of the biblical God, we cannot always predict a personal deity's future actions, especially when our knowledge about the factors involved in those actions are limited. If miracles happened with absolute regularity, we would view them as part of the course of nature; their occurrence beyond providence in nature allows them to function more specifically as signs revealing God's activity and character.[18, 19]

5.3 ROMAN CATHOLIC EXAMPLES

A defining characteristic of many Catholic miracles is the element of intercession. While saints have healed people directly during their lifetimes, very often it is after their deaths that miracles are claimed through prayer. Intercessory prayer is an element in all of the miracles of the Saints and at the Shrine of Lourdes.

16. Keener, *Miracles*, 762.

17. Prayer, and the not coincidental timing of prayer are the essential elements which places various naturalistic explanations into the realm of the implausible. This point is foundational in overcoming the God of the gaps objection. And is perhaps the lynchpin to the entire evidential argument from miracles!

18. Keener, *Miracles*, 740–41.

19. The irregularity of miracles points away from both the God of the gaps and an unknown naturalistic force objections.

While intercessory prayer does not have as strong a presence within many Protestant denominations, its origins are nevertheless biblical (Jas 5:16, Rev 5:8, John 15:17, 2 Cor 1:11, Luke 23:34, 1 Sam 7:5–9). Martin Luther himself defended the Magnificat and intercessory prayers to Mary. In Luther's commentary on the Magnificat he states: "That is why I said Mary does not desire to be an idol; she does nothing, God does all. We ought to call upon her that for her sake God may grant and do what we request. Thus also all other saints are to be invoked, so that the work may be every way God's alone."[20] According to Catholic apologist and theologian Dave Armstrong, this view is "Very Catholic! Luther understands biblical paradox: God does all; at the same time (without contradiction) He uses us to do it."[21]

5.3.2 Vatican Process of Authentication (*Medica Consulta*)

Non-Catholic authors such as Jacalyn Duffin and Ruth Cranston are very impressed by the lengths which the Catholic Church goes to in order to validate miracles. Duffin is a hematologist who describes herself as an atheist. Duffin first became interested in possible Catholic miracles after evaluating medical results of a patient who was cured of leukemia after praying to a future saint.[22] Ruth Cranston is a Protestant reporter who developed an interest in Lourdes after hearing about numerous miracles occurring there, which she decided to investigate firsthand.

Duffin summarizes her ten years of research in her text *Medical Miracles: Doctors, Saints, and Healing in the Modern World* (2008). Duffin relays the numerous safeguards which the Catholic Church uses during their authentication process.[23] For instance, the church encourages the sick to continue going to doctors as long as there is any possibility of a medical cure. And, if there is a claim of a cure through prayer, it is immediately scrutinized by a team of world class doctors. She states that these doctors: "were looking for hard evidence of diagnosis, dire prognosis, and unexplained cure. The Vatican takes all this very seriously. It was always insisting

---

20. Luther, "Commentary on the Magnificat," 164.
21. Armstrong, *Proving the Catholic Faith*, 121.
22. Thavis, *Vatican Prophecies*, 184–85.
23. See Congregation for the Saints, "New Laws," lines 1–200.

on up-to-date medicine, it was always insisting on medical corroboration. And it didn't much care if the doctor was a believer or not."[24, 25]

Cranston's account is of value as she writes using an ethnographic approach as a Protestant outsider. Cranston was primarily interested in the details of the authentication process. In particular, she was concerned with the possibilities of fraud and psychosomatic conditions. In her research, she found that all groups of pilgrims are accompanied by at least one doctor who is given a certificate by the pilgrim's primary doctor certifying their condition. If a person then claims to be cured, the doctor immediately informs the Lourdes Medical Bureau so that they can begin an evaluation.

Once the Bureau is given the case, they first rule out all cases where there is no immediate organic change. They are looking for cases such as "the healing of malignant tissue, the restoration of wasted nerves and muscles, the sudden knitting of chronic bone fractures."[26] Cases which are inconclusive are dropped. Cases passing initial evaluation are referred to local physicians. These physicians monitor and test the alleged cures for at least one year; before referring them back to Lourdes for more testing and evaluation by the Bureau itself. The Bureau is comprised of medical doctors from numerous specializations. Likewise, they come from a wide range of religious backgrounds. As one bureau director noted: "Jews, Moslems, Buddhists, Hindus, Protestants of all sects, have been among our colleagues; atheists and unbelievers, too. It's this study of the cures by men of such different viewpoints that guarantees our good faith."[27]

If the Lourdes Medical Bureau decides that the cure is outside of the laws of nature; it is forwarded to another panel of twenty physicians and surgeons in Paris. This panel either drops the case, or declares it as having no scientific explanation. Only cases passing all of these steps are finally referred to the Vatican's Canonical Commission; to be evaluated as a possible miracle. The Commission evaluates the possible cure according to the criteria which includes:

1. That the malady was grave and not improving under medication.

---

24. Thavis, *Vatican Prophecies*, 187–88.

25. Pope Urban VIII originally developed the criteria for establishing miracles and reserved the canonization of saints to the Holy See in 1625. Previous to Urban local bishops were able to canonize saints. See Ott, "Pope Urban VIII," loc. 662499–662611 of 700382.

26. Cranston, *A Protestant Looks at Lourdes*, loc. 168–175 of 385.

27. Cranston, *A Protestant Looks at Lourdes*, loc. 168–175 of 385.

2. That the cure was instantaneous, with no period of convalescence.
3. That the cure was perfect, and that there was no relapse.[28]

According to Ruth Cranston's text *The Miracle of Lourdes*, each year over six million people visit Lourdes in hopes of obtaining a miracle. Since its inception in 1858, there have been over 7000 claims of miracles. Yet only sixty-nine have been authenticated by the church. This is not however because the Bureau believes that such a small number of cures have actually occurred. Rather, it is because of the stringent and lengthy process (described above), which it undergoes in authenticating official miracles, which dismisses all but the most verifiable. Additionally, the number of possible miracles is probably much higher, as many are cured and never seek to have their case authenticated, as they do not wish to have the publicity. Still others cannot begin the authentication process as doctors will often refuse to release medical records to the Bureau.[29]

Nevertheless, the Medical Bureau at Lourdes has catalogued complete records on over 1200 cures which it recognizes as "inexplicable under natural laws." According to Cranston: "In addition it has notations and material concerning some 4000 other cases that are very probably complete and genuine cures. This may seem a small number, in view of the many thousands who come. But ten such cures—or even one—would be equally dumb-founding."[30] The five criteria which a case must satisfy for authentication are:

1. An absence of a curative agent (Such as drugs or injections and special treatments for example).
2. Instantaneousness.
3. Suppression of convalescence.
4. Irregularity of the method of healing.

---

28. Cranston, *A Protestant Looks at Lourdes*, loc. 168–175 of 385.

29. In the case of Dr. Alexis Carrel his mere presence at the grotto was cause for concern. After his name was mentioned as a witness to a cure he wrote an article detailing his observations. Although he remained agnostic on what he had seen, the fact that he did not dismiss the possibility of a miracle led to him being removed from his university teaching position. He subsequently authored the text *The Voyage to Lourdes* wherein he details his observations of the alleged miracle. See Carrel, *The Voyage to Lourdes*.

30. Cranston, *A Protestant Looks at Lourdes*, loc. 168–175 of 385.

Documented Cases of Modern Special Divine Action

5. Function restored without function of the organ—still incapable of accomplishing it.[31]

According to Cranston, any one of these five characteristics would place a cure outside of the boundaries of known medical science and thus would rule out natural causes. This is the label which is given to such cures when they are referred to the Vatican theologians for further evaluation: "outside the known bounds of science." These finding are just as shocking to the scientists and doctors preforming evaluations as they too are sceptics. Many of these doctors are non-Catholics, some are even atheists. Nevertheless, they are willing to follow the cases and evidence where it leads. They conclude that much of what they see in these cures, including the *instantaneousness*, violates all the known laws of science and medicine. For instance, Dr. Guinier, a four-year member of the Lourdes medical board, states: "Microbes are annihilated. . .carcinomas vanish, tubercle bacilli exist no more; gangrenous bones are reformed, severed nerves joined together, wounds cicatrized. Sometimes this happens in a few seconds, sometimes in a few hours, but so rapidly that we can say that factor *time* has disappeared, consequently the cure has operated beyond the laws of biology."[32]

5.3.2 Lourdes (Leg Healing Example)

The Cases of Francis Pascal and Rose Martin are typical of the sixty-nine authenticated miracles. Pascal was a three-year-old who had been blinded and partially paralyzed due to meningitis. Martin had inoperable cervical cancer which had spread throughout her body and left her nearly comatose. Both people, along with thousands of others, were instantly and unexplainably cured after bathing in the waters at Lourdes.[33]

While these cases have their sceptics (as all miraculous claims do); no case has gained such notoriety and caused so much debate as the case of Pieter De Rudder. De Rudder's case is the eighth authenticated case from Lourdes and is labeled as "Lourdes' most discussed miracle."
While working on an estate in Belgium De Rudder's left leg was crushed by a falling tree. The accident was severe, and both the tibia and fibula were crushed below the kneecap. Dr. Affenear set the bones in starched

---

31. Cranston, *A Protestant Looks at Lourdes*, loc. 126 of 385.
32. Cranston, *A Protestant Looks at Lourdes*, loc. 127 of 385.
33. Martin, *Pilgrims Guide to Lourdes*, 31.

bandages. Several weeks later when he removed the bandages, he saw that the ends of the bones were "swimming in pus" and had not begun to knit. Rather, the ends had become necrotic and black in color. Several other physicians looked at the bones and all agreed that the leg must be amputated. De Rudder refused and became bedridden.[34]

Seven years later the owner of the estate called in a specialist named Dr. van Hoestenberghe of Stahille. The doctor noted an open wound still present and a one-inch visible gap between the bones. He stated: "He had endured this break for eight years. The lower part of the leg could be turned in any direction. The heel could be lifted so as practically to fold the leg in half. The foot could be twisted until the heel was in front and the toes at the back."[35] This doctor also recommended amputation; which De Rudder again refused.

Upon hearing of miracles at a shrine in Oostacker, dedicated to Our Lady of Lourdes, De Rudder made a pilgrimage there to seek a miracle. After arriving, another pilgrim accidently bumped into his leg causing Pierre intense pain. De Rudder looked at the statue of the virgin and said:

> "Asking pardon for my sins and begging Our Lady of Lourdes for the grace to be able to earn a livelihood for my wife and children". Then suddenly he felt a strange sensation and was upset, shaken, agitated. Forgetting his crutches, inseparable companions for the last eight years, he rose, walked through the rows of pilgrims and knelt in front of the statue of Mary. Then, astonished to find himself kneeling, he cried, "I am on my knees! O my God!" Getting to his feet he walked again, needing no help. His wife cried out, "What are you doing?" Then like a bolt came the realization, and she fainted.[36]

The cure was instant, full, and without a medical explanation. It was covered in numerous newspapers throughout Europe. De Rudder had numerous witnesses including medical doctors who could attest to his condition both before and after his trip to the shrine. Several doctors from all around Europe came to examine and speak with De Rudder. While many were convinced by the mountain of evidence authenticating the healing; there remained sceptics.

De Rudder worked on the estate for the final twenty-three years of his life. After his death, Dr. Hoestenberghe (the specialist who had examined him before his cure), exhumed his body and amputated his legs. Today, the

34. This summary is culled from Glynn, *Healing Fire of Christ*, loc. 1879–1962 of 3157.
35. Glynn, *Healing Fire of Christ*, loc. 1900 of 3157.
36. Glynn, *Healing Fire of Christ*, loc. 1925 of 3157.

original bones are displayed in the University of Louvain. Copper reproductions are displayed at Lourdes.

In Dr. E. Le Bec's *Medical Proof of the Miraculous*,[37] Dr. Le Bec concludes that the case must be a miracle; as there is no scientific explanation for what occurred. The cure was instant and would have required five grams of phosphate of lime to add the two inches of bone which instantly appeared. A person's blood stream only contains 1.6 grams. Le Bec states: "Both the instantaneous nature of the cure and the amount of phosphate of lime suddenly appearing cannot be explained medically. Medical literature has no such examples."[38] Additionally, the muscles and tendons would have atrophied after eight years, and would have required months and years of therapy. Instead: "In a matter of seconds the almost dead-leg Pierre was walking briskly without any sign of abnormal gait..."[39]

5.3.3 Saints (Duffin's Slide Analysis Example)

Jacalyn Duffin works as a hematologist at Queens College in Ontario. She recalls being asked to review some bone marrow slides in 1987. The slides were from 1978 and 1979 and she assumed that the patient was dead, and that the review was part of a lawsuit. This assumption was based upon the readings which showed a relapse of leukemia following an initial treatment. Duffin knew that a leukemia relapse after an initial treatment meant certain death.[40]

After submitting her report to the physician, she was informed that the report was not part of a lawsuit, rather it was being sent to the Vatican for the Canonization Trial of Marie-Marguerite d'Youville. The slides had come from a woman healed of leukemia after praying to Marie and represented the third miracle attributed to the future saint. Duffin as an atheist was perplexed by the situation. She did not believe in God or miracles; yet she had no explanation for why the patient had been cured after a relapse.

This occurrence sparked Duffin's interest in the Vatican's authentication process, as well as in the phenomenon of medical miracles. Duffin's text *Medical Miracles: Doctors, Saints, and Healing in the Modern World*

---

37. See Le Bec, *Medical Proof of the Miraculous*.

38. Glynn, *Healing Fire of Christ*, loc. 1925 of 3157.

39. Glynn, *Healing Fire of Christ*, loc. 1946–1965 of 3157.

40. This summary is culled from: Duffin, "Pondering Miracles," A21, and Duffin, *Medical Miracles*, 3–9.

(2009), is the culmination of Duffin's ten years of research on the topic. During this time, she spent hundreds of hours using the Vatican's archives to research over 1400 miracles used in the canonization process during the years 1588 to 1999.[41] Her findings help to shed light on a process which is often seen as being cloaked in secrecy.

Duffin found that the church often has to demure to physicians during the canonization process. Physicians are seen as the experts in the early stages. Due to this, the vast majority of miraculous claims are dismissed. Duffin states that: "For the canonization process, happy outcomes do not automatically qualify as miracles. Even when good evidence establishes that the patient appealed to God or a saint at a crucial moment, recovery is not considered miraculous if any chance remains that it might have occurred naturally or through human intervention."[42]

93% of the miracles authenticated during this time frame (1588–1999), were medical. They included recoveries from paralysis, resurrections from the dead, and instantaneous cures from terminal diseases. Almost all cases included testimony from physicians who were familiar with the patients. Often, the physicians testifying were not believers and were totally at a loss to explain what they had observed.[43] Similarly, the woman involved in Duffin's slide analysis is still alive forty years later. Duffin as a scientist and an atheist admits that she has no explanation for this.[44] Duffin's experience is just one of thousands of such examples of the miracles recorded in the Vatican's archives of the saints.[45]

5.4 CRITICAL EVALUATION

5.4.1 Naturalistic Explanations

Often claims of miracles can be dismissed due to naturalistic explanations (e.g., psychosomatic, misdiagnosis, fraud, remission, etc.). The cases cited

---

41. Duffin, "Pondering Miracles," A21.
42. Duffin, *Medical Miracles*, 5.
43. Duffin, *Medical Miracles*, 115.
44. Duffin, "Pondering Miracles," A21.
45. There are between 7000–10,000 blessed persons and saints. The estimate of modern saints who underwent the full process instituted in the 1600s is about 1200. *The Roman Martyrology* is seen as one of the more definitive though not exhaustive Vatican sources on the topic. See Catholic Church, *Roman Martyrology*. See also: Cruz, *Lives of the Saints*.

in this chapter were chosen as they render naturalistic explanations to be highly improbable. For instance, in Dr. Crandall's case, the naturalistic explanation involves dismissing all of the available evidence for a highly implausible alternative.

Dr. Crandall's case received local and national media attention. One of the sceptics was an OB/GYN who acted as a consultant to a national news program. The naturalistic explanation he offered was that the patient had never actually flat lined; but rather, had a subtle heartbeat during the forty minutes he was thought dead. Dr. Crandall correctly labeled this alternative hypothesis as grasping at straws. As Keener notes:

> The team had "tried to revive him for forty minutes using standard American Heart Association protocols," and this resuscitation could not have happened naturally. Even the information in the media reports support Crandall's verdict: the darkening of the extremities and the unanimous verdict of those actually present in the emergency room, including renowned cardiologist Crandall, makes the more skeptical alternative seem forced compared with the more obvious interpretation.[46]

I would add, that even if the sceptic's theory were allowed, this could explain the possibility of the resuscitation. However, a heartbeat which would be so subtle as to be undetectable would not be strong enough to provide adequate amounts of oxygen to the brain. Thus, the patient would have suffered severe brain damage. The fact that the patient fully recovered without any brain damage defies any plausible naturalistic explanation(s). The fact that the resuscitation occurred immediately in response to prayer; raises its apologetical value exponentially.

Similarly, the doctors from the Lourdes Medical Bureau are able to dispense with the common skeptical objection of *unknown natural forces*. As Cranston notes:

> One of the favorite explanations of Lourdes cures by rationalist doctors is that they are produced by "unknown natural forces"— unknown today, but whose laws may be uncovered tomorrow. Most of the doctors at the Medical Bureau discount this theory. They point out that the action of the forces of nature is always uniform and unchanging. The law of gravity, for example, works in exactly the same way for everybody. If "unknown natural forces" were responsible for Lourdes cures, they would have to act the

---

46. Keener, *Miracles*, 578.

same for all persons under similar conditions. But the exact opposite is true. The "unknown forces" act neither constantly nor uniformly. They act today, but not tomorrow; for some people, but not for others. One of the baffling things about Lourdes cures is their extreme variability and unpredictability.[47, 48]

5.4.2 Science and Testimony

Keener notes that even in cases which defy naturalistic explanations, the anti-supernaturalist will always be able to come up with an alternative explanation. However, in doing so, they are not following the evidence where it leads. Rather, they are being disingenuous in their clinging to their *a priori* presuppositions.[49] Keener argues that we allow for testimonies and the observations from reliable witnesses in all other disciplines within the academy; then why should this change when the subject of the supernatural is discussed? It is only within the confines of western academia, that many hold to the unproven enlightenment presuppositions so tightly that they dismiss *a priori* the testimony of hundreds of millions of people.[50] This of course is not being scientific (following the evidence to where it leads); but rather, it is being closed minded in positing ontological naturalism *a priori*.

Swinburne offers a similar critique with his epistemological tools of credulity and testimony:

- The Principle of Credulity—accept what you see as true unless you have a good reason not to.
- The Principle of Testimony—accept what eyewitnesses/others say as true unless you have a good reason not to.[51]

5.4.3 Good Faith Skepticism

There will always be those who will not be convinced not matter what evidence is produced. There will always be alternate hypotheses and

---

47. Cranston, *A Protestant Looks at Lourdes*, loc. 369–375 of 385.

48. The non-uniformity of the Lourdes cures is of the utmost importance in dismissing possible naturalistic explanations. In the cases cited by Keener prayer was the vital element. In Lourdes, it is prayer coupled with the healing properties of the water.

49. Keener, *Miracles*, 579.

50. Keener, *Miracles*, 579.

51. For a fuller discussion see Richard Swinburne's discussion on epistemic justification as an *a priori*, see *Existence of God*, 123–27.

explanations to claims of miracles. No miracle will ever rise to the absurdly high level of proof demanded by the most ardent sceptic. It is for these reasons that I developed the tool of good faith skepticism in chapter 2. In short, this form of skepticism does place the burden of proof on the apologist. However, it also accepts the evidence wherever it leads, and only places the demand of *more probable than not* on the claims of Special Divine Action.

In the above examples, the phenomena deify any plausible naturalistic explanation(s). They are simply outside the bounds of all that we know about science and medicine. Some sceptics will then argue that our knowledge of science is incomplete, and that there are probably unknown naturalistic explanations. However, the element of prayer and the lack of uniformity in these cases, as well as the instantaneousness of the healings makes these explanations highly improbable! Far beyond mere coincidence! These elements, in these cases, make a conclusion of supernatural intervention (i.e., Special Divine Action), far more probable than not.

5.5 CONCLUSION

In conclusion, of the hundreds of millions of people throughout the world who claim to have experienced a miracle, a very small percentage of these miracles have scientific documentation. However, the cases which have scientific and medical documentation do strongly point towards a conclusion of supernatural intervention (Special Divine Action). Differences of opinion usually come down to the level of proof required. Keener readily admits none of the miracles will ever meet the highest degrees of proof required by many sceptics who echo Hume's dictum of "extraordinary claims require extraordinary evidences." However, the miracles documented by Keener, the Vatican, and elsewhere point towards some type of involvement from a supernatural power as being far more likely than not. Thus, the criteria of good faith skepticism can be easily satisfied. That is, when the good faith sceptic looks at these miracles, he will conclude that the probability of Special Divine Action is far more probable than not.

This conclusion that God has provided ample evidence of both his existence and interaction in the world is not new. It will be of importance in the next chapter on the interpretation of miracles. In many ways, this *general revelation* points towards the nature of God and his willingness to reveal himself to all.[52] As Vatican II's *Constitution of the Catholic Faith* summarizes:

> In order that the homage of our faith may be in harmony with reason God has willed to add to the interior aids of the Holy Spirit exterior proofs of His revelation, that is, divine facts, particularly miracles and prophecies, which, demonstrating with evidence the almighty power and infinite knowledge of God, afford in behalf of divine revelation very certain signs suitable to the intelligence of all (Const. on the Catholic Faith, chapter 2).[53]

---

52. General revelation is knowledge about God which is available to all through observation and reasoning about nature and the universe.

53. Devivier, *Christian Apologetics*, loc. 2225 of 8995.

Chapter 6

Interpretive Framework

6.1 INTRODUCTION

"Like every miracle that ever was, it is a sign from beyond this world, pointing us to the God beyond this world, to the God who came into this world to lead us back to himself and who is himself the way back."[1]
—Eric Metaxas

In the previous chapter, it was established that there is enough evidence to reasonably conclude that modern medical miracles do occur. While this evidence may not convince the hardened sceptic, it does rise to the level of proof required in chapter 2 to overcome good faith skepticism (i.e., more probable than not). However, the question still remains that even if the sceptic accepts that miracles do occur, the obvious next question is; why? And perhaps, more often, as in the case of suffering; why not?

John Polkinghorne has stated that the theological consistency of divine action is a larger dilemma than the science behind a miracle. Science merely asks how things happen; but brackets out "why?" Answering this becomes the task of the Christian theologian/apologist. The argument from evil/suffering has become a favorite amongst modern atheists.[2]

---

1. Metaxas, *Miracles*, 87.

2. The argument simply stated is why would an all good God allow for suffering to occur? This is of primary importance to this chapter as God does allow suffering to occur; but at times alleviates suffering via miracles. The question in this context becomes one of understanding God's reasons for both action and inaction.

In this chapter, I will first examine the interpretative frameworks established by Jeffrey John, Jon Ruthven, Heidi Baker, and Roman Catholicism which seek to answer the question: "why God preforms miracles?" Jeffrey John's answer of *deeper meaning* will be explicated and evaluated in light of scripture. Ruthven's *Kingdom of God* answer will be analyzed more heavily within the context of the current Renewal movement. Heidi Baker's view of salvation as being connected to physical healing will also be given. Finally, the Catholic view of healing as exorcism will be explicated. Francis MacNutt's healing ministry will be highlighted as an example of the Catholic Charismatic Revival.[3] The list of scholars chosen is by no means exhaustive or even necessarily representative. Rather, I have chosen scholars whose work provides both unique theological insights, as well as strong connections to modern occurrences of Special Divine Action.

Next, I will address the second question of why God refuses to do miracles; within the context of Christian theodicy. This will entail differentiating Christian miracles from supernatural occurrences in pagan religions. The concept of *divine providence* will be offered as the overarching motif for interpretation. Examining Special Divine Action within the framework of Christian theodicy will help lay the foundation for my Renewal apologetic in the final chapter.

6.2 JEFFREY'S "DEEPER MEANING" INTERPRETIVE FRAMEWORK

When examining the New Testament, we see several instances wherein Christ refused to perform signs and wonders for those who demanded them. For instance, Christ refused to perform any signs and wonders when tempted by Satan in the desert (Matthew 4:11). Nor would he perform signs and wonders at the demands of the Pharisees (Mark 6:4). Jesus refused to

3. While Francis MacNutt's healing ministry could have been included in chapter 5's discussion on documented modern medical miracles; I chose to include it here instead for the following reasons: 1. MacNutt's ministry tends to cause healings which occur over time and thus lack the instantaneous nature necessary to be of apologetical value. 2. MacNutt's ministry tends to deal a lot with mental healings instead of physical. Thus, the charge of psychosomatic causes could easily be raised. 3. Finally, MacNutt has not made the effort to catalogue the medical documentation needed to prove his cases as authentic as this appears not to be a goal of his ministry. Nevertheless, theological MacNutt's insights are of considerable value. Additionally, since the Catholic Charismatic Revival makes up a substantial percentage of the Renewal movement, the healings occurring within the movement are worthy of theological examination.

INTERPRETIVE FRAMEWORK

use signs and wonders as some sort of sideshow to his message. Christ used signs and wonders to convey a message; often understanding the full meaning of his signs and wonders requires theological reflection to comprehend the deeper meanings involved.

Jeffrey John's text *The Meaning in the Miracles* (2001), provides a theological analysis of several New Testament signs and wonders. John's thesis is that the signs and wonders of Jesus cannot be taken at just face value, rather they always had a deeper meaning and significance. They truly were signs pointing towards something else. In the following sections, I will examine three types of deeper meanings contained in the signs and wonders of Jesus.

6.2.1 Served to Authenticate Jesus as Messiah

Jesus often used signs and wonders to authenticate his messiahship. This was a necessary part of his ministry, as he was claiming many capabilities which his critics (e.g., scribes and Pharisees), viewed as blasphemous. For instance, Christ claimed to have knowledge from God (John 5:21–23; John 6:40), to be the son of God (John 6:40; John 10:30–33), and to have the ability to forgive sins (Mark 2:10–11; John 8:23–24). His critics challenged him on all three claims; and he used his ability to perform signs and wonders to both authenticate his message and refute his critics.

The signs and wonders which Jesus preformed were a sign for the less spiritual to accept his message. This is part of why Jesus was at times hesitant to perform signs and wonders for those who asked with the wrong intentions. Jesus would have preferred that the people believe his message just by faith. But, he knew that there were many doubting Thomases who needed to see signs and wonders. To such people Jesus would state: "If I am not doing the works of my Father, then do not believe me; but if I do them, even if you do not believe in me, believe in the works, so that you may know and understand that I am in the Father and the Father in me" (John 10:38).

Despite seeing signs and wonders performed right before their eyes, the scribes and Pharisees still would not believe that Jesus was the messiah due to their hardened hearts (Mark 8:17–18; Isaiah 6:9–10).[4] Rather, they accused him of being a magician causing signs and wonders by the power of the devil (Matthew 12:24). This point is of extreme importance, as their stubbornness is similar to that of modern sceptics clinging to their naturalistic presuppositions. No amount of evidence can persuade those whose

4. John, *Meaning in Miracles*, 20.

hearts are hardened. This is why the good faith skeptic must be the target for intellectual persuasion.

6.2.2 Importance of who was Healed (Sinners, Outcasts)

According to Jeffrey John, the people that Jesus chose to heal often were the outcasts of Jewish society. They were considered ritually unclean, meaning that they could not even enter the temple. These same people were ostracized by the religious rulers of the day. They included lepers, tax collectors, gentiles, the blind and the deaf.[5] The mere fact that Jesus even spoke with them, let alone healed them, is an indication that his signs and wonders needed to be viewed at a deeper level. They signified an abolishment of the current social order, a massive paradigm shift.[6] These signs and wonders pointed towards the creation of the new covenant and the accompanying social order.

6.2.3 Importance of Why They Were Healed (Faith, Repentance)

Jesus would not perform signs and wonders for those who sought them out as some sort of magic show; rather, he performed healings for those who showed genuine repentance. Jesus often first spoke with those who sought out his healings, to see what their motivations were. In the Gospels time and again we hear Jesus tell those that he had healed: "Go and sin no more, your faith has saved you" (Luke 17:19, Luke 18:42). John concludes:

> All the Gospel miracles of Jesus healing the blind and deaf are to be interpreted in terms of this theology of revelation: their point is not medical but spiritual and theological. Whatever history may lie behind the stories of individual healings, their meaning and importance in the evangelists' mind is a universal, symbolic one: these miracles are about the potential of us all to be healed of our age-old, inherited spiritual deafness and blindness.[7]

---

5. John, *Meaning in Miracles*, 18.
6. John, *Meaning in Miracles*, 10.
7. John, *Meaning in Miracles*, 22.

6.3 THE ESSENCE OF THE GOSPEL (HEALING AND SALVATION)

6.3.1 Kingdom of God (Ruthven)

According to Jon Ruthven, the *Kingdom of God* is the central essence of both the miraculous and Christ's message. Ruthven states:

> Jesus' central mission in the New Testament is to inaugurate the kingdom "in power" and "in word and deed" (Lk. 4:23–27; 24:19). His signs and wonders are not mere "signs," in the English sense of extrinsic value, "pointing" to the truth of the "gospel" or its bearer. Rather, miracles manifest the essential core activity of his mission: to displace the physical and spiritual ruin of the demonic kingdom by the wholeness of the Kingdom of God.[8]

According to Jon Ruthven, the Reformers fundamentally misunderstood the purpose of miracles by viewing them as a means of authenticating the gospel. Ruthven states: "They didn't understand that miracles don't prove the gospel—they are the gospel."[9] This misunderstanding is because: "Crucially, traditional Protestantism fails to grasp the central essence of the biblical message: that "the kingdom of God does not consist of talk but of miracle power"-that" your faith not rest on persuasive words of 'wisdom,' but on God's miracle power" (1 Cor 4:19–20; 2:4–5, cf. Rom 1:16; 1 Thes 1:5; 1 Pet 1:5)."[10] . Failure to understand this, or embracing cessationism leads towards a truncated gospel.[11] As Ruthven states:

> Warfield's soteriology, a Calvinistic ordo salutis limited to the problem of sin, is also unbiblical in that it fails to grasp the holistic nature of salvation, including healing, revelation, and deliverance from demonic power. His eschatology is flawed in that he fails to see that the work of the Kingdom of God (alternately, the Spirit of God), as biblically described, that is, that the exalted Christ bestows charismata provisionally in this age as a "down payment," the "first fruits," or a "taste of the powers of the age to come.[12]

---

8. Ruthven, *Cessation of the Charismata*, 100 101.
9. Ruthven, *Protestant Theology*, 31.
10. Ruthven, *Protestant Theology*, 301.
11. Ruthven, *Cessation of the Charismata*, 94.
12. Ruthven, *Cessation of the Charismata*, 103–4.

Ruthven's appeal to the Kingdom of God, and the age to come, in terms of the charismata is also of interest. Because, it points towards miracles as a means of the expansion of the kingdom of God; as well as a foreshadowing of the age to come, when Christ will conquer evil and the powers of darkness in full. Thus, when God allows for miraculous healings to occur today, he is both expanding his kingdom power over darkness; as well as indicating his strength to conquer disease, sickness, and death. This will be accomplished in full in the coming kingdom.

Salvation, according to Ruthven, is not limited to the Calvinist concept of *Ordo Salutis* (Order of Salvation). Rather, salvation includes many other components: "including healing, revelation, and deliverance from demonic power."[13] This is of importance to this discussion, as we will see in the following sections, salvation and miraculous healings often occur together. This happens both in the context of contemporary miracles on the mission field, as well as throughout church and biblical history. Ruthven states that: "In any case, salvation, at least in the Gospels, always refers first to physical healing or exorcism!"[14]

6.3.2 Salvation=Healing (Heidi Baker)

In the modern context, missionaries from the third world often see miraculous healings with incredible frequency. There are numerous reasons for this. The usage of miracles as a means to authenticate the gospel in unevangelized areas is perhaps the most widely accepted. The belief held by Keener and others, that God is acting as a loving father, and heals those who lack appropriate medical care, is another possible cause. Mozambique, as the poorest country in the world, would certainly qualify for this explanation. Rolland Baker states that in Mozambique there is only one doctor per 40,000 people. Since sanitation and immunizations are greatly lacking; and thus, half of all children are dead by the age of five.[15]

However, the most obvious and often overlooked interpretation, is the view held within various spiritual warfare models: salvation and miraculous healings often occur simultaneously with the deliverance from the demonic.[16] The expansion of the Kingdom of God is largely done at the in-

---

13. Ruthven, *Cessation of the Charismata*, 104.

14. Ruthven, *Protestant Theology*, 30.

15. Baker, *Always Enough*, 15–22.

16. For a full discussion of the various models of spiritual warfare see Beilby and Eddy, *Understanding Spiritual Warfare*.

dividual level by the salivation of individual believers. Often, the unbeliever is afflicted by a demonic presence which can cause physical ailments. Heidi Baker, who has severed as a missionary in Africa for decades, believes that healing is frequently accomplished by deliverance from demonic powers. "'It's not very pretty,' admits Baker, describing the physical manifestations of writhing and vomiting that often accompany deliverance. 'We gently work with the person and ask, "Would you like to be set free? If you trust in Jesus the demons have no hold." If the person works with us then the demons leave within minutes.'"[17]

In the Baker's experience, salvation, deliverance, and healing always occur simultaneously. This is probably due to her unique context within Mozambique and the poverty, pagan rituals, and demonic strongholds[18] which are present there.[19] For instance, Baker states that in recent years 100% of the deaf in the Chiure area of Mozambique have been healed through prayer.[20] This strengthens her belief in salvation as a means of physical healing.

Fr. Jack Ashcroft notes that in scripture Christ makes it clear that some illnesses are caused by sin (John 5:14), while others are not (John 9:1–3). Since the body is the temple of the lord (1 Cor 3:16–17), then it can come under demonic attack. But illness can also be a way which God deals with personal sins (e.g., Miriam in Numbers 12). He concludes that: "Illness exists because of the original sin of Adam and eve. Although all illness is in the world because of sin, it does not mean everyone who is suffering is doing so because of personal sins. Sacred Scripture reveals various reasons for illness."[21]

6.3.3 Healing as Exorcism (Catholicism)

Ruthven's view of salvation, as a freeing from evil and physical infirmity, is not unique. Within Catholicism, the Sacrament of Baptism has traditionally been viewed as a means of exorcism. The pre-Vatican II Sacrament

---

17. Brierley, "80 Miracles," lines 75–78.

18. While Mozambique is predominately Catholic, like most of the global south various pagan practices persist such as ancestor worship and animism. This is perhaps why Baker and other missionaries experience such strong spiritual battles while evangelizing.

19. Elisha Baker gives an extensive account of the hardships experienced by her family for their ministry in Mozambique see Baker, *Keeping the Fire*, loc. 43–82 of 1627.

20. Stafford, "Miracles in Mozambique," 19–26.

21. Ashcroft, *Real Exorcist*, 2:1.

included an exorcism of the church itself before preforming the Sacrament proper.[22] Much of this is derived from Catholic theology which views the soul and the Sacraments as phenomena which are both material and immaterial simultaneously (matter and form).[23]

When speaking of the soul, such terms as "stained," or "habitus," are often used by Catholic theologians.[24] The implication of this is that when the soul is not in a state of grace, it is afflicted with the demonic, and this affliction can often be manifested in physical disease and infirmities. Thus, when grace is infused into the believer, via the Sacraments, they are freed from these various spiritual and physical afflictions. In short, obtaining a state of grace is often accompanied by miracles of healing. This type of healing comes from the banishment of the demonic presence from the life of the believer.

Within Catholicism, the infusions of grace are obtained via the sacramental system. Healing is often obtained in the Sacrament of the *Anointing of the Sick*. The passage which best encapsulates the Sacrament, and its justification, is found in the book of James which states: "Is anyone among you sick? Then he must call for the elders of the church and they are to pray over him, anointing him with oil in the name of the Lord; and the prayer offered in faith will restore the one who is sick, and the Lord will raise him up, and if he has committed sins, they will be forgiven him" (Jas 5:14–15). According to Scheeben:

> The effects of the sacrament are thus described by the Council of Trent: "The thing (res) here signified is the grace of the Holy Ghost, whose anointing cleanses away sins, if there be any still to be expiated, as also the remains of sins; and raises up and strengthens the soul of the sick person, by exciting in him a great confidence in the mercy of God, whereby the sick person, being supported, bears more easily the inconveniences and pains of his illness, and more readily resists the temptations of the devil, who lieth in wait for his heel (Gen. 3: 15); and at times obtains bodily health when expedient for the welfare of the soul" (sess. xiv. ch. 2). Here, then, are three effects enumerated: (1) remission of sin; (2) strengthening of the soul; (3) restoration of health.[25]

22. McHugh and Callan, *Catechism of the Council of Trent*, loc. 2988 of 9018.

23. The matter and form of a sacrament are Aristotelian categories. Matter is the physical aspect of the sacrament. In the case of the anointing of the sick, oil is the matter. The form is the supernatural grace which is to be infused to the believer via the sacrament (anointing of the sick); e.g., healing. For a fuller discussion of these aspects of a sacrament see Scheeben, *Manual of Catholic Theology*, loc. 13465–13680 of 16884.

24. Aquinas, *Summa Theologia: Question 86*.

25. Scheeben, *Manual Catholic Theology*, loc. 16740–16745 of 16884.

Finally, we have insight from the Catholic exorcist Fr. Gabrielle Amorth. Amorth believes that any Christian has the power to cast out demons as evidenced in (Luke 10:1–18).[26] Furthermore, as Christians, we should not have divisions in this warfare. Christ reprimanded the apostles for forbidding another Christian from casting out demons (Mark 9:38–40).[27] Father Amorth laments that members of the Catholic Renewal movement originally encountered resistance from the church hierarchy when they said prayers for deliverance. In fact, Amorth believes that the Catholic Church could learn a lot from the Pentecostals and various other sects when it comes to spiritual warfare. He believes that the Catholic Charismatic Revival and their deliverance services can provide a valuable resource for Catholics afflicted by the demonic, when there are no exorcists available.[28] This is of importance according to Amorth as there are some illnesses which cannot be healed by natural remedies:

> The devil is at the root of every illness, suffering, sin, death—they are all consequences of sin. But there are also ills that are directly provoked by the evil one. The Gospel mentions some such cases: the woman who was stooped for eighteen years (paralysis?) and a deaf-mute. In both instances, a satanic presence caused the sickness, and the Lord healed them by expelling the demons. The rule of thumb that I sketched before is very useful—if an illness has an evil origin, there is no drug that will cure it, while prayers and exorcisms will.[29]

6.3.3.1 Francis MacNutt's Healing Ministry

Francis MacNutt (1925-) originally planned on becoming a doctor and healing others through medicine. However, when he was drafted for WWII in 1944 (ten days before he was to begin medical school), these plans were derailed. After the war, he entered seminary and was ordained as a Roman Catholic priest in the Dominican order in 1956—eventually earning a PhD in theology at the Aquinas Institute.[30]

26. Amorth, *Exorcist Tells His Story*, 166.
27. Amorth, *Exorcist Tells His Story*, 174.
28. Amorth, *Exorcist Tells His Story*, 172–74.
29. Amorth, *Exorcist Tells His Story*, 154.
30. MacNutt, *Healing*, loc. 36 of 3445.

Once MacNutt was a priest, he did not think of himself as worthy to be an instrument for God's healing. So, when a friend of his asked him to come to his house, and pray for his partially blind son; he refused as he did not want to hurt his friend with further disappointment.[31] However, he was aware of the miracles performed by the saints on an almost daily basis, and was a bit troubled that priest did not/could not perform such miracles. MacNutt states:

> Years later, when I entered the Dominican Order and read the lives of the saints with all the fervor of those seminary days, I couldn't help but wonder why healing seemed an everyday occurrence in the saints' lives and yet we were never encouraged to pray for such things. We got the impression that praying for healing was presumptuous, like pretending to be a saint—which I certainly was not. We were not worthy of extraordinary manifestations of God's power.[32]

However, during the 1960s, through contact with Pentecostal friends, he became associated with the Catholic Charismatic Revival and was spirit baptized. Subsequently, he spoke in tongues and became a faith healer. His spirit baptism was through the influence of Agnes Sanford; who also predicted that he would be a means of spreading the Catholic Charismatic Revival worldwide. This prediction came true, as MacNutt has spread the Revival into thirty nations, and his 1974 text *Healing* has sold over one million copies.[33]

However, his expansion of the Catholic Charismatic Revival ended in 1980 when he left the priesthood to get married.[34] Now excluded from the Revival, MacNutt and his wife Judith (also a faith healer), were welcomed by various mainline Protestant denominations. Within these groups, they continued their healing crusades. The Catholic Church eventually granted the MacNutt's a dispensation for their marriage in 1994. Afterwards, Francis was again able to receive the Sacraments in the Catholic Church.[35] Today he remains the president emeritus of Catholic Healing Ministries. His numerous books on healing include: *Healing* (1974), *Power to Heal* (1992), *The Prayer that Heals* (1981), *Overcome by the Spirit, Deliverance from Evil Spirits (1995), Homosexuality: Can It Be Healed?* (2001), and *The Healing Reawakening (2005).*

31. MacNutt, *Healing*, loc. 40 of 3445.
32. MacNutt, *Healing*, loc. 38–41 of 3445.
33. Grady, "Priest with Healing Hands," lines 49–54.
34. Grady, "Priest with Healing Hands," lines 65–66.
35. Grady, "Priest with Healing Hands," lines 127–28.

In MacNutt's writings we see three distinct themes about physical and mental healing:

1. Freedom from suffering.
2. Deliverance from the demonic.
3. The power of prayer.

6.3.3.1.1 Freedom from Suffering

Christianity in general, and Roman Catholicism in particular, have a long history of embracing suffering. There certainly are biblical and theological reasons for embracing a theology of the cross and suffering. However, MacNutt believes that the general message of the New Testament is that sin and suffering are caused by evil; and that we have victory over suffering through Christ. MacNutt states:

> The real problem for anyone who adopts an exclusively cross-centered spirituality, who embraces all suffering as God's will, is what to make of the gospels where over and over we read that Jesus "cured them all" (e.g., Mt 12:16). How do we account for the fact that everywhere in the gospel Jesus treated sickness as an enemy? Why, today, do we accept sickness as a friend, as God's will?[36]

Additionally, like Ruthven, MacNutt does not see signs and wonders as a mere means of authentication of the messiahship of Christ, nor the anointing of the apostles. Rather, MacNutt sees the signs and wonders contained in scripture as an integral part of the gospel message:

> The healing of Jesus, then, is essential to the gospel. Jesus' healings are not merely "signs and wonders" outside the teachings, pointing to the truth of the gospel; they are part of the very gospel message itself! To deny this is, in effect, to deny the gospel to change it from good news into good advice which lacks the power to transform us into a new creation. In short, Jesus did not heal people to prove that he was God; he healed them because he was God.[37]

---

36. MacNutt, *Healing*, loc. 840–842 of 3445.
37. MacNutt, *Healing*, loc. 1029–1032 of 3445.

6.3.3.1.2 Deliverance from the Demonic

According to MacNutt, many in need of healing, especially mental problems such as depression, are in need of deliverance from the demonic. While actual full possessions requiring formal exorcisms are rare; demonic oppression is common. MacNutt's *Deliverance From Evil Spirits: A Practical Manual* (2009),[38] is a practical manual for the laity dealing with demonic oppression in their lives or the lives of others. Deliverance from the demonic via the healing of depression is not of apologetical value as it can be challenged as psychosomatic. However, there is a wide body of research showing the improved physical and mental health of Christians.[39]

According to Judith MacNutt, there is a fundamental misunderstanding of the relationship between healing and deliverance which makes many healings only temporary. According to Judith: "In some denominations you'll find an understanding of deliverance ministry, but they have no clue about inner healing. Yet 90% of all demonic activity is based on trauma or wounding. Many will cast a demon out of someone, but they won't do the inner healing work that heals the wound, so the demon comes back."[40]

This lack of understanding of healing and deliverance in the modern church is part of a long process where the two disciplines have witnessed a slow and steady decline since the apostolic age. This is covered more extensively in MacNutt's text *The Nearly Perfect Crime: How the Church Almost Killed the Ministry of Healing* (2005) which details the importance of the act of healing and the importance of signs and wonders as the principle means of evangelism for the early church.[41]

6.3.3.1.3 The Power of Prayer

MacNutt believes that prayer is the primary method through which healings occur. However, the types of healing prayer which MacNutt engages in (soaking prayer), usually does not give instant results. Thus, these healings are of lesser value apologetically. Additionally, soaking prayer is controversial within conservative Christian circles, as it is seen as a possible means

---

38. See MacNutt, *Deliverance from Evil Spirits*.
39. See Brown, *Testing Prayer*.
40. Grady, "Priest with Healing Hands," lines 183–86.
41. MacNutt, *Nearly Perfect Crime*, reprinted in 2006 as: MacNutt, *Healing Reawakening*.

for demonic contact.[42] Regardless of the controversy, MacNutt believes that his methods have statistics on their side. MacNutt states that while less than 1% of attendees at his healing crusades are healed, 20% are healed with longer individual prayers over time.[43]

6.3.3.1.4 MacNutt's Conclusion

MacNutt also offers a harsh critique for various Christian denominations in America. He believes that the Catholic Church has quenched and "domesticated" the Holy Spirit by not being more open to the Charismatic Revival. Additionally, he believes that the most fundamental aspect of the faith (salvation in Christ), is often ignored by the American Catholic church. He states: "How often I meet young people who say, "I used to be a Catholic, but now I'm a Christian." What they seem to be saying is that their training merely made them conscious of rules and doctrines. They claim that it was only after they began to move outside Catholic circles that they found a personal relationship with Jesus and a new life."[44]

MacNutt's criticism of mainline Protestant churches is no less severe. He states: "Most mainline Protestants in this country don't realize they are outnumbered. They still see charismatics and Pentecostals as fringe groups. They don't realize that the main centers of Christianity 25 years from now will not be Rome, Geneva and New York but New Delhi, Lagos and other exotic centers."[45] MacNutt's strong views about the church leadership missing these dramatic changes tend to make him unpopular with those in charge. But, they are not his target audience, he is trying to reach: "the people in the pews--anyone who's hungry to know more about the deeper things of God."[46, 47, 48] MacNutt concludes: "In this country the move of the

42. For more on the dangers of soaking prayer and its connections to occultism see Yungen, *A Time of Departing*.

43. Grady, Priest with Healing Hands," lines 33–34.

44. MacNutt, *Healing*, loc. 851–853 of 3445.

45. MacNutt, *Healing*, loc. 851–853 of 3445.

46. MacNutt, *Healing*, loc. 851–853 of 3445.

47. For more on how liberalism has infected the post Vatican II Roman Catholic Church in America see Rose, *Goodbye to Good Men*. Rose explains how many seminaries systematically discriminated against seminarians who held to orthodox beliefs and created an artificial shortage of priests.

48. For more on the growth of the Charismatic Revival in the third world see Cleary, *Latin America Saved*, and, Cleary, *Charismatic Catholicism*.

Holy Spirit has been domesticated."[49] By contrast: "In other parts of the world it's growing so explosively that the largest group of Christians next to the Roman Catholics are the Pentecostals."[50]

6.4 THEODICY

"This leads to the third point: that for God to be glorified, it sometimes means first allowing something unpleasant to transpire."[51]

—ERIC METAXAS

"The presence of God is veiled because, when you think about it, the naked presence of divinity would overwhelm finite creatures, depriving them of the possibility of truly being themselves and freely accepting God. A recurring theme in this book is that, out of love, God has self-limited the exercise of divine power to give creatures the space to be themselves and, as we shall discuss when we come later to evolution, even to "make themselves."[52]

—POLKINGHORNE

6.4.1 Why Does God Refuse?

The problem of evil/suffering (theodicy) is one of the major objections to the Christian faith which Christian apologists have to overcome. Plantinga defines theodicy as the answer to the question of "why God permits evil?"[53] In the context of Special Divine Action, the question can be more appropriately framed as: "why does God permit physical suffering? Why does he not heal all?" Catholicism has a rich history of theologians addressing human suffering as a means of sanctification. However, the Renewal movement, with its emphases on divine healing and sanctification as a means of physical healing, is currently lacking in this regard.

49. Grady, "Priest with Healing Hands," line 55.
50. Grady, "Priest with Healing Hands," lines 55–57.
51. Metaxas, *Miracles*, 91.
52. Polkinghorne and Beale, *Questions of Truth*, 11.
53. Plantinga, *Knowledge and Christian Belief*, 116. For a full discussion of Plantinga's views see Plantinga, *God, Freedom, Evil*.

The two major Christian views on theodicy are the Augustinian and the Irenaean. The Augustinian view states that evil is like a parasite affecting the good, like rust on iron, or rot on a tree. Evil is caused by men choosing the lesser of the good, due to their freewill.[54, 55] The Irenaean view is that since man was born imperfect, he must grow in order to reach spiritual perfection. God does not intervene in the removal of our suffering; as it is both necessary for our growth, and is caused by sin, due to our freewill. Thus, suffering is necessary as a means of soul making.[56] What both views have in common is that they accept that since suffering is part of God's plan, it will not always be removed. When looking at the biblical text we see that suffering can serve a multitude of purposes within God's providence.

If one looks at the scriptural witness, we see a dichotomy emerge in terms of human suffering and prosperity. In the Old Testament, wealth and freedom from suffering were seen as blessings from God (Prv 10:22). However, God did at times bring misfortune as a corrective upon both individuals as well as the nation of Israel itself (Amos 3:13–15). In the New Testament, we are told by Christ that suffering for his sake will be rewarded greatly in heaven (Matthew 5:11–12). The apostles felt glorified in suffering for their faith (Acts 5:41). Almost all of the New Testament apostles were eventual martyred after spending years of persecution, attempted stonings, and imprisonment.

While God may not desire this degree of suffering from all, he does allow it in the case of some. Certainly, it can be argued, that those closest to God, often suffer the most. Understanding this concept, as well as the relative rarity of miracles, helps us to come to an understanding of why God often refuses to perform a miracle.

6.4.1.1 *Problem of Evil*

According to the philosopher Michael Tooley, the problem of evil argument consists in seven linked parts as a *reductio* argument. These parts are:

---

54. Augustine, *On Grace and Freewill,* loc. 191–201 and 838–853 of 939.

55. Augustine's view is known as the privation of the good. This view originated with Clement of Alexandria in the second century and can also be found in Augustine's *Enchiridion*. Clement's writing is fragmented and was not done in a systematic way. For this reason, many scholars trace his importance to have been his influence on Origen. For these reasons, the secondary source compilations are the most practical option to study his works. See Floyd, *Clement Problem of Evil*.

56. Hicks, "Soul Making Theodicy," 262–73.

1. If God exists, then God is omnipotent, omniscient, and morally perfect.
2. If God is omnipotent, then God has the power to eliminate all evil.
3. If God is omniscient, then God knows when evil exists.
4. If God is morally perfect, then God has the desire to eliminate all evil.
5. Evil exists.
6. If evil exists and God exists, then either God doesn't have the power to eliminate all evil, or doesn't know when evil exists, or doesn't have the desire to eliminate all evil.
7. Therefore, God doesn't exist.[57]

Tooley evaluates this argument as logically sound. However, he acknowledges that any of the premises may be challenged as false. But, he believes ". . .that when one conceives of God as unlimited with respect to power, knowledge, and moral goodness, the existence of evil quickly gives rise to potentially serious arguments against the existence of God."[58] Premise number six is what must be challenged. This premise presupposes that no good can come from suffering. However, within a Christian framework, suffering can bring about several good ends including:

1. Correction of sin.
2. Healing as an evidence of Christianity.
3. Looking towards God for salvation.

Of course, these are just some challenges which can be readily observed at the individual level. Within the larger framework of salvific history (panoply), there is a lot of suffering for some greater good. For instance, the martyrdom of the saints and the apostles, and the crucifixion of Jesus himself. This suffering had a specific purpose, and was not necessarily normative, or even normal. But, the sufferings of these individuals was not in vain. Additionally, any inquiries into theodicy, must eventually juxtapose the finitude of man with the infinitude of God. The reasons why we suffer may be beyond our limited and finite intellect (Isaiah 45:9; Romans 9:20–21).

---

57. Tooley, "The Problem of Evil," lines 41–48.
58. Tooley, "The Problem of Evil," lines 59–61.

6.4.1.2 Theodicy: Divine Providence/Freewill/Foreknowledge

"There are only two kinds of people in the end: those who say to God, 'Thy will be done,' and those to whom God says, in the end, 'Thy will be done.'"[59]
—C.S. Lewis

The different views of divine providence are perhaps the foundation of the question of theodicy. In fact, as framed by Gundry, the problem of evil is actually a subset within the larger question of divine providence. In his text *Four Views on Divine Foreknowledge* (2011), Gundry attempts to show the four major views and their points of convergence and divergence. According to Dennis Jowers, the four major views are: ". . . the open view, the simple-foreknowledge view, the middle-knowledge view and the Augustinian-Calvinist view."[60] Within these four views, the authors (Paul Kjoss Helseth, William Lane Craig, Ron Highfield, and Gregory A. Boyd), agree on the areas of divine transcendence, divine intervention, and the veracity of scripture. There is disagreement in the areas of freewill, divine omniscience, and the problem of evil.

An additional nuance, according to R. C. Sproul, is the distinction between providence and foreknowledge. Sproul states: "Providence is not the same thing as God's foreknowledge or prescience. Foreknowledge is His ability to look down the corridors of time and know the outcome of an activity before it even begins. Nevertheless, it is appropriate to use the word providence with reference to God's active governance of the universe, because He is indeed a God who sees."[61] Sproul makes these distinctions while upholding a traditional Augustinian-Calvinist theology. Sproul concludes: "God does not overlook even the slightest detail in the universe. Rather, He governs the universe in total awareness of everything that is happening within it."[62]

Divine Foreknowledge: Four Views (2001) by James Beilby and Paul Eddy specifically addresses the issue of divine foreknowledge. According to the authors the major issues are:

> First, and most immediately, there is the question of the nature and mode of God's foreknowledge. Second, in the eyes of many, there

---

59. Lewis, *Great Divorce*, 66–67.
60. Jowers, *Divine Providence*, loc. 32–33 of 4906.
61. Sproul, *Does God Control Everything*, 9.
62. Sproul, *Does God Control Everything*, 11–12.

are important implications for the question of the nature of divine sovereignty (i.e., whether God's sovereignty operates in a general or in a particular and meticulous fashion). Finally, there are direct implications for the question of the nature of human freedom (i.e., whether humans possess compatibilistic or libertarian freedom). Further, each of these theological questions plays an essential role in the articulation of a stance on the "problem of evil."[63]

6.4.1.2.1 THE OPEN VIEW

"According to its adherents, God knows the future partly as a realm of possibilities, not exclusively as settled facts."[64] Usually the knowledge that God is lacking is exactly what humans will do with their freewill. Therefore, God has to work his providence out around these unknown variables.

6.4.1.2.2 THE SIMPLE FOREKNOWLEDGE VIEW

God is omniscient. Being omniscient, God is all knowing of both the past and the future and does not make mistakes. "God's knowledge contains no gaps that must await future developments before they can be filled in. Because most Christians understand God's omniscience this way, most subscribe to the doctrine of divine foreknowledge: God has complete and infallible knowledge of the future."[65]

6.4.1.2.3 THE MIDDLE KNOWLEDGE VIEW (MOLINIST)

This view is that God knows what anyone of his creatures will do in any given situation. Thus, while humans have freewill, God is able to exercise his providence due to his knowledge of their actions in a given situation. This is referred to as knowledge of counterfactuals, or middle knowledge. As William Lane Craig summarizes: "God can-by decreeing to place just those persons in just those circumstances-bring about his ultimate purposes through free creaturely decisions."[66]

---

63. Beilby and Eddy, *Divine Foreknowledge*, loc. 23 of 3003.
64. Beilby and Eddy, *Divine Foreknowledge*, loc. 28–31 of 3003.
65. Beilby and Eddy, *Divine Foreknowledge*, loc. 761–766 of 3003.
66. Beilby and Eddy, *Divine Foreknowledge*, loc. 1499 of 3003.

6.4.1.2.4 The Augustinian/Calvinist View

This view holds to the strongest form of divine foreknowledge. God is not the author of evil, rather evil is a "causal force arising from a deficiency—that God is not and could not himself be the author of, though he willingly permits it."[67] God did remove his hand of protection and allow for evil to enter the world. Though he foreknew his creatures, they still have the freewill to act; but God knows their actions and decisions ahead of time.[68]

6.4.1.3 C.S. Lewis

6.4.1.3.1 The Problem of Pain

"Why, then, did God give them freewill? Because freewill, though it makes evil possible, is the only thing that makes possible any love, or goodness or joy worth having."

—C.S. Lewis

"I willingly believe that the damned are, in one sense, successful, rebels to the end; that the gates of hell are locked on the inside."[69]

—C.S. Lewis

In C.S. Lewis's seminal text *The Problem of Pain* (1940),[70] Lewis argues against the position that a good God could not permit suffering. Lewis begins by summarizing the problem of pain in a simpler form than the one listed above by Tooley. Lewis states: "If God were good, He would wish to make His creatures perfectly happy, and if God were almighty He would be able to do what He wished. But the creatures are not happy. Therefore God lacks either goodness, or power, or both.' This is the problem of pain, in its simplest form."[71]

Lewis then argues that it is Christianity itself which creates the problem of pain rather than solving it. It is the belief in the all-powerful and loving God of the Bible which causes the evil and suffering in the world to

---

67. Beilby and Eddy, *Divine Foreknowledge*, loc. 2221 of 3003.
68. Beilby and Eddy, *Divine Foreknowledge*, loc. 2381 of 3003.
69. Lewis, *Problem of Pain*, 127.
70. Lewis, *Problem of Pain*.
71. Lewis, *Problem of Pain*, 17.

be an apparent contradiction; at least at a superficial level. Lewis states: "In a sense, it creates, rather than solves, the problem of pain, for pain would be no problem unless, side by side with our daily experience of this painful world, we had received what we think a good assurance that ultimate reality is righteous and loving."[72]

Lewis goes on to define God's love for us as something more than just mere kindness. Rather: "He has paid us the intolerable compliment of loving us, in the deepest, most tragic, most inexorable sense."[73] And this deep love means denying many of our request. When God denies some of our requests it is because: "When we want to be something other than the thing God wants us to be, we must be wanting what, in fact, will not make us happy."[74]

Finally, Lewis believes that God uses pain and suffering as a way of correcting us when we are failing to live as he intended us to live. Lewis states: "But pain insists upon being attended to. God whispers to us in our pleasures, speaks in our conscience, but shouts in our pain: it is His megaphone to rouse a deaf world. A bad man, happy, is a man without the least inkling that his actions do not 'answer', that they are not in accord with the laws of the universe."[75] But, in the end, due to our freewill, we must choose which path we will take.

Lewis prefaces his text by stating:

> If any real theologian reads these pages he will very easily see that they are the work of a layman and an amateur. Except in the last two chapters, parts of which are admittedly speculative, I have believed myself to be restating ancient and orthodox doctrines. If any parts of the book are 'original', in the sense of being novel or unorthodox, they are so against my will and as a result of my ignorance.[76]

It is obvious that his theodicy is based upon the Irenaean view of life as a soul making process. Despite his humility and simplicity, *The Problem of Pain* accomplishes an important and profound purpose; it presents the Irenaean theodicy in a clear and concise way which all can understand. This is the genius of Lewis.

72. Lewis, *Problem of Pain*, 15.
73. Lewis, *Problem of Pain*, 34.
74. Lewis, *Problem of Pain*, 47.
75. Lewis, *Problem of Pain*, 92.
76. Lewis, *Problem of Pain*, 1.

6.4.1.3.2 A Grief Observed

C.S. Lewis married Joy Davidman in 1956. She died of bone cancer four years later in 1960. Lewis himself died of renal failure a mere three years later on 11/22/1963. The death of his wife had a profound effect on Lewis. He wrote the text *A Grief Observed* (1961)[77] under the pseudonym N.W. Clerk; so that he could unleash his true feelings without fear of tarnishing his earlier works. The text was republished after his death, under his real name, and later became the inspiration for the *Shadowland* movies (1985, 1993).[78]

In the text, Lewis describes the self-pity and loathing which he initially experienced following his wife's death.[79] Lewis also describes the initial anger which he felt towards God. However, as he went through the grieving process he begins to once again accept his earlier views on theodicy from his earlier text *The Problem of Pain*. And, to once again accept that he was suffering for things which were beyond his understanding. Lewis states: "When I lay these questions before God I get no answer. But rather a special sort of 'No answer'. It is not the locked door. It is more like a silent, certainly not uncompassionate, gaze. As though He shook his head not in refusal but waving the question. Like, 'Peace, child; you don't understand.'"[80]

Lewis' answer here shows that some of God's plans, which include our suffering, are beyond our understanding. Lewis builds upon this to ponder if some of our theology and philosophy is so misguided that it is ultimately nonsensical to God? Lewis continues: "Can a mortal ask questions which God finds unanswerable? Quite easily, I should think. All nonsense questions are unanswerable. How many hours are in a mile? Is yellow square or round? Probably half the questions we ask—half of our great theological and metaphysical problems—are like that."[81]

6.4.2 Miracles in Other Religions?

Christianity is not the only religion to claim miracles. Other religions such as Hinduism and Islam claim to have holy men today capable of performing

---

77. See Lewis, *A Grief Observed*.

78. For more on C. S. Lewis' personal life and the background for *A Grief Observed*, see Sibley, *Shadowlands*.

79. Lewis, *A Grief Observed*, 1.

80. Lewis, *A Grief Observed*, 33.

81. Lewis, *A Grief Observed*, 33.

miracles. Additionally, many religions have shrines and holy places where miracles are claimed to have occurred.[82] Sceptics of the miraculous, as well as religious pluralists (those who reject the exclusive truth claims of Christianity), often point towards these supernatural occurrences in other religions to disprove exclusivistic claims of the miraculous by Christians. However, supernatural occurrences in other religions do not negate the miraculous claims of Christians; nor do they deny Christianity its rightful place as the sole means of salvation.

First, the Bible never denies that the supernatural exists in other religions. Rather, Christianity affirms that demons are able to do supernatural works.[83] The New Testament mentions in several places (e.g., 2 Thes 2:9–12) the lying signs and wonders which the devil can use to deceive those who are perishing. Jesus himself was accused of doing demonic works by the Pharisees. The demon possessed slave girl in the Book of Acts (Acts 16:16–24), who was used by her owner as a fortune teller, is another example of this.

Second, there is a fundamental theological difference between the miracles found in other religions and those performed by Christians. According to Geisler:

> A True Miracle Always Brings Glory to God. Occult "magic" brings glory to the magician, and psychosomatic "cures" to the one who performs them. Satanic delusions (see 2 Thess. 2: 9; Rev. 16: 14) are lies (2 Thess. 2: 9) that do not glorify the God who cannot lie (Titus 1: 2; Heb. 6: 18). A True Miracle Brings Good to the Natural World. The resurrection is the ultimate example. It reverses death and brings back the good of life (see Rom. 8). Healing restores the body to the way God made it, which was "good" (Gen. 1: 27– 31). Even "negative" miracles are good in that it is good for God's justice to defeat sin.[84]

Third, miracles can be done through the power of the devil or his demons in order to cause confusion. Satan as the ruler of the world's pagan religions can perform supernatural acts in order to mislead people into thinking that God is operating in that religion. As Catholic apologist Matt Nelson states:

---

82. Stafford, *Miracles*, 127.

83. To be more specific, many scholars label the works of Angels and demons as preternatural (beyond nature); reserving the term supernatural (outside of nature) as solely for the works of God.

84. Geisler, *Big Book Christian Apologetics*, 338.

A non-divine supernatural explanation may also explain apparent miracles. Satan is cunning and deceitful and wants to generate religious confusion. He may therefore conduct false apparitions or manipulate the physical world in an attempt to trick someone into thinking that God is the one acting. Demonic forces could also be the source behind a person's supernatural abilities.[85]

Lastly, the spiritual hierarchy which can be claimed by Christianity, is unique amongst the world's religions. Just as Paul demonstrated the power of God over Satan by exorcising the slave girl, so too does the supernatural power of Christianity reign supreme over the power exercised by "miracle workers" in other religions. It is common to hear from Christian missionaries returning from the third world, that the local witch doctors or priests from some indigenous religion, become frustrated that their magic would not work in the presence of a Christian.

6.4.3 Divine Providence = Multitude of Reasons

When scholars attempt to interpret signs and wonders, they often look at the various functions which they serve. Jeffrey John looks for the *deeper meaning*, Ruthven for the *Kingdom of God*, and Baker looks at *deliverance from the demonic*. While there is truth to all of their views, we see in scripture that God used signs and wonders to perform numerous functions. Additionally, the direct purposes of signs and wonders are sometimes implied in scripture; at other times, they are explicitly stated (Mark 2:10). As Jack Deere notes:

> The first thing that I noticed is that there are very few direct statements in the New Testament regarding the purpose of miracles. I never found a statement to the effect that "God gave miracles in order to. . .." I discovered that the purpose of miracles is sometimes indicated by "function" words accompanying the miracles themselves. Mark, for example, says that miracles "confirm" (Mark 16:20). John says that they "testify" (John 5:36). Peter says that Jesus was "accredited" by miracles (Acts 2: 22). At other times the purpose of a miracle must often be inferred from the context or from the result of the miracle.[86]

However, Deere does find two clear purposes for miracles in the New Testament:

85. Nelson, "Do Miracles Happen," lines 45–50.
86. Deere, *Strangers to Fire*, 121.

Renewal Apologetics

1. To confirm the relationship of Jesus to the father; as the son of God.
2. To authenticate the message of grace given by Jesus as the messiah.[87]

So, what is the overarching pattern to all of the signs and wonders both within the Bible and church history? Divine providence. God uses signs and wonders to achieve his purposes, for his own reasons, sometimes known only to him. God interacts and injects signs and wonders into the physical universe; as he is not bound by the natural laws, which he himself created.

God's providence can at times be a source of frustration to those who are suffering. However, we need to have faith that in is infinite wisdom he is doing what is best not only for us, but for the entirety of his creation. We need to understand that we are limited and finite, but God is not. Thus, we need to look to the very words of Christ when he said: "but not my will, but your will be done" (Luke 22:42).

Within this motif of divine providence as the foundation for all signs and wonders, the answers to the questions of theodicy and the interpretation of signs and wonders can become clearer. The short answer to the question: "why God chooses to heal only sometimes?" Is that God uses his role as our heavenly father to help us, his children, whenever possible. However, this help cannot interfere with his overall plans.[88] Sometimes signs and wonders are an integral part of his plans.

An understanding of the necessity of prayer; is of importance in order to understand the purpose of signs and wonders. As stated in scripture: "Ask, and it shall be given you; seek, and you shall find; knock, and it shall be opened unto you" (Matthew 7:7). This is because we have a heavenly father who loves us. As Christ states: "If you then, being evil, know how to give good gifts unto your children, how much more shall your Father who is in heaven give good things to them that ask him" (Matthew 7:11)? Signs and wonders are almost always performed as an answer to a prayer. In this way, God as a loving father, is answering a request from one of his children. Since direct appearances of the divine are extremely rare, prayer is the mechanism by which God is able to communicate with his children.

However, sometimes the answer to a prayer is no. Just as God refused to remove the cup of suffering from Christ, so too must we suffer at times

---

87. Deere, *Strangers to Fire*, 121–22.

88. For more on this biblical/apologetical motif see the argument for the probability of miracles see Geisler, *Big Book Christian Apologetics*, 317–18.

within God's plans. But, we suffer with the knowledge that God is omnipotent and benevolent. Therefore, we can know that we will not suffer in vain. And, that if it is within his plans, the suffering can be removed by our prayers for healing.

6.5 CONCLUSION

Signs and wonders serve several functions which help to convey the Christian message. First, they serve an evidential function. One reason why Jesus preformed signs and wonders was to prove that he was the son of God. The apostles preformed signs and wonders to authenticate both the Gospel message; as well as their divine authority/mandate to preach the Gospel. However, as has been shown, it would be wrong to restrict signs and wonders to the evidential level (e.g., cessationism), as they severe many other valuable functions as well. Signs and wonders are an integral part of the Christian message throughout scripture.

The three main functions of signs and wonders are:

1. Signs of God's interaction with the world.
2. A way for God to heal those whom he chooses.
3. A method for the expansion of the kingdom of God.

Additionally, this chapter has shown that the role that the miraculous plays in other religions is very different from that which it plays in Christianity. Miracles in other religions tend to point towards the person performing the miracle and not towards an ultimate divine authority. The power by which non-Christian supernatural works are performed is demonic in origin. It is for this reason that Christian apologists do not have an insurmountable obstacle when faced with non-Christian supernatural works. Miracles in the Christian worldview are the very mechanism through which God interacts with his creation. Counterfeit miracles in other religions are how the devil causes confusion.

In summary, in this chapter, four major interpretive frameworks were examined. First, Jeffrey John's deeper meaning framework which views miracles as being signs which point towards something more profound. John cites the role of faith and repentance as well as the healing of outcasts and sinners as examples of this deeper, more profound meaning. Second, Ruthven's Kingdom of God view of the miraculous was examined. Ruthven sees miracles as a means of divine foreshadowing as God conquers sin, disease, death, and darkness. Baker's view of miracles as a means of expelling the demonic, causally related to salvation, was also examined. Finally, the Roman Catholic view of healing as exorcism was presented and examined. While all of these interpretive frameworks are biblically valid, they are not complete as God uses signs and wonders for a multitude of purposes in scripture. Therefore, the one key defining characteristic for signs and wonders is divine providence. God uses signs and wonders for his purposes, within his plans, to bring glory to him.

In the final chapter, a full evidential Renewal apologetic will be defined. This apologetic will also serve as a polemic within Christianity, and as an interpretative tool for scripture. This apologetic will be based upon the preceding chapters, but will also include eschatological elements such as the Great Apostasy and End Times harvest as answers for the dramatic increase in Special Divine Action within our era. Finally, my interpretive tool of *Realized Renewal Eschatology* (Section 7.3) will seek to bring clarity to these dramatic movements of God during the past century.

Chapter 7

Apologetical Significance of Modern Miracles

"The nineteenth century is the last time when it was possible for an educated person to admit to believing in miracles like the virgin birth without embarrassment."[1]

—Richard Dawkins

"I will never tire of repeating this: rationalism and materialism have polluted a segment of theologians, and their influence on both bishops and priests has been profound."[2]

—Fr. Gabrielle Amorth

In a recent discussion with a cessationist Christian, I argued that I could give him several examples of blessings which have occurred in my own life despite nearly impossible odds that they would have occurred by chance alone. Is this absolute and definitive proof of Special Divine Action? No, but it points in that direction with a very high degree of probability. Phenomena which occur through Christian prayer, and lack plausible naturalistic explanations, are the very foundation for an evidential apologetic for Christianity. While he did not discount this, he nevertheless refused to

---

1. Dawkins, *God Delusion*, 187.
2. Amorth, *Exorcist Tells His Story*, 174.

renounce cessationism until he himself experiences something which he considers miraculous.

While writing this book, and having engaged in countless hours of intellectual debate and discussions with atheists, agnostics, and cessationists; I have come to realize that unbelief in Special Divine Action and Christianity is not really an intellectual issue, rather it is a spiritual one. That is, the evidence supporting a belief in Special Divine Action and theism is significantly stronger than the skeptical position. Unfortunately, many atheists and sceptics are like the Pharisees in the New Testament; whose hardened hearts would not allow them to believe no matter what signs and wonders Jesus preformed in front of them (Mark 3:5; Ephesians 4:18). Sceptics will defend the most implausible of naturalistic explanations, since the alternative is to allow for the existence of God.

Interestingly, many of the strongest opponents of Christianity were once Christians themselves. Many professional atheist debaters such as Farrell Till and Dan Barker were once conservative Christian pastors. Often, they came to renounce their faith not due to a logical process, but rather an emotional one. Having adopted a false theology that Christians are never to experience any hardship in their lives, when some hardship and suffering occurs, they blame God for not protecting them. This is why an understanding of theodicy is vital for all Christians (see chapter 6).

So, is this ultimately a fruitless endeavor? No. However, apologists must simply understand who their efforts should be directed towards. Many agnostics and atheists have reached their present condition merely due to their secular education. Their worldview is more a product of years of indoctrination into secularism than it is a well-reasoned and informed conclusion. Critical thinking and logic are often not taught, even at the university level. The theistic position is usually ignored if not outright ridiculed and mocked during this process. This is why Christian apologists must venture into secular universities for intellectual debates.[3] It is clear that often the students have never heard the evidences for Christianity first hand. They often do not know that there are Christian scholars represented in all fields of the academy. Christians have usually been maligned by their secular teachers and professors as uneducated fools. This is why there is such a strong need for Christian apologists!

3. Dr. Ravi Zacharias frequently recounts how his presentations at the most liberal universities fill up the auditorium and even have crowds outside listening. It is a common occurrence for former agnostics/atheists to adopt theism after hearing it defended by Zacharias or other apologists.

Apologetical Significance of Modern Miracles

However, apologists should not view such debates, nor any areas of their scholarship, as merely an intellectual endeavor. Rather, all must be viewed in light of the supernatural, as a means of expanding light into darkness; expanding the kingdom of God. Thus, the apologist must pray not only for victory in debate, and divine insight in scholarship, but also that God will soften the hearts of those who are obstinate to his message. Pray that God will shine the light of truth into the darkness of those who are blinded by worldly philosophies and pagan belief systems. This will cause Renewal to break out through the apologist.

7.1 EVIDENTIAL VALUE OF MODERN MIRACLES

The current status of modern Christian apologetics is largely shaped by the quality (or lack thereof) of its opponents. While the mid-twentieth century saw vibrant debates between scholars such as C.S. Lewis and Bertrand Russell;[4] many/most of the current debates lack this quality. This is largely due to the popularity of the New Atheists who use rhetoric, insult, and mockery instead of argumentation.[5] While these rhetorical tactics will suffice for those already committed to atheism, it does not convince the educated, open minded sceptic who is able to see through such tactics. This is perhaps why the New Atheists such as Richard Dawkins often refuse to engage in open debates with world class Christian apologists such as Dr. William Lane Craig.[6]

---

4. For a summary of this debate see Wielenberg, *God and the Reach of Reason*.

5. Arguments equating the theistic position with a belief in the flying spaghetti monster are indicative of this trend. The demand that the burden of proof is so heavily on the theistic position as to provide complete and overwhelming evidences (i.e., extraordinary claims require extraordinary evidences) rather than the more probable than not (i.e., good faith skepticism); is yet another example of their disingenuous argumentation.

6. William Lane Craig is considered by many to be the world's best Christian apologist. Richard Dawkins is viewed by many as the best atheist debater. However, Dawkins has thus far refused to engage in open debate with Craig. Craig has extended numerous invitations to debate Dawkins at Oxford, Cambridge, Liverpool, Birmingham, Manchester, Edinburgh, Glasgow and Bristol. Dawkin's refuses to debate Craig by citing him as unimportant; and an advocate of Old Testament genocide—based upon his literal interpretation of Deuteronomy. This argument is seen as a mere diversionary tactic by most observers. Dawkin's outlined his argument which caused Craig to debate an empty chair in, Dawkins, "Why I Refuse to Debate Craig."

7.1.1 Christian Explanations Are More Plausible

Recalling the standard of *good faith skepticism* (chapter 2), this book has not sought to prove that the theistic argument based upon modern miracles is absolute; rather, that it is more probable than not. What has been shown thus far (particularly in chapters 2 through 4), is that it is the naturalistic explanations of modern miraculous phenomena that stretch the bounds of credulity. Similarly, it is when researchers apply the usual rules of scientific analysis, and allow for testimonies from reliable sources (e.g., American medical doctors and nurses), that the occurrence of modern miracles becomes far more probable than not. As John Polkinghorne states:

> There are no knock-down arguments for the existence of God—or, for that matter, for divine nonexistence—in the sense that it would be completely irrational to deny them. The question is too deep for a 2 + 2 = 4 kind of proof response. Yet there are good motivations for belief in God, sufficient for many of us to commit ourselves to betting our lives on them. The claim is not that atheists are stupid, for that is clearly not the case, but that theism explains more than atheism ever could, making intelligible what otherwise would have to be treated as merely a happy accident.[7]

7.1.2 Modern Miracles can be Argued for Evidentially

While various philosophical arguments (e.g., classical apologetics)[8] and intelligent design are the current status quo of most debates on theism; this book has shown that this need not be the case. Arguments based upon modern miracles are less abstract than those of classical apologetics. And, unlike other evidential arguments (e.g., the empty tomb); modern miracles can be examined, evaluated, and argued for on a contemporaneous basis.

---

7. Polkinghorne and Beale, *Questions of Truth*, 14.

8. The three main arguments of classical apologetics are: the teleological argument, the cosmological argument, and the ontological argument—all three are philosophically abstract in nature. For more details about these arguments see Geisler, *Baker Encyclopedia Christian Apologetics*.

7.1.3 Birth of Renewal Apologetics (Evidential)

While there have been Christian apologists such as John Lennox and Richard Swinburne who have argued for and defended the occurrence of modern miracles; what has been lacking thus far is a full and comprehensive Renewal apologetic based upon modern miracles. The previous chapters have helped to form the argument which I will now summarizes in the next section. Additionally, I will add my own development, the epistemological tool of *Realized Renewal Eschatology* (Section 7.3.2) as an important contribution to Renewal theology, Renewal hermeneutics, and Renewal eschatology.

7.2 MIRACLES AS THE FOUNDATION OF RENEWAL APOLOGETICS

The worldwide Renewal movement began at the beginning of the twentieth century. The twentieth century also witnessed many end-times occurrences such as the re-founding of Israel (prophetic fulfillment), and the Great Apostasy. These occurrences, while not exclusive to the Renewal movement, do have much greater emphases within the movement, particularly in the areas of Renewal theology and Renewal eschatology.

The twentieth century has been one of great harvest as Christianity changed from a first world religion (global north), to a third world religion (global south). The gospel was heard for the first time throughout many African and Asian countries, as well as in other remote areas across the globe. Not suffering from a secular/naturalistic worldview, those in the third world who heard the gospel expected to see signs and wonders firsthand; and the Holy Spirit delivered. The signs and wonders contained in scripture have been displayed on mission fields throughout the world in the twentieth and early twenty-first centuries. These signs and wonders have served as a means to authenticate both the message and the messenger. Additionally, the signs and wonders occurring in the lives of new believers have served as an added witness to the authenticity of the gospel message. Through signs and wonders, the power of God is displayed over both the natural and supernatural realms.

7.2.1 Personal Salvation via Renewal (Deliverance from the Demonic)

God's power is important not only in terms of the miraculous; but also, for the salvation experience itself. Salvation historically was understood as a supernatural experience. Often viewed as beginning in baptism, wherein, the Holy Spirit was seen as driving out any demonic presence from the new Christian. Thus, in the occurrence of salvation, God was seen as using the Holy Spirit to "Renew" his child, to break curses, and to drive out the demonic. This type of salvation accompanied by physical healing is consistent with the biblical model,[9] as well as the modern witness of many third world missionaries such as Heidi Baker. Baker's testimony that once an unbeliever comes to accept Christ, they are physically healed of their aliments within minutes is consistent with the numerous examples seen in scripture.[10] Additionally, exorcists such as Malachi Martin,[11] and Fr. Gabriele Amorth,[12] recount numerous instances wherein possessed people are healed physically after being freed of the demonic.

7.2.2 Evangelism via Miracles

In the spreading of the gospel, God uses the Holy Spirit as a means of authenticating both the message and the messenger as He "Renews" the afflicted, and removes their sicknesses. While evangelism in the west is often an intellectual process, in the third world, unbelievers expect to see signs and wonders as a means of authenticating the messenger. Evangelists and missionaries who lack the ability to perform signs and wonders are not seen as authentic. God does accommodate this worldview, and delivers accordingly, in order that the gospel may be spread. Missionaries who have never performed a miracle while living in the west often return from the third world having preformed numerous healings; often to their own surprise.[13]

---

9. Ruthven, *Protestant Theology*, 30.
10. Brierley, "80 Miracles," lines 75–78.
11. See Martin, *Hostage to the Devil*.
12. See Amorth, *Exorcist Explains Demonic*.

13. See Baker, *Always Enough*. Heidi Baker's testimony that 100% of the deaf were healed in certain districts of Mozambique is evidence of this phenomenon. There are several possible implications from this phenomenon: 1. That there are more illnesses caused by the demonic in the 3rd world. 2. There are more healings to help spread the gospel in the 3rd world. 3. God heals more where the need is the highest due to a lack of medicine (echoes Keener).

Those suffering in spiritual bondage are usually living in areas which could be described as demonic strongholds, especially within the 10/40 window. As new believers are saved from the demonic by the renewing and sanctifying presence of the Holy Spirit, they become a vessel for the Renewal of their communities as well. The presence of the Holy Spirit in them allows for cleansing and exorcism of the demonic from their community. Thus, the new converts infused with the Holy Spirit "Renew" the land.

7.2.3 Realized Renewal Eschatology

Realized Renewal Eschatology-[14] Interpreting end-times scripture in light of experience and events from our twenty-first century context. This is a valuable tool for Renewal exegesis as we see scripture fulfilled right before our eyes on a daily basis in the world. Additionally, this tool will serve as a foundation for a Renewal apologetic for the reasons below.

Exegetes of Scripture ignore the world around them at their own peril. While theological interpretations of the book of Revelations are debatable, numerous prophecies fulfilled during the past century are of great significance hermeneutically and eschatologically. For instance, the Renewal movement, and the spread of the gospel via signs and wonders into the third world, has simultaneously coincided with the Great Apostasy in the first world. The re-founding of Israel (1948), with all of its prophetic fulfillments, occurred almost simultaneously with the emergence of nuclear weapons (1945); which are capable of destroying the earth by fire (2 Peter 3:4–12; Revelation 20:9; Malachi 4:1).

We live in a time where the prophecies of Joel 2:28 and Acts 2:17 (Spirit poured out on all flesh) are occurring simultaneously with the destructive prophecies in Revelation about the Great Apostasy. This dichotomy makes the spread of Renewal/Charismatic Christianity, and the Gifts of the Spirit, the method which God has chosen to save the most numbers of souls (End-Time Harvest) before the return of Christ.

---

14. Realized Renewal Eschatology is built upon the concept of realized eschatology formulated by C. H. Dodd and popularized by N. T. Wright. Realized eschatology is the view that eschatological passages in the New Testament were being fulfilled contemporaneously in the ministry and work of Jesus and the disciples. This stands in stark contrast with the more common premillennial interpretations which view eschatological prophecies as future events. Realized eschatology can be seen as a form of preterism. For a fuller discussion of these views see Wright, *Revelation*.

Miracles are foundational to Christianity. It is through miracles that God shows us his love and character. Miracles show the desire of God to heal those who are repentant. They show the means which God wants us to seek after him, with humility and prayer. But perhaps most importantly miracles *Renew!* They "Renew" the individual receiving them. They "Renew" the faith of those who witness them. And, most importantly, they spread the kingdom of God. God knows that there are many who would not have believed unless they saw miracles (John 10:38; John 20: 24–29). But, it is also through miracles that God promulgates Renewal and redemption worldwide. It is for this reason that God is using miracles for his final plans.

With this interpretive tool (Realized Renewal Eschatology), I will now examine several key end-times occurrences and Renewal motifs. We will see that viewing scripture in light of modern events helps to provide clarity in many theological/eschatological debates. It will also become apparent that God is using Renewal as a key component in his end-times plans.

7.2.3.1 Apostasy/Renewal Dichotomy (The Great Apostasy/End Time Harvest)

> *"At that time if anyone says to you, 'Look, here is the Christ!' or, 'There he is!' do not believe it. For false Christs and false prophets will appear and perform great signs and miracles to deceive even the elect—if that were possible."*
>
> MATTHEW 24:23–25

On the surface, it would seem counter intuitive that a *Great Renewal* would be taking place simultaneously with a *Great Apostasy*. However, in terms of various eschatological patterns, this is exactly what can be witnessed during the last hundred years. God used twentieth century inventions such as radio, television, and the internet to spread the gospel to remote regions of the world. One popular interpretation of (Matthew 28:16–20) is that Christ will return once the gospel has been spread to every tongue, tribe, and nation. Many missiologists believe that this can/will occur within the next one to two generations.

Simultaneously, one can tell that we are living in the end-times due to the Great Apostasy which has afflicted the western church. Ideas such as inclusivism, abortion, homosexuality, etc. which were anathema throughout church history, are now seen as debatable by many modern, liberal theologians who see scripture as "unclear" on these issues. These scholars usually deny biblical inerrancy/infallibility in practice, and do not see scripture as authoritative and foundational in their epistemologies. Rather, the very foundations of the Christian faith, are seen as a fluid vessel, open to various "communal" interpretations (excluding both dogma and doctrine) in the postmodern/post-foundational era. This is truly a time wherein God is separating the wheat from the chaff, as he pulls in his last Great Harvest (Matthew 13:30; Luke 3:17).

One only has to look at the current backlash against historical orthodox beliefs (i.e., the Nicene Creed, the Apostles Creed, etc.) to see that beliefs which have survived for 1900 years in the west have come under a heavy assault within the past century even within "conservative" Christianity. The adoption of a postmodern worldview (first in philosophy, next in theology), has made it so that any foundational knowledge or truth claims are heavily disputed.[15] Even the very language, logic and reason being used is assaulted within this framework. Strong beliefs against abortion, divorce, homosexuality, etc. which were nearly universal 100 years ago are now in the minority. These occurrences were prophesized 2000 years ago as the Great Apostasy.

There are numerous passages contained in scripture which predicted the present state of the church. For instance, we are told that: "For the time will come when they will not endure sound doctrine; but after their own lusts shall they heap to themselves teachers, having itching ears" (2 Timothy 4:3). And, "Now the Spirit speaketh expressly, that in the latter times some shall depart from the faith, giving heed to seducing spirits, and doctrines of devils;" (1 Timothy 4:1) (See also: Matthew 24; 2 Thessalonians 2:4; 2 Timothy 3:1–9).

The Great Apostasy and end-times anticipation have been a focal point of the Renewal movement since the beginning. Within classical Pentecostalism, many early denominations believed that they were within a generation of the return of Christ. Within Catholicism, many traditionalist Catholics view Vatican II as the beginning of the Great Apostasy.[16] The

---

15. For an in-depth discussion of this see Penner, *Christianity and Postmodern Turn*. See also: Erickson et al., *Reclaiming the Center*.

16. Examples of traditionalist Catholics include Sedevacantists (Chair of Peter is empty) e.g., Society of Saint Pius V (SSPV), Sedeimpeditists (Cardinal Giuseppe Siri was the truly elected Pope in 1958), and the various Latin Mass groups e.g., Society of Saint Pius X (SSPX). These various groups reject the various reforms made during the Vatican II council including the adoption of the Novus Ordo—vernacular mass. However, it is

Renewal Apologetics

Catholic Charismatic Revival has placed much more of an emphasis on the participation of the laity since the hierarchy is often seen as oblivious to the contemporaneous dynamic work of the Holy Spirit.[17]

7.2.3.2 End-Time Harvest (Acts 2:17; Joel 2:28)

"And this gospel of the kingdom will be preached in the whole world as a testimony to all nations, and then the end will come."
Matthew 24:14

"The Holy Spirit is working overtime in the 20th century. There have been more miracles and more martyrs in the 20th century than in all the previous centuries of human history combined."[18]
—Peter Kreeft

For most of the last two millennia, since Christ gave the Great Commission, there have existed many tribes and nations which were inaccessible due to logistical and geographical difficulties. Even today, there are many unreached people groups within the 10/40 window due to these same reasons; as well as the prohibition of Christian evangelism by Islamic, Hindu and other religious belief systems.

However, first the radio, and now the internet, have been able to transcend many of these geographical and legal boundaries. Many unreached people groups have heard the gospel and the name of Jesus for the first time, not through a missionary visiting their village; but through a missionary on the radio, television or the internet. These technologies will make it possible for the gospel to be preached to the entire world sometime in the twenty-first century.[19]

---

the New Theology (*Nouvelle Théologie*) contained in the Vatican II documents of Lumen Gentium and *Gaudium et Spies* which emphasized Karl Rahner's concept of the Anonymous Christian (i.e., inclusivism) which is perhaps the casus belli (cause of war) for the various groups. Cf. Pius XII, "Humani Generis," Paul VI, "Lumen Gentium," and, Paul VI, "Gaudium et Spies."

17. For a summary of the importance of the Catholic Charismatic Revival see Cleary, *Latin America Saved*. See also: Cleary, *Charismatic Catholicism*.

18. Kreeft and Nevins, *Charisms*, loc. 103–105 of 483.

19. Various groups such as the Joshua Project and Empower 21 are attempting to fulfill the Great Commission during the twenty-first century by translating the bible into

Apologetical Significance of Modern Miracles

Many Renewalists have interpreted the prophesies contained in Joel 2:28 and Acts 2:17–18 to have been a reference to the twentieth century Renewal movement and the reemphasis on the gifts of the spirit:

> *"It will come about after this that I will pour out My Spirit on all mankind; and your sons and daughters will prophesy, Your old men will dream dreams, Your young men will see visions." (Joel 2:28)*
>
> *"And it shall come to pass in the last days, says God, I will pour out of my Spirit upon all flesh: and your sons and your daughters shall prophesy, and your young men shall see visions, and your old men shall dream dreams: And on my servants and on my handmaidens I will pour out in those days of my Spirit; and they shall prophesy" (Acts 2:17–18).*

The significant changes in denominations and demographics of the twentieth century certainly shows the prominence of the Renewal movement. While the church in the west has become stagnant and is lacking in orthodoxy; the church in the third world has exploded! According to peter Kreeft, during the 1980s Cardinal Ratzinger said that: "We were living in the "Pentecostal hour" of the church and at the time he spoke that in the 1980s, Pentecostalism comprised only 6% of Christianity. Now we're at an astonishing 25%—600 million—in the world's fastest growing movement."[20] Most of these members of the Renewal movement are in the global south which now represents 61% (1.3 billion) of all Christians worldwide.[21] Within Catholicism, Renewal has been seen as the mechanism which has cured the ills of nominalism and declining numbers.[22] During Vatican II it was declared that: "The Charismatic Movement will fulfill itself when it disappears into the rest of the church, like a mighty river that waters a desert."[23]

---

several thousand languages spoken by the remaining unreached people groups. While this is sometimes accomplished by actual missionaries, many are being reached through radio, internet, and various digital technologies. See Mandryk, *Operation World*.

20. Kreeft and Nevins, *Charisms*, loc. 96–99 of 483.

21. As cited by Pew, the common usage the global north consists of the developed countries including the USA, Canada, Europe, Australia, New Zealand and Japan. The global South includes the rest of the world. The global north in 1900 contained 80% of the world's Christians. Today it only contains 40% and many of those are nominal. See Pew Research Center, "Global Christianity."

22. For an in-depth discussion on this see Cleary, *Latin America Saved*.

23. Kreeft and Nevins, *Charisms*, loc. 111–113 of 483.

One advantage the cultures within the global south have over the global north is that they are largely traditional societies. Thus, living out the *natural law* of God, written on the hearts of men (Rom 2:15), is natural rather than countercultural. Additionally, since they never adopted an enlightenment/secular worldview, they are much more open to the miraculous. God has used this openness to prove his power via miracles. As Kreeft notes: "You don't see many miracles in Europe and Christianity is dying in Europe; you see enormous miracles in Africa and in China and Christianity is growing by leaps and bounds there."[24] The people see the power of God over darkness and convert. Jack Hayford concludes of this end time's dichotomy:

> Today, the Bible's prophecies of the end times declare the challenge between, on the one hand, the increasing enterprises of evil and dark powers that corrupt humanity, and the inky blackness of hell's demons surfacing for the final conflict (see 1 Timothy 4: 2; 2 Timothy 3: 1– 5, 13; Revelation 9: 1– 21). On the other hand are those who answer Christ's call as the Lord of the Church for us to overcome (see 1 John 5: 4– 5)! The darkness is deepening—but the Word of God sounds a trumpet blast of faith-inspiring promise: Where sin abounds, grace much more abounds![25]

7.2.3.3 Refounding of Israel

"Frederick the Great, King of Prussia, once asked his chaplain, 'Give me a sure proof of the inspiration of the Holy Scriptures.' The chaplain answered, 'It is the Jew, Your Majesty.' The Jews and their miraculous history are another proof of the truth of biblical prophecy."[26]

—RICHARD WURMBRAND

There are numerous end-times prophecies about modern Israel contained in both the Old Testament and the New Testament. The restoration of Israel after the Jews were banished from the land and scattered to the ends of the earth for 2000 years was highly improbable. However, this did occur by the hand of God when in 1948 God brought the Jews back to their

---

24. Kreeft and Nevins, *Charisms*, loc. 107–109 of 483.
25. Hayford, *Penetrating the Darkness*, 14.
26. Wurmbrand, *Answer to Atheist's Handbook*, loc. 1731–1733 of 2564.

ancient homeland. The refounding of Israel is perhaps the greatest example of fulfilled prophecy from an apologetical standpoint. The occurrence is modern, specific, and immune to challenges of ex post facto authorship; since the predictions were made over 2000 years ago. A few examples of these prophecies are:

1. Jeremiah 38: 38–40 (enlargement of Jerusalem).
2. Ezekiel 37:21–22 (Israel reestablished as a nation).
3. Jeremiah 16:14–15 (2nd Israel more impressive than first).
4. Ezekiel 4:3–6 (Reestablishment of Israel).
5. Ezekiel 34:13 (People of Israel return to their own land).
6. Jeremiah 31:10 (God would watch over the people of Israel).
7. Leviticus 26:3; 7–8 (Israel's army would be disproportionately powerful).
8. Deuteronomy 30:3–5 (The fortunes of the people of Israel would be restored).[27, 28]

7.2.3.4 Destruction by Fire (Nuclear Weapons)

The invention of nuclear weapons (1945) occurred almost simultaneous with the refounding of Israel (1948). Nuclear weapons have strong eschatological implications. While their development helped to bring an end to WWII and to catapult the USA into becoming the world's first superpower, it came at a cost. Within ten years the USSR had the same technology and became engaged in a battle for supremacy for the next fifty years (the cold war). Today, there are nine nations with nuclear weapons.[29] There are numerous other rogue states and terrorist groups seeking out the ability to become nuclear powers. At a naturalistic level, it seems probable that a nuclear war will occur in the twenty-first century. It is actually amazing that one has not occurred yet. This is where divine providence and the hand of God must be seen as a restraining force. God is preventing the destruction of the world, until his end times harvest is complete. However, an eventual nuclear war does seem probable and would fulfill

---

27. For more examples see Konig and Konig, *100 Prophecies*, 19.
28. See Also: McDowell, *Evidence Demands a Verdict*.
29. Kristensen and Norris, "Status of World Nuclear Forces," lines 16–18.

many end-times prophecies citing the destruction of the world by fire (2 Pet 3:4-12; Rev 20:9; Mal 4:1).

Additionally, many scholars have interpreted the names of Gog and Magog (Rev 20:7-8) to reference Russia and Syria for decades previous to the current Syrian civil war (2011-present).[30] These same scholars believe that the battle of Armageddon will be fought in northern Israel where the prophecy of Zechariah will be fulfilled: "And this shall be the plague where with the LORD will smite all the people that have fought against Jerusalem; Their flesh shall consume away while they stand upon their feet, and their eyes shall consume away in their holes, and their tongue shall consume away in their mouth" (Zech 14:12).

7.3 RENEWAL AS POLEMIC

Thus, when we view the four preceding phenomena in light of Realized Renewal Eschatology, we discover that not only are modern miracles an apologetic capable of bringing non-Christians to have faith in Christ; but the argument can also be effectively used as a polemic within Christianity as well. Renewal Christianity is the fastest growing type of Christianity because it is the most biblically based. Renewal is also the mechanism for the end-times harvest being used by God!

7.3.1 Renewal as Discernment (Miracles Separate the True from the False Church!)

"The Charismatic Movement will fulfill itself when it disappears into the rest of the church, like a mighty river that waters a desert."[31]
— VATICAN II DECLARATION

In Bible based churches which honor God, miracles occur. In churches where evangelism and faith and are lacking, there will be a simultaneous lacking of miracles. Miracles will occur far more often in the growing and vibrant church than in a stagnant one. This is because authentication is one of the most important functions of miracles. Thus, when members are

---

30. Hagee predicts an invasion of Israel by Russia and various Islamic nations. See Hagee, *Jerusalem Countdown*.

31. Kreeft and Nevins, *Charisms*, loc. 111–113 of 483.

engaged in evangelism, particularly in unevangelized areas, God will allow more miracles to occur, as a means of authenticating the gospel message as well as the messenger (evangelist/missionary). Additionally, Christians with pure hearts, will make many petitions to God as they believe that he can heal them. This is the reason why third world converts, not suffering from western secularism, believe in the power of God so much more; and why God delivers miracles so strongly in their lives.

7.3.2 Renewal as Hermeneutic (Miracles Refute Cessationism & Theological Liberalism)

The occurrence of modern signs and wonders refutes two widely held theological methods of biblical interpretation: theological liberalism and cessationism. Theological liberals believe that biblical signs and wonders did not occur as they violate their naturalistic worldview. The signs and wonders of Scripture are metaphors or myths containing a hidden truth. One must demythologize the Scripture in order to arrive at its kernel of truth.[32] The fact that signs and wonders do occur now, refutes this view of Scripture.

The Cessationist position that signs and wonders ceased at the end of the apostolic age is refuted by the occurrence of modern signs and wonders. Therefore, while scriptural passages such as 1 Cor 13:8–12 can be used as a proof text for the cessationist position, correct interpretation must not be done in a textual vacuum. Exegetes must look towards the rest of scripture, tradition, and experience. The phenomenon of modern medical miracles preformed within a Christian context refutes the cessationist position.

7.3.3 Renewal as Providence (Eschatology)

In recent scholarship, many have proposed positions such as open theism,[33] and the weak God[34] concept, which are at odds with traditional Christian orthodoxy and its views on divine providence. Additionally, the prophetic fulfillments being witnessed in the end times refute these positions as well. If one thing can be gleamed theologically from the twentieth century, it is that God's promises are fulfilled via his providence. The refounding of

---

32. For more on this method see Bultmann, *New Testament and Mythology*.
33. For more on open theism see Pinnock, *Openness of God*.
34. For more on the weak God concept see Caputo, *Weakness of God*.

Israel, along with the end times harvest, and the Renewal movement, are perhaps the greatest examples of these prophetic fulfillments. All of this was accomplished by divine providence; the providence of an omniscient and omnipotent God.

Conclusion

This book has led to numerous theological, scientific, and apologetical implications and conclusions; which I will briefly summarize below. While both Christian and secular scholars may debate some of these conclusions, the one prescient point, which seems beyond debate, is that this entire project is but an initial foray into these areas. There needs to be a lot more research into the phenomenon of modern medical miracles. As well as scholarship in the development of Renewal apologetics.

C 1 THEOLOGICAL IMPLICATIONS

This study has highlighted numerous theological implications for Christian scholars of all stripes; not just Renewalists. I will now briefly summarize the three most important of these in the following sections.

C 1.1 Miracles show the Character of God (Power/Love)

Chapter 5 (history) and chapter 6 (interpretation) showed how miracles reveal the character of God. God has his providential plans, and has set up natural and scientific laws. But God is not bound by the laws of the universe as he is the creator of the universe. If God is able to answer a prayer request from one of his children, and it does not violate his providential scheme or the framework of his plans, then God at times will allow for a breakthrough of grace (Meister Eckhart);[1] and a miraculous healing will occur.

Interestingly, God has allowed for the twentieth and twenty-first centuries to be a time of great healing, particularly in the third world. God knew the dominate worldview ahead of time, and that the gospel could

---

1. See Eckhart, *Breakthrough*.

only be spread effectively with miracles. Subsequently, God has allowed for hundreds of millions of miracles to occur there.

C 1.2 God has used Miracles throughout History (Cessationism Refuted)

The theological position of cessationism is largely in retreat at the beginning of the twenty-first century. This is due in part to cessationism being theologically unsound (i.e., proof texting; not viewing scripture in light of scripture).[2] However, it is largely the Renewal movement, and the millions of modern miracles, which have caused evangelical scholars to reexamine their theology and adopt a more open position towards post-biblical miracles. A cursory examination of church history will show that cessationism clearly violates 2000 years of church history and its post-biblical miracles.

C 1.3 Miracles show that God is both Imminent and Transcendent (Uses his power to Renew)

Theologians have long argued whether God is imminent or transcendent. The case of modern miracles shows that God is both. God's imminence is seen as he interacts closely and specifically with the person that he wishes to heal. This healing is either the result of the person themselves, or someone else praying to God as an intercessor.

Miraculous phenomena also show God's transcendence for two reasons:1. In the case of answered prayer, God transcends the natural laws and boundaries of the universe as he injects a one-time supernatural act.[3]
2. In the case wherein a prayer request is denied, God is asserting his providence and salvific plans as paramount in the denial. God allows for bad things to happen in order to bring about a greater good.

---

2. One of the foundations of the historical grammatical method is interpreting scripture as a collective whole (e.g., The Whole Counsel of God). Scripture must not be broken into small pebbles, but rather must remain as a solid and cohesive rock (Reinhard Bonnke). For more on the historical grammatical method see Elwell, *Evangelical Dictionary of Theology*, and Geisler, *Biblical Inerrancy*. For a fuller discussion of biblical interpretation also involving canon, creed and patristics see Hahn, *Canon and Biblical Interpretation*.

3. This is the view/definition of a miracle held by Richard Swinburne. See Swinburne, *Existence of God*.

CONCLUSION

C 2 SCIENTIFIC IMPLICATIONS

In modern culture, science and faith are often seen as being at odds with one another. This book has shown that historically (previous to the twentieth century), this was not the case. Additionally, this book has shown that true science as opposed to scientism, must allow for supernatural explanations to scientific problems. This will be more fully examined in the following three sections.

C 2.1 Science and Faith are not in Conflict

Chapter 2 (epistemology), showed that there is no set scientific method of enquiry, rather there are various systems of methods. Previous to the enlightenment, God and the supernatural were not banished from the list of plausible explanations in scientific enquiry. In fact, most of the major areas of science were discovered by Bible believing Christians. It was only during the enlightenment, when many scientists began to reject science in favor of scientism (i.e., methodological naturalism); that the gulf between science and faith began to emerge.

C 2.2 A Priori Naturalism (Scientism) is not Scientific

As was shown in chapters 2, 3, and 4; there is no scientific reason to posit naturalism as an *a priori* for any scientific methodology. Positing ontological naturalism, or engaging in methodological naturalism, necessarily taints any scientific enquiry; since the researcher is not following the evidence wherever it leads. Many, if not most, scientific enquiries will still have naturalistic explanations, due to the relative rarity of miracles. However, to eliminate miracles and the supernatural *a priori* is not only illogical, it is unscientific.

C 2.3 Science must allow for Divine Interaction

Scientists must remain open minded and follow the evidence where it leads (see chapters 2 through 4). The Lourdes Medical Bureau is an excellent example of this. Far from being an insular group of Catholics, the Bureau purposefully recruits scientists from all faiths, and even includes atheists amongst its ranks. In doing so, they hope to be able to follow the evidence wherever it leads. Their final determination is not that a miracle has occurred (that is left up to the theologians), but rather, that something has occurred outside the bounds of known science. For this, Special Divine Action is one possible explanation.

C 3 FUTURE TRAJECTORIES

While writing this text, I often felt like I was just scratching the surface of many important topics; and indeed, I was. To fully address all of the topics encountered will require a full series of texts on Renewal apologetics. Nevertheless, I do feel that this study has accomplished its original purposes of evaluating the apologetical value of modern miracles and subsequently establishing an evidential Renewal apologetic. Hopefully, this work will serve as a foundation for what will soon develop into a series of works on the topic of Renewal apologetics.

C 3.1 Bayesian Analysis of Modern Miracles

One possible future project would be an evaluation of modern miracles via Bayesian analysis.[4] Bayesian analysis would yield similar, though more technical, results than my own tool of good faith skepticism. Tim and Lydia McGrew have offered a road map to this endeavor with their chapters on "The Reliability of Witnesses and Testimony to the Miraculous"[5] and "The Argument from Miracles."[6] These two works examine the probability of the New Testament miracles and the Resurrection of Jesus Christ via Bayesian analysis. However, like many apologetical endeavors, the focus is only on the Bible. Modern evidence of God, which may be more convincing to the sceptic, exists today in the form of modern Special Divine Action.

---

4. Bayesian analysis is considered a cornerstone for modern probabilistic reasoning. Based upon the original journal article Bayes, "An Essay toward Solving a Problem in the Doctrine of Chances," 370–418. In short, Bayes theorem shows if the likely outcome of a given scenario is above 50% (i.e., more likely than not). For further explanation, as well as technical examples of Bayesian analysis, see Stone, *Bayes' Rule*, and, Joyce, "Bayes' Theorem." Examples of Bayesian analysis in regard to special divine action include: De-Poe, "Bayesian Approach Confirming Miracles," 229–38; Earman, "Bayes, Hume and Miracles," 293–310; and, Holder, "Hume Miracles: Bayesian Interpretation," 49–65.

5. McGrew, "Reliability of Witnesses," 46–63.

6. McGrew, "Argument from Miracles," 593–662.

C 3.2 Empirical Examination of Catholic Miracle Documentation

My research into the documentation of Catholic miracles has relied upon the research of others. One day, I hope to be able to visit the Vatican archives and empirically evaluate the evidence from Lourdes and other modern miracles, from a Renewal perspective. This endeavor would yield yet another text in a series on Renewal apologetics.

C 3.3 More Development in the Theology of the Miraculous

Perhaps the largest gap in scholarship which this survey has exposed is the need for the development of a Renewal theology of the miraculous. As shown in chapters 4 and 6, we are perhaps far past merely proving that miracles occur; but we are in only in the initial stages of explaining their meanings in terms of Renewal scholarship. Certainly, we can stand on the shoulders of giants and look at the explanations of Augustine and Aquinas. But, we are living in the age of the end-times harvest, the Great Apostasy, and the Renewal movement. This all coincides simultaneously with the unprecedented occurrences of hundreds of millions of miracles worldwide. Scholars should examine these occurrences to develop a deeper Renewal theology of the miraculous.

Bibliography

Amorth, Gabriele. *An Exorcist Explains the Demonic: The Antics of Satan and His Fallen Army of Angels*. Manchester, NH: Sophia, 2016.

———. *An Exorcist Tells His Story*. San Francisco: Ignatius, 1999.

Anderson, Alan. *An Introduction to Pentecostalism*. New York: Cambridge University Press, 2014.

Aquinas, Thomas. *Contra Gentiles*. Kindle ed. Seattle: Amazon Digital Services, 2010.

———. *Summa Theologia*. Seattle: Amazon Digital Services, 2011.

Armstrong, Dave. *Proving the Catholic Faith is Biblical*. Manchester, NH: Sophia, 2015.

Ashcroft, Jack. *The Real Exorcist: Spiritual Warfare Methodology*. Vol. 2. North Charleston, SC: Create Space, 2013.

Audi, Robert. "Contemporary Foundationalism." In *The Theory of Knowledge, Classical and Contemporary Reading*, edited by Louis P. Pojman, 206–13. Belmont, CA: Wadsworth, 1993.

———. *Epistemology: A Contemporary Introduction*. New York: Routledge, 2011.

Augustine. *Against the Epistle of Manichaeus, Called Fundamental*. Translated by Phillip Schaff. Kindle ed. Seattle: Amazon Digital Services, 2011.

———. *The City of God*. Translated by Marcus Dods. New York: Catholic Way, 2015.

———. *Confessions*. Translated by E. B. Pusey. Kindle ed. Seattle: Amazon Digital Services, 2012.

———. *Enchiridion on Faith, Hope and Love*. Kindle ed. Seattle: Amazon Digital Services, 2011.

———. *On Grace and Freewill*. Translated by Peter Holmes. Kindle ed. Seattle: Amazon Digital Services, 2011.

———. *Revisions*. Vols 1 and 2. Translator Boniface Ramsey. Hyde Park, NY: New City, 2010.

Baker, Heidi, and Rolland Baker. *Always Enough: God's Miraculous Provision among the Poorest Children on Earth*. Grand Rapids: Chosen, 2003.

Baker, Rolland. *Keeping the Fire: Sustaining Revival through Love: The Five Core Values of IRIS Global*. Kent, UK: River, 2015.

Bayes, T. "An Essay Toward Solving a Problem in the Doctrine of Chances." *Philosophical Transactions of the Royal Society of London* 53 (1764) 370–418.

Beilby, James, and Paul Eddy, eds. *Divine Foreknowledge: Four Views*. Downers Grove, IL: InterVarsity, 2001.

———. *Understanding Spiritual Warfare: Four Views*. Grand Rapids: Baker Academic, 2012.

Bibliography

Bergo, Bettina. "Emmanuel Levinas." https://plato.stanford.edu/archives/sum2015/entries/levinas/.

Bernard, Claude. *An Introduction to the Study of Experimental Medicine*. New York: Dover, 1957.

Bock, Darrell L. *Who Is Jesus? Linking the Historical Jesus with the Christ of Faith*. New York: Simon and Schuster, 2012.

Brierley, Justin. "Around the World in 80 Miracles." 2014. http://www.premierchristianity.com/Past-Issues/2014/May-2014/Around-the-World-in-80-Miracles.

Broussard, Karlo. *20 Answers—Miracles*. El Cajon, CA: Catholic Answers, 2016.

Brown, Candy Gunther. *Testing Prayer*. Cambridge, MA: Harvard University Press, 2012.

Bultmann, Rudolf. *The New Testament and Mythology: And Other Basic Writings*. Minneapolis: Fortress, 1984.

Burton, Chris, ed. *Traditional Catholic Rites of Exorcism: (English)—Volume 1: 1614 De Exorcizandis Obsessis A Daemonio in the Rituale Romanum*. Seattle: Amazon Digital Services, 2017.

Butler, Joseph. *The Analogy of Religion*. Hartford: Samuel G. Goodrich, 1819.

Cabal, Ted. *The Apologetics Study Bible*. Nashville: Holman, 2007.

Came, Daniel. "Richard Dawkins's Refusal to Debate Is Cynical and Anti-Intellectualist." *The Guardian*, October 11, 2011. https://www.theguardian.com/commentisfree/belief/2011/oct/22/richard-dawkins-refusal-debate-william-lane-craig.

Caputo, John D. Caputo. *The Weakness of God: A Theology of the Event*. Bloomington: Indiana University Press, 2006.

Carrel, Alexis. *The Voyage to Lourdes*. Fraser, MI: Real View, 1994.

Catholic Church. *The Roman Martyrology*. London, UK: Aeterna, 2014.

Chandler, Jake, and Victoria Harrison eds. *Probability in the Philosophy of Religion*. New York: Oxford University Press, 2012.

Clarke, Adam. *Adam Clarke's Commentary on the Bible*. Nashville: Abingdon, 1997.

Cleary, Edward L. *How Latin America Saved the Soul of the Catholic Church*. Mahwah, NJ: Paulist, 2010.

———. *The Rise of Charismatic Catholicism in Latin America*. Gainesville: University of Florida Press, 2011.

Congregation for the Causes of Saints. "New Laws for the Causes of Saints." http://www.vatican.va/roman_curia/congregations/csaints/documents/rc_con_csaints_doc07021983_norme_en.html.

Craig, William Lane, and J. P. Moreland. *Philosophical Foundations for a Christian Worldview*. Downers Grove, IL: InterVarsity, 2003.

Cranston, Ruth. *The Miracle of Lourdes*. New York: Doubleday, 1998.

———. *A Protestant Looks at Lourdes*. New York: McGraw Hill, 1955.

Cruz, Joan Carroll. *Mysteries, Marvels, and Miracles in the Lives of the Saints*. Charlotte, NC: Tan, 1997.

Davis, Richard B. "Can There Be An 'Orthodox' Postmodern Theology?" *JETS* 45/1 (March 2002) 111–23.

Dawid, P., and D. Gillies. "A Bayesian Analysis of Hume's Argument Concerning Miracles." *Philosophical Quarterly* 39 (1989) 57–65.

Dawkins, Richard. *The God Delusion*. New York: First Mariner, 2008.

———. "Why I Refuse to Debate William Lane Craig." *The Guardian*, October 20, 2011. https://www.theguardian.com/commentisfree/2011/oct/20/richard-dawkins-william-lane-craig.

Bibliography

Deere, Jack. "Were Miracles Meant to Be Temporary?" In *Strangers to Fire: When Tradition Trumps Scripture*, edited by Robert W. Graves, 117–34. Woodstock, GA: The Foundation for Pentecostal Scholarship, 2014.

DePoe, John M. "Vindicating a Bayesian Approach to Confirming Miracles: A Response to Jordan Howard Sobel's Reading of Hume." *Philosophia Christi* 10/1 (2008) 229–38.

Devivier, Walter. *Christian Apologetics: A Defense of the Catholic Faith*. New York: Lex De Leon, 2003.

Driscoll, John T. "Miracle." In *The Catholic Encyclopedia*, edited by Charles G. Herbermann et al. New York: Catholic Way, 2014.

Duffin, Jacalyn. *Medical Miracles: Doctors, Saints, and Healing in the Modern World*. New York: Oxford University Press, 2009.

Duffin, Jacalyn. "Pondering Miracles: Medical and Religious." *New York Times*, September, 6, 2016, A21.

Dyrness, William A., and Veli-Matti Karkkainen, eds. *Global Dictionary of Theology*. Downers Grove, IL: InterVarsity, 2008.

Earman, John. "Bayes, Hume and Miracles." *Faith and Philosophy* 10/3 (1993) 293–310.

Eckhart, Meister. *Breakthrough: Meister Eckhart's Creation Spirituality*. New York: Doubleday, 1980.

Elwell, Walter A., ed. *The Evangelical Dictionary of Theology*. Grand Rapids: Baker Academic, 2001.

Elwell, Walter A., and P. W. Comfort. "Miracles." In *The Tyndale Bible Dictionary*, 900–902. Wheaton, IL: Tyndale, 2001.

Erickson, Millard J., Paul Helseth, and Justin Taylor, eds. *Reclaiming the Center: Confronting Evangelical Accommodation in Postmodern Times*. Wheaton, IL: Crossway, 2004.

Floyd, W. E. Gregory. *Clement of Alexandria's Treatment of the Problem of Evil*. Oxford: Oxford University Press, 1971.

Fumerton, Richard. "Foundationalist Theories of Epistemic Justification." 2010. https://plato.stanford.edu/archives/sum2010/entries/justep-foundational/.

Geisler, Norman L. *The Baker Encyclopedia of Christian Apologetics*. Grand Rapids: Baker, 1998.

———. *Biblical Inerrancy: The Historic Evidence*. Matthews, NC: Bastion, 2013.

———. *The Big Book of Christian Apologetics: An A to Z Guide*. Grand Rapids: Baker, 2012.

———. *Christian Apologetics*. Grand Rapids: Baker, 2013.

———. *If God, Why Evil? A New Way to Think About the Question*. Grand Rapids: Baker, 2011.

Gilson, Etienne. *The Christian Philosophy of Saint Thomas Aquinas*. South Bend: Notre Dame University Press, 1994.

———. *Thomist Realism and The Critique of Knowledge*. San Francisco: Ignatius, 2012.

———. *The Unity of Philosophical Experience*. San Francisco: Ignatius, 1999.

Glynn, Paul. *The Healing Fire of Christ: Knock, Lourdes, Fatima*. San Francisco: Ignatius, 2003.

Gould, Steven J. *Rocks of Ages: Science and Religion in the Fullness of Life*. New York: Ballantine, 2002.

Grady, J. Lee. "The Priest with Healing Hands." https://www.charismamag.com/site-archives/351-features/heroes-of-the-faith/1269-the-priest-with-healing-hands.

Graves, Robert W., ed. *Strangers to Fire: When Tradition Trumps Scripture*. Woodstock, GA: The Foundation for Pentecostal Scholarship, 2014.

Bibliography

Grudem, Wayne, ed. *Are Miraculous Gifts for Today? (4 Views).* Grand Rapids: Zondervan, 2011.

Gundry, Stanley, ed. *Four Views on Divine Providence.* Grand Rapids: Zondervan, 2011.

Gundry, Stanley, and Steven B. Cowan, eds. *Five Views on Apologetics.* Grand Rapids: Zondervan, 2010.

Habermas, Gary, and Michael Licona. *The Case for the Resurrection of Jesus.* Grand Rapids: Kregel, 2004.

Hagee, John. *Jerusalem Countdown: A Warning to the World.* Lake Mary, FL: Frontline, 2007.

Hahn, Scott, and Benjamin Wiker. *Politicizing the Bible: The Roots of Historical Criticism and the Secularization of Scripture,* 1300–1700. New York: Herder and Herder, 2013.

Hahn, Scott, et al., eds. *Canon and Biblical Interpretation.* Scripture and Hermeneutics 7. Grand Rapids: Zondervan, 2010.

Hawking, Stephen. *The Grand Design.* New York: Bantam, 2012.

Hayford, Jack. *Penetrating the Darkness: Discovering the Power of the Cross Against Unseen Evil.* Bloomington, MN: Chosen, 2011.

Hick, John. "Soul Making Theodicy." In *The Problem of Evil,* edited by Michael Peterson, 262–73. South Bend, IN: University of Notre Dame Press, 2017.

Hilgevoord, Jan, and Jos Uffink. "The Uncertainty Principle." 2016. https://plato.stanford.edu/archives/win2016/entries/qt-uncertainty/.

Holder, R. D. "Hume on Miracles: Bayesian Interpretation, Multiple Testimony, and the Existence of God." *British Journal for the Philosophy of Science* 49 (1998) 49–65.

Hume, David. *An Enquiry Concerning Human Understanding.* Oxford: Oxford University Press, 2007.

———. *The Natural History of Religion.* Kindle ed. Seattle: Amazon Digital, 2011.

Hutchinson, Ian. *Monopolizing Knowledge.* Belmont, MA: Fias, 2011.

Ingram, Chip. *The Invisible War: What Every Believer Needs to Know About Satan, Demons, and Spiritual Warfare.* Grand Rapids: Baker, 2015.

John, Jeffrey. *The Meaning in the Miracles.* Grand Rapids: Eerdmans, 2004.

Jowers, Dennis W. "Introduction." in *Four Views on Divine Providence,* edited by Stanley Gundry, loc. 27–369 of 4906. Kindle ed. Grand Rapids: Zondervan, 2011.

Joyce, James. "Bayes' Theorem." 2008. https://plato.stanford.edu/archives/fall2008/entries/bayes-theorem/.

Kaiser, Walter C., Jr. *Recovering the Unity of the Bible: One Continuous Story, Plan and Purpose.* Grand Rapids: Zondervan, 2009.

Kant, Immanuel. *The Critique of Practical Reason.* Kindle ed. Seattle: Amazon Digital, 2012.

———. *The Critique of Pure Reason.* Translated by J. M. D. Meiklejohn. Kindle ed. Seattle: Amazon Digital, 2011.

———. *Prolegomena to Any Future Metaphysics.* Translated by Paul Carus. Overland Park, KS: Digireads, 2011.

Keating, Karl. "Scott Hahn on the Politicized Bible." September 1, 1996. https://www.catholic.com/magazine/print-edition/scott-hahn-on-the-politicized-bible.

Keener, Craig. *Miracles: The Credibility of the New Testament Accounts.* Grand Rapids: Baker, 2011.

Kennedy, D. James. *Why I Believe.* Nashville: Thomas Nelson, 2005.

Konig, George, and Ray Konig. *100 Prophecies: Ancient Biblical Prophecies That Foretold the Future.* Fraser, MI: Create Space, 2008.

Kramer, Heinrich, and Jacob Sprenger. *Malleus Maleficarum*. Translated by Montague Summers. Overland Park, KS: Digireads, 2012.
Kreeft, Peter. *Angels and Demons: What Do We Really Know About Them?* San Francisco: Ignatius, 1995.
Kreeft, Peter, and Dave Nevins. *Charisms: Visions, Tongues, Healing, etc.* Pennsauken, NJ: BookBaby, 2013.
Kristensen, Hans M., and Robert S. Norris. "Status of World Nuclear Forces." May 2019. http://fas.org/issues/nuclear-weapons/status-world-nuclear-forces/.
Kuhn, Thomas. *The Structure of Scientific Revolutions*. Chicago: University of Chicago Press, 2010.
Le Bec, E. *Medical Proof of the Miraculous: A Clinical Study*. London: Forgotten, 2015.
Lennox, John C. *God's Undertaker: Has Science Buried God?* Oxford: Lion, 2009.
———. *Gunning for God: Why the New Atheists are Missing the Target*. Grand Rapids: Lion Hudson, 2011.
———. *Miracles: Is Belief in the Supernatural Irrational?* Cambridge, MA: Veritas Forum, 2013.
Levine, Michael. "Review of *Hume's Abject Failure: The Argument Against Miracles*, by John Earman." *Hume Studies* 28 (2002) 161–67.
Lewis, C. S. *An Experiment in Criticism*. Cambridge: Cambridge University Press, 1961.
———. *A Grief Observed*. London: Faber & Faber, 1964.
———. *Mere Christianity*. New York: Harper Collins, 2009.
———. *Miracles*. New York: Harper Collins, 2009.
———. *The Problem of Pain*. New York: Harper Collins, 2009.
Lewis, C. S., and E. M. W. Tillyard. *The Personal Heresy*. New York: University of Oxford Press, 1939.
Longman, Tremper, III, and Raymond B. Dillard. *An Introduction to the Old Testament*. Grand Rapids: Zondervan, 2009.
Lunn, Nicholas P. *The Original Ending of Mark: A Case for the Authenticity of Mark 16:9–20*. Eugene, OR: Wipf & Stock, 2014.
Luther, Martin. "Commentary on the Magnificat." In *Works of Martin Luther* 3, translated by Albert T. W. Steinhaeuser. Grand Rapids: Baker, 1982.
Maas, Anthony. "Resurrection of Jesus Christ." http://www.newadvent.org/cathen/12789a.htm.
MacArthur, John. *Charismatic Chaos*. Grand Rapids: Zondervan, 1992.
———. *Strange Fire*. Nashville: Thomas Nelson, 2013.
———. *The Truth War: Fighting for Certainty in an Age of Deception*. Nashville: Thomas Nelson, 2008.
MacDonald, William. *Bible Believer's Commentary*. Nashville: Thomas Nelson, 1995.
MacNutt, Francis. *Deliverance From Evil Spirits: A Practical Manual*. Grand Rapids: Baker, 2009.
———. *Healing*. Notre Dame: Ave Maria, 2001.
———. *The Healing Reawakening: Reclaiming our Lost Inheritance*. Grand Rapids: Chosen, 2006.
———. *Homosexuality: Can It Be Healed?* Grand Rapids: Chosen, 2006.
———. *The Nearly Perfect Crime: How the Church Almost Killed the Ministry of Healing*. Grand Rapids: Chosen, 2005.
Mandryk, John. *Operation World: The Definitive Prayer Guide to Every Nation*. Downers Grove, IL: InterVarsity, 2010.

Bibliography

Martin, Malachi. *Hostage to the Devil: The Possession and Exorcism of Five Contemporary Americans.* New York: Harper One, 1999.

Martin, Sally. *Every Pilgrims Guide to Lourdes.* London: Hymns Ancient and Modern, 2005.

McDowell, Josh. *Evidence That Demands a Verdict: Historical Evidences for the Christian Faith.* Nashville: Thomas Nelson, 1999.

McGrew, Timothy. "Miracles." http://plato.stanford.edu/archives/spr2013/entries/miracles.

McGrew, Timothy, and Lydia McGrew. "The Argument from Miracles." In *The Blackwell Companion to Natural Theology*, edited by William Lane Craig and J. P. Moreland, 593–662. New York: Blackwell, 2009.

———. "The Reliability of Witnesses and Testimony to the Miraculous." In *Probability in the Philosophy of Religion*, edited by Jake Chandler and Victoria Harrison, 46–63. Oxford: Oxford University Press, 2012.

McHugh, John A., and Charles J. Callan, eds. *The Catechism of the Council of Trent (1566).* New York: Joseph F. Wagner, 1923.

McNeal, T. R. "Miracles, Signs, and Wonders." 1991. https://www.studylight.org/dictionaries/hbd/m/miracles-signs-wonders.html.

Mendel, Gregor. *Experiments in Plant Hybridization.* New York: Cosimo Classics, 2008.

Metaxas, Eric. *Miracles: What They Are, Why They Happen, and How They Can Change Your Life.* New York: Penguin, 2014.

Mill, John Stuart. *On Liberty.* Kindle ed. Seattle: Amazon Digital Services, 2016.

Moreland, J. P. "Four Degrees of Postmodernism." In *Come Let Us Reason: New Essays in Christian Apologetics*, edited by William Lane Craig and Paul Copan, loc. 388–692 of 6393. Kindle ed. Nashville: B&H, 2012.

Morris, Henry M. *Men of Science: Men of God.* Green Forest, AK: Master, 2007.

Moser, Paul ed. *The Oxford Handbook of Epistemology.* New York: Oxford University Press, 2002.

Nash, Ronald H. *Worldviews in Conflict: Choosing Christianity in a World of Ideas.* Grand Rapids: Zondervan, 1992.

Naugle, David K., Jr. *Worldview: The History of a Concept.* Grand Rapids: Eerdmans, 2002.

Nelson, Matt. "Do Miracles Happen in Non-Christian Religions?" https://www.catholic.com/magazine/online-edition/do-miracles-happen-in-non-christian-religions.

Newbigin, Lesslie. *Proper Confidence: Faith, Doubt and Certainty in Christian Discipleship.* Grand Rapids: Eerdmans, 1995.

Noll, Mark A., et al., eds. *When God and Science Meet: Surprising Discoveries of Agreement.* Washington, DC: National Association of Evangelicals, 2015.

Ott, Michael. "Pope Urban VIII." In *The Catholic Encyclopedia.* New York: Catholic Way, 2014.

Owen, D. "Hume versus Price on Miracles and Prior Probabilities: Testimony and the Bayesian Calculation." *Philosophical Quarterly* 37 (1987) 187–202.

Oxford Divine Action Project. "Special Divine Action." https://sda.bodleian.ox.ac.uk/sda/#!/about?id=191.

Paley, William. *Evidences for Christianity.* Kindle ed. Seattle: Amazon Digital Services, 2011.

Parigi, Paolo. *The Rationalization of Miracles.* New York: Cambridge University Press, 2012.

Bibliography

Paul VI. "Gaudium et Spies (Papal Encyclical)." December 7, 1965. http://www.vatican.va/archive/hist_councils/ii_vatican_council/documents/vat-ii_const_19651207_gaudium-et-spes_en.html.

———. "Lumen Gentium (Papal Encyclical)." November 21, 1964. http://www.vatican.va/archive/hist_councils/ii_vatican_council/documents/vat-ii_const_19641121_lumen-gentium_en.html.

Penner, Myron B., ed. *Christianity and the Postmodern Turn: Six Views*. Grand Rapids: Brazos, 2005.

Petre, Marian, and Gordon Rugg. *The Unwritten Rules of PhD Research*. New York: McGraw Hill, 2010.

Pew Research Center. "Global Christianity—A Report on the Size and Distribution of the World's Christian Population." 2011. http://www.pewforum.org/2011/12/19/global-christianity-exec/.

Pinnock, Clark, et al. eds. *The Openness of God: A Biblical Challenge to the Traditional Understanding of God*. Grand Rapids: InterVarsity Academic, 1994.

Pius XII. "Humani Generis (Papal Encyclical)." August 12, 1950. http://w2.vatican.va/content/pius-xii/en/encyclicals/documents/hf_p-xii_enc_12081950_humani-generis.html.

Plantinga, Alvin. *God, Freedom, and Evil*. Grand Rapids: Eerdmans, 1989.

———. *Knowledge and Christian Belief*. Grand Rapids: Eerdmans, 2015.

———. *Where the Conflict Really Lies: Science, Religion and Naturalism*. New York: Oxford University Press, 2011.

Plato. *The Republic*. Translated by Benjamin Jowett. Kindle ed. Seattle: Amazon Digital Services, 2012.

Polanyi, Michael. *Personal Knowledge: Towards a Post-Critical Philosophy*. Chicago: University of Chicago Press, 2015.

Polkinghorne, John C. *Science and Providence: God's Interaction with the World*. West Conshohocken, PA: Templeton, 2005.

Polkinghorne, John C., and Nicholas Beale. *Questions of Truth*. Louisville, KY: Westminster John Knox, 2009.

Raatikainen, Panu. "Gödel's Incompleteness Theorems." https://plato.stanford.edu/archives/spr2015/entries/goedel-incompleteness/.

Ratzsch, Del, and Jeffrey Koperski. "Teleological Arguments for God's Existence." https://plato.stanford.edu/archives/win2016/entries/teleological-arguments.

Robart, Harley A. *Miracles We Have Seen: America's Leading Physicians Share Stories They Can't Forget*. Deerfield Beach, FL: Health Communications, 2016.

Rooker, Mark F. "Dating Isaiah 40–66: What Does the Linguistic Evidence Say?" *Westminster Theological Journal* 58 (1996) 303–12.

Rose, Michael S. *Goodbye to Good Men: How Liberals Brought Corruption into the Catholic Church*. New York: Regenery, 2015.

Ross, Hugh. "Anthropic Principle: A Precise Plan for Humanity." 2001. https://www.reasons.org/explore/publications/facts-for-faith/facts-for-faith/2001/12/31/anthropic-principle-a-precise-plan-for-humanity.

———. "Fulfilled Prophecy: Evidence for the Reliability of the Bible." 2003. https://www.reasons.org/explore/publications/tnrtb/read/tnrtb/2003/08/22/fulfilled-prophecy-evidence-for-the-reliability-of-the-bible.

Russell, Bertrand. *Human Knowledge: Its Scope and Limits*. Abingdon, UK: Routledge, 2009.

Bibliography

———. *Why I Am Not a Christian*. Kindle ed. Seattle: Amazon Digital Services, 2016.
Ruthven, Jon. *On the Cessationism of the Charismata: The Protestant Polemic on Post-Biblical Miracles*. Tulsa, OK: Spirit and Word, 2011.
———. *What's Wrong with Protestant Theology?* Tulsa, OK: Spirit and Word, 2013.
Rydelnik, Michael, and Michael Vanlaningham, eds. *The Moody Bible Commentary*. Chicago: Moody Bible Institute of Chicago, 2014.
Scheeben, Matthias Joseph. *A Manual of Catholic Theology*. New York: Lex De Leon, 2013.
Sibley, Brian. *Shadowlands: The True Story of CS Lewis and Joy Davidman*. London: Hodder, 2013.
Sire, James W. *Naming the Elephant: Worldview as a Concept*. Downers Grove, IL: InterVarsity, 2015.
———. *The Universe Next Door*. Downers Grove, IL: InterVarsity, 2009.
Sobel, J. H. "Hume's Theorem on Testimony Sufficient to Establish a Miracle." *Philosophical Quarterly* 41 (1991) 229–37.
———. "On the Evidence of Testimony for Miracles: A Bayesian Interpretation of David Hume's Analysis." *Philosophical Quarterly* 37 (1987) 166–86.
Sproul, R. C. *The Consequences of Ideas: Understanding the Consequences that Shaped Our World*. Wheaton, IL: Crossway, 2000.
———. *Does God Control Everything?* Sanford, FL: Reformation Trust, 2012.
———. "The Witness of Matthew." https://www.ligonier.org/learn/articles/witness-matthew/.
Stafford, Timothy. *Miracles: A Journalist Looks at Modern Day Experiences of God's Power*. Bloomington, MN: Bethany, 2012.
———. "Miracles in Mozambique." *Christianity Today* (May 2012) 19–26.
Stenger, Victor. "Hawking and the Multiverse." https://www.huffingtonpost.com/victor-stenger/hawking-and-the-multivers_b_713744.html.
Stokes, Philip. *Philosophy 100 Essential Thinkers: The Ideas That Have Shaped Our World*. London: Arcturus, 2012.
Stone, James V. *Bayes' Rule: A Tutorial Introduction to Bayesian Analysis*. Berlin: Sebtel, 2013.
Swanson, J., and O. Nave. *New Nave's Topical Bible*. Oak Harbor, WA: Logos Research Systems, 1994.
Swinburne, Richard. *The Existence of God*. Oxford University Press: Oxford, 2004.
———. "Miracles." *Philosophical Quarterly* 18/73 (October 1968) 320–28.
Thavis, John. *The Vatican Prophecies: Investigating Supernatural Signs, Apparitions, and Miracles in the Modern Age*. New York: Penguin, 2015.
Thomas, J. Harold. "The Authorship of the Book of Isaiah." *Restoration Quarterly* 10/1 (1967) 46–55.
Tooley, Michael. "The Problem of Evil." https://plato.stanford.edu/archives/fall2015/entries/evil/.
Via, Dan O. *What is New Testament Theology?* Minneapolis, Fortress, 2002.
Voorhis, Troy Van. *Certainty: Is Science All You Need?* Cambridge, MA: Veritas Forum, 2014.
Walton, John H., and Craig Keener eds. *NIV Cultural Backgrounds Study Bible*. Grand Rapids: Zondervan, 2016.
Ward, Michael. "C. S. Lewis and the Art of Disagreement." https://home.isi.org/cs-lewis-and-art-disagreement.
Warfield, B. B. *Counterfeit Miracles*. Whitefish, MT: Kessinger, 2010.

Wielenberg, Erik J. *God and the Reach of Reason: C. S. Lewis, David Hume and Bertrand Russell*. Cambridge: Cambridge University Press, 2007.

Wildman, Wesley. "A Counter Response on the Divine Action Project." *Theology and Science* 3/1 (2005) 17–29.

Wilken, Robert Louis. *The First Thousand Years: A Global History of Christianity*. New Haven, CT: Yale University Press, 2012.

Williams, Rodman J. *Renewal Theology: Systematic Theology from a Charismatic Perspective*. Grand Rapids: Zondervan, 1996.

Winters, Anne Case. *Reconstructing a Christian Theology of Nature*. New York: Routledge, 2007.

Wittgenstein, Ludwig. *Philisophico Logicio Tractatus*. New York: Harcourt Brace, 1922.

Wood, D. R. "Miracles." In *New Bible Dictionary*, edited by I. Howard Marshall et al. Downers Grove, IL: InterVarsity, 1996.

———. "Resurrection." In *New Bible Dictionary*, edited by I. Howard Marshall et al. Downers Grove, IL: InterVarsity, 1996.

Wright, N. T. *Revelation*. Downers Grove, IL: InterVarsity, 2012.

Wurmbrand, Richard. *The Answer to the Atheist's Handbook*. Bartlesville, OK: Living Sacrifice, 2002.

Yungen, Ray. *A Time of Departing: How Ancient Mystical Practices Are Uniting Christians with the World's Religions*. Silverton, OR: Lighthouse Trails, 2006.

Zacharias, Ravi, and Vince Vitale. *Jesus Among Secular Gods: The Countercultural Claims of Christ*. New York: FaithWords, 2018.

www.ingramcontent.com/pod-product-compliance
Lightning Source LLC
Chambersburg PA
CBHW051741230426
43670CB00012B/2114